What people are

Our Eternal E

Our Eternal Existence: A Metaphysical Perspective of Reality, by David V. Gaggin, is a well written and researched book which delves deeply into belief versus science. Religion and Science have both become inflexible as followers of each are unbending in their assumption they are correct. However, as David demonstrates, before arriving at any conclusions, one must examine the whole picture.

As an attorney I have a mind trained in analytical thinking and skepticism. *Our Eternal Existence* appeals to both of these aspects of my being and that is why I highly recommend and endorse *Our Eternal Existence* as an authoritative classic in the field of metaphysics.

Mark Anthony JD, Psychic Explorer, author of the bestsellers *The Afterlife Frequency*, *Evidence of Eternity* and *Never Letting Go*

What David has written here is nothing less than an encyclopedia of spirituality. If you are seeking answers for... Who am I? Where am I? Why am I here? ... you will be rewarded with a codex of spiritual knowledge to answer these questions, and this book is like a guidepost with signs pointing in the relevant and researched directions to guide your spiritual path. This is an easy-to-read, concise, spiritual book that is appropriate for people who are already on a spiritual path as well as those who are just starting out. I thoroughly enjoyed reading it.

Miki Jacobs, psychic, medium, spiritual teacher, and bestselling author of *Soul Secrets*

This extraordinary and engaging work provides an illuminating roadmap for the spiritual aspirant. It answers many questions that 'seekers' ask and points their thinking process in an extremely helpful direction.

Ron and Mary Hulnick, Founding Faculty and Co-Directors of the University of Santa Monica, and bestselling authors of *Loyalty To Your Soul* and *Remembering the Light Within*

Our Eternal Existence is a remarkable book. David Gaggin has done the research and assembled information from numerous sources and times to present a unified view of the metaphysical and physical universes. This is a book of wisdom and a catalyst for change.

Ken Elliott, author of *Manifesting 1,2,3: and You Don't Need #3*

Gaggin's scientific background lends itself to *Our Eternal Existence* by revealing complex spiritual secrets that anyone can understand, bridging how science, religion, and philosophical concepts intertwine with metaphysical ideas often dismissed. Gaggin's *Our Eternal Existence* is a sign of hope that our species is evolving to realize that 'spirit,' the human spirit, is to be revered like the mind and body, and can positively change our world when they are in union.

Laura Lee, host of the *Radio Medium Laura Lee* show

Our Eternal Existence

A Metaphysical Perspective of Reality

Our Eternal Existence

A Metaphysical Perspective of Reality

David Gaggin

6TH BOOKS

Winchester, UK
Washington, USA

JOHN HUNT PUBLISHING

First published by Sixth Books, 2023
Sixth Books is an imprint of John Hunt Publishing Ltd., No. 3 East St., Alresford,
Hampshire SO24 9EE, UK
office@jhpbooks.com
www.johnhuntpublishing.com
www.6th-books.com

For distributor details and how to order please visit the 'Ordering' section on our website.

Text copyright: David Gaggin 2021

ISBN: 978 1 80341 293 1
978 1 80341 294 8 (ebook)
Library of Congress Control Number: 2022945034

A CIP catalogue record for this book is available from the British Library.

Design: Lapiz Digital Services

UK: Printed and bound by CPI Group (UK) Ltd, Croydon, CR0 4YY
Printed in North America by CPI GPS partners

We operate a distinctive and ethical publishing philosophy in
all areas of our business, from our global network of authors to
production and worldwide distribution.

Contents

Preface

My first book, *The Endless Journey*, provides a broad perspective on the nature of reality and why we are here. *Our Eternal Existence* is a more in-depth discussion on who we are, how the universe works, and how we fit into it. It expands on the concepts that I described in *The Endless Journey*.

The purpose of this book is four-fold. 1) To challenge your ideas about who you are and the nature of your reality. There is a tremendous amount of information that contradicts the theories of mainstream science and the various religions, yet most people have never been exposed to these ideas. If we consider ourselves knowledgeable about the nature of our world, we need to be open to contradictory views. We don't need to agree with them, we just need to consider them. 2) To help people who are struggling with various aspects of their lives. Health, wealth and happiness are within everyone's reach if they know how to achieve them. 3) To provide a basis for an ethical standard of conduct that is not based on religious fear, but rather on the inherent benefits of equality and mutual self-interests of all humanity. 4) To help people realize that each human is a divine being with a purpose and not a soulless entity living here by chance as science asserts, or that people are separate from the divine as mainstream religions proclaim.

Science, religion, and metaphysics each view the world from different perspectives, and each has created their own view of reality. Science assumes that our physical environment is all that exists, and all knowledge can be learned by examining it. As a result, science concludes that consciousness arose from the complexity of physical matter. Conversely, mainstream religions assume that there is a spiritual reality behind the physical universe and that truth has been given to mankind by various deities.

1

Metaphysics believes consciousness came before matter and is the source of all reality, to include the physical universe. In other words, matter is the result, not the source, of true reality. Metaphysics aligns with religion in that it views the physical universe to only be a portion of total reality. However, metaphysics asserts that over time much of the original information provided to the religious founders has been distorted beyond recognition. It also believes that the original information is available to us through other sources.

Our Eternal Existence views reality from a metaphysical perspective.

Sources

Many great geniuses have attributed their inspiration and wisdom to spiritual sources, yet mainstream science has refused to accept this possibility. However, quantum mechanics and ESP experiences have uncovered phenomena that not only support these assertions but contradict the very basis of our understanding of the laws of physics. More and more scientists are considering alternative theories of reality that better explain our existence.

The information in *Our Eternal Existence* comes from a multitude of spiritual sources that are assisting mankind's evolution. I have simply interpreted, filtered, and condensed the abundance of available information and presented it in a more concise manner than is presently available elsewhere. Although I received some of the information first-hand through mediums and channels, the largest portion of it by far comes from others who have channeled it both in recent times and throughout history.

Mediums, psychics and channels are common sources of spiritual information. Knowledge has been continually given to mankind since the beginning of human history and it is available to anyone who seeks it.

Convincing yourself that channeled information can be valid is the first order of business for anyone who seriously wants to understand their true nature. If you are new to metaphysics it helps to start by convincing yourself that the spiritual world exists and the easiest way to do this is to communicate with it. A good way to begin is to find an authentic medium, and there are many available. If possible, use a recommendation from a trusted friend. Then pick a deceased person with whom you had a close and positive relationship. Parents, grandparents, a spouse, siblings, children, and close friends are good choices. Provide the medium with minimal details about yourself and the spirit you want to communicate with. Names and relationships are all you need to disclose. The spirit will usually have things it wants to tell you so it will do most of the communicating through the medium. The spirit also knows you need convincing that they are really the one you are communicating with so they will provide the relevant information that you will need. If the medium is capable, you will have no trouble being convinced that you are talking to your chosen person. They will use terms, refer to situations, and discuss various topics that have special meaning to only you. If you are not satisfied with the results then try another medium.

My daughter has always been psychic to some extent and actually knew something was going to happen to her mother nine months before my wife suddenly died. Subsequent to her mother's death, she focused on expanding her psychic capabilities. She had a reliable psychic teach her how to channel her mother through 'automatic writing.' This is a technique in which the spirit actually takes over control of the channel's hand to communicate in writing. She became quite skilled and the family has been able to communicate with my deceased wife numerous times. Once I was even able to ask her for assistance in identifying the location of the source of a leak on the roof of my house that I had been attempting to locate for months.

She identified the location to be on the side of the chimney above the wet bar. Armed with this information I looked at the area and found a hairline crack that I had never noticed at the exact location where she said it would be. There was no way my daughter could have known this information as she did not live in my house and had never been on my roof.

Knowledge requires discernment and that is a personal task. Plato said that for an idea to be considered knowledge it must be believed, true, and reasonable. No one can convince anyone else what knowledge is. We need to determine it for ourselves.

The deeper we probe reality, the more our views will evolve. The knowledge required to create this universe is far beyond man's ability to comprehend. But as we evolve, this wisdom will slowly open up to us. The concepts in this book should not be seen as the final word on anything, but more as a starting point.

Foreword

By Shepherd Hoodwin

No matter what our level of consciousness is, we each still have to deal with the life of the body, including relationships, health, finances, etc. No one is immune from the myriad challenges of being human.

The way we frame them, however, makes all the difference. *Our Eternal Existence* offers us a way of viewing life that can free us from the repressive burdens of culturally imprinted ways of interpreting existence. We can begin to see ourselves as we truly are: creators in training who are exploring new ways that love, truth, and beauty can be manifested. We can increasingly live with respect for all beings and their paths. The expansive picture David Gaggin paints can help us live not just as a human but as a human being, an eternal being temporarily enlivening a human vehicle because we chose to, in order to grow, evolve, and create.

Humanity faces vast, even existential challenges today. It would be easy to become depressed by what we read and hear daily in the news. We, of course, do need to pay attention and take constructive action. But a larger view can help us to do so without losing hope or becoming overwhelmed by what is required.

Any activism that we feel called to participate in can help, but the greatest thing we can contribute is to raise our own vibration to be more harmonious with the love that created the universe. We cannot directly change other people or control their choices, but higher vibrations are more powerful than lower ones. Shining light into the world to the best of our ability offers a role model, seen or unseen, to others, and raises the overall vibration of humanity.

Perhaps the key insight of this book is that we aren't merely the personality that we know ourselves to be. We are that, but also something much larger. On a personality level, we may seek love, but truly we *are* love. As we live more from this truth, we are not only a greater force for good, but true happiness becomes possible.

Introduction

If you do not change direction, you may end up where you are heading.

Lao Tse

Is it possible that ancient wisdom was given to the early Eastern and Western philosophers and then lost over the millennia? If so, is it returning to us through the scientific theories of quantum mechanics, relativity, and the teachings of spiritual entities like Michael and Seth?

If you are frustrated with religion but know intuitively that science's atheistic view of the world cannot be correct, then there are other avenues to pursue. *Our Eternal Existence* is based on the teachings of well-respected channels like Jane Roberts, Edgar Cayce, and Shepherd Hoodwin, plus others too numerous to mention. In addition, it considers the latest scientific theories concerning the creation of the universe and the nature of reality. It is a story of how an omnipotent intelligence, which is all loving and all virtuous, created a universe that simultaneously benefits and supports every creature in existence.

Our Eternal Existence is based on five principles, which we will discuss in detail. 1) There is an overwhelming body of evidence that a spiritual reality supports the physical universe. 2) The physical world is an illusion in that it is not what it appears to be. It is an illusion created for our benefit and with our help. 3) The only thing that exists is the mind of the Universal Consciousness, and both we and the rest of nature are part of that mind. 4) With the essence of everything being a mind, then thoughts are not only the true power in the universe, they are the only power. 5) It is our thoughts that control our lives and cause both our comforts and our difficulties.

Mankind is being shown that consciousness is the basis of reality. We see ourselves as physical bodies living in a physical

7

world and separate from each other and our environment. When a disturbance occurs, we consider it a solitary event, and if we are not directly involved, we don't think it has any effect on us. But reality is very different than this. All things, from an atom to a distant galaxy, including you and I, are tied together through a web of consciousness. We are multidimensional beings and our consciousness exists outside of what science calls our four-dimensional space-time continuum. We live in an illusion that makes what our senses perceive very different from true reality.

Each of us is endowed with remarkable powers, but our naivety causes us to misuse them to our detriment. Inadvertently we have developed personal habits that cause us to squander the very capabilities we are here to learn to master. Because we do not understand the nature of our reality, our good intentions can just as easily create problems as solve them.

To improve our lives we need to change what we think. But changing our beliefs is not an easy task. We have each created a personal reality that is both ingrained within us, and frequently misdirected. In order to change our beliefs and improve our lives, we need to understand: who we are; where we are; and why we are here. We cannot change our life unless we understand our reality and the control we have over it.

When mankind eventually learns the universe's secrets, science, religion and philosophy will be a single subject. Metaphysics is presently the closest body of knowledge available to us for the pursuit of that goal.

Section I

The Unseen Universe

Chapter 1

Aspects of Metaphysics

Real knowledge is to know the extent of one's ignorance.
Confucius

Key Concept: The world is not as it appears to be.

'Woo Woo,' Blasphemy or Reality

Is spirituality just a 'woo woo' subject or is it reality? Metaphysics tells us that the physical world is a creation of the spiritual world. It describes an amazing reality, highly organized, and lovingly supporting every creature in existence. But science considers it 'woo woo,' and religion considers it blasphemy, each for their own reasons.

Science

Mainstream science allocates the entire subject of spirituality to the trash bin, claiming it does not exist. It struggles with spirituality for the following reasons:

1. Science believes that all knowledge comes from the physical environment. Because its present instruments cannot detect the spiritual world, it assumes it does not exist.
2. Science's root assumption is that the physical universe is a self-created reality. This allows them to postulate the Big Bang Theory and the physical creation of consciousness, two fundamental suppositions that are unsubstantiated.
3. Science is in its infancy. Even with the huge strides that it has made in the last century, its 'knowledge' has a half-life of about 18 months. In a thousand years science will be telling us a completely different story about reality.

11

Mainstream scientific theories are unable to explain any form of extrasensory perception (ESP), so they pretend it does not exist. By claiming the creation of the universe was an accident, science can conveniently focus on explaining how the universe works without any attempt to tell us why. The most tragic outcome of science's physical model of reality results in an amoral doctrine, which science is fostering. If there is no greater purpose than simply living this life, where is the motivation to improve ourselves and indeed the world in general. Ethics has no place in scientific philosophy, and we see the result of that in our school curriculums where ethics is nonexistent. Science tells us their doctrine is 'truth,' but they fail to point out that it is only 'truth' when reality is viewed from a totally physical perspective. If a moral spiritual world lies behind the physical exterior, then science's physical focus may actually be retarding mankind's evolution, not assisting it. Our technology has outpaced our emotional maturity. Most people who have succeeded financially in this life can attest that acquiring 'things' is not the answer to happiness. Our civilization needs a philosophy with deeper insights into our true nature.

Religion
Religions see God as separate and apart from both mankind and nature. God is seen as the creator who expects perfection out of Its subjects. In contrast to science, instead of searching for truth, religion claims it has already found it. Many religious leaders fear that contradictory facts will expose fatal gaps in their doctrines. Blind faith for the fearful is their chosen recourse. New information contradictory to doctrine is causing great difficulty for major religions. Unless they embrace the search for spiritual truth before science comes to its senses, religion will find itself outside mainstream society with only cult status. The old guard is too embedded in their ways to change so it will be up to the young to salvage the institutions. The unwillingness

of religion to pursue spiritual truth is condemning them, not only to spiritual ignorance, but to the inevitable rejection by their followers.

Philosophy

Over two thousand years ago the great Greek and Eastern philosophers sought truth from spiritual sources and verified it by searching within themselves. Ancient philosophy was based on moral principles that mankind could follow and be proud to adhere to. But the truth they found has been disparaged by both science and religion. Western religions were the instigators in the demise of Greek philosophy because it contradicted their teachings. With philosophy out of favor, science took over the lead role of rational thought.

Philosophy today has become a search for truth through logic. But the logic philosophers use to find truth is distorted by the illusion in which we live. They have abandoned their pursuit of ethics and have followed science ever deeper into the physical illusion.

Philosophy needs to lead science and religion, not follow them. Without the proper philosophical framework to guide them, science will remain lost in the illusion and religion will continue pushing its dogma. Philosophy needs to provide an ethical standard that will tell mankind why we exist and what our purpose is. Science can then discover how the universe works, and religion can guide us on how we can maximize our time on earth.

Metaphysics

Both science and religion have contributed a great deal to the development of mankind, but each has created its own baggage. So far these two pillars of social thought have chosen to ignore the massive amount of contradictory information that undermines their main premises. The Internet has brought easy access to information and the misconceptions are being increasingly disseminated and challenged. The general public is demanding better explanations for theories that make little sense. The 'spooky' world of quantum theory is not spooky at all when one considers a universe that stretches beyond the physical one we see. Once science learns the true nature of matter, quantum theory will prove to be a fairly accurate but incomplete description of how consciousness manifests in the physical universe.

Metaphysics is the philosophy that both science and religion need to help put meaning into our lives. Metaphysics is the only body of knowledge that is investigating spirituality, and consciousness is at the center of its theories.

A Paradigm Shift

There are a number of reasons why we need a paradigm shift: First and foremost, mankind needs to believe that life has meaning. If life has no meaning it leads to despair, desperation and chaos. Religion has always understood this, which is still its greatest appeal and probably its greatest asset. The older and wiser amongst us realize that a meaningless life makes no sense and they are searching for more realistic answers. When we think life has no purpose, it is easy to lose our way. But life does have meaning and we each have an individual purpose. It is important to understand our individual contribution to the whole, and see the power and majesty that we are all a part of.

Secondly, science created a model of reality using the physical world as its basis and is now attempting to draw conclusions about its nature. But if reality's source and power is not physical, science's model will always be insufficient. Concepts like Quantum Mechanics and Relativity Theory are causing the physical models to be widely challenged. When ESP phenomena are considered the troubles science faces increase exponentially.

Thirdly, metaphysics provides a philosophy that answers the questions science and religion do not address. Metaphysical principles show us that our physical reality is an illusion. It presents a consistent and logical picture of reality, to include a rationale that is an amazingly 'good news' story. Life is not an accident nor is it a punishment. It is simply an important step in our evolution.

A paradigm based on metaphysical principles provides a guide for how to treat each other and improve our lives. Metaphysical principles are not new to mankind. They encompass all the ancient religious beliefs, but without the added dogma. They also provide a structure and direction for science to pursue, which will address all the phenomena that we encounter, both spiritual and physical. The information comes from many sources starting as far back as the oral traditions before the beginning of recorded history and continues up to our present day. Many great minds from both Eastern and Western cultures have contributed in some significant way. Each provided different aspects of the story, sometimes offering new concepts and other times validating previous ideas.

Seekers of knowledge who have read Plato, Blavatsky, Ouspensky, Cayce, Hall, Emerson, Hoodwin, Roberts, etcetera often struggle to understand how these 'apparently' conflicting models all fit together. However, each explains reality from a valid, although different, perspective. Efforts to grasp bits and pieces of the story can be extremely complicated and confusing. In order to understand why we are here we need to look at the world differently.

Spiritual Reality

Down through the ages, untold numbers of mystics, psychics and channels have received inputs from spiritual sources in regards to various aspects of reality. In an attempt to describe reality, each spiritual source used a simplified model to explain the concepts. It is impossible for a human or even the spiritual sources that provide this information to fully understand the complete nature of reality. Its complexity is beyond mankind's ability to comprehend. The details of the workings of the Universal Consciousness are far beyond human understanding. But this does not mean we cannot understand key concepts at a simplified level. Each model that has been given to mankind provides a specific and often unique insight into some aspect of reality. They all contribute to pulling back the 'veil of the illusion,' which broadens our understanding of who we are and our purpose. Each new insight offers another view of reality for our consideration. Knowing that no model will ever be complete, the best we can do is try to understand those aspects that can most readily improve our lives.

For example, the models presented by the channeling of the Michael entity (via Shepherd Hoodwin) and the Seth entity (via Jane Roberts) are good examples. They both present different models of reality, which on the surface seem to be contradictory. But under closer scrutiny, these two models are not at all contradictory. Much of the confusion arises because reality is extremely complex and the models explaining them, by necessity, need to be highly simplified for mankind's level of understanding. Only the simplifications make the models appear different.

From the times of Plato and Socrates and onward through the ages, figures such as Leonardo da Vinci, Sir Isaac Newton, Nikola Tesla, Albert Einstein and many other geniuses have been impacted by the principles of metaphysics. Inevitably they have told us that intuition received from inner sources was the source of their insights. Their perceptions were received in a similar manner as the sources for this book received their information.

Ethics

When we search for truth, there is one ultimate standard that we need to test the doctrine against. No model of reality can possibly be true if it does not incorporate an ethical standard for mankind to live by. It is inconceivable that mankind was placed in this universe with no moral guidelines to follow.

Historically, religions were created to provide people with moral guidance as the spiritual world realized its critical importance to society. As mankind became more sophisticated, religions should have as well. All religions were founded on the bases of ethical principles. But over the millennia the parochial views of many religious leaders changed the moral codes into dogmas and rituals, which have slowly caused them to lose their value as science has become more prevalent. The Seth entity says that Christianity was supposed to provide mankind with an understanding of the inner self that we could use as a moral foundation for future evolution, but it was not properly accomplished by those that followed Christ. The original principles were correct but the implementation was badly distorted. Fifty years ago the Seth entity said that religions would fall into chaos, which we can see is beginning to happen today. Seth predicted that by 2075 a new set of principles will be available for mankind to follow, which will greatly improve our living conditions. I do not know how accurate this timetable is because predictions are only probabilities, but change for the better is likely.

Science, on the other hand, makes no pretense in offering an ethical standard. With no belief in the afterlife, science forms its own dogma, which is based on a world created by happenstance. Survival of the fittest is an apt principle for the creation of a material society, and it offers mankind no incentive to live a noble life.

In contrast, there is an ethical standard of conduct that mankind is being taught by the spiritual world. It is a personal standard that requires no formal organization to implement, but it does require a good deal of insight to fully understand. In time mankind will learn to embrace these standards because eventually we will realize that the chaos in our world is the result of ignoring them.

Spirituality vs Metaphysics

Spirituality and metaphysics are difficult concepts to understand because the terms mean different things to different people. We commonly think of spirituality as separate from our physical life. It is something other than the material world we know, but we are not quite sure what that 'other' really is. We consider ourselves to be spiritual when we pray or attend church or maybe even meditate. This type of thinking is highly limiting and contributes to the hardships of life by making us think we are separate from nature and the divine.

Spirituality needs to be seen from a broader perspective. Since humans are spirits having a physical experience, then everything we do is a spiritual experience. Life consists of a continual series of spiritual experiences. Even our most mundane tasks are spiritual lessons. We learn from everything we do and everything we think.

Metaphysics is the search for the ultimate reality of life, which happens to have a spiritual source. So I see spiritual and metaphysical reality as virtually interchangeable. They both describe reality as we experience it from our earthly perspective. Who are we? Why are we here? Where were we before this life? Where will we go when we die? What is our true nature? These are all spiritual and metaphysical questions. Realizing that there is nothing in our lives that is not spiritual helps us understand that we are both part of nature and part of the divine. However, I like the term metaphysical because it does not have the multitude of connotations that the term spirituality does.

The creation of the universe was not an accident nor is our presence in it an accident. Some highly developed intelligence spent a lot of effort to create this universe and it is inconceivable that it was created without a very important purpose. Life becomes a lot easier when we understand that purpose.

Our Eternal Existence describes a paradigm that is consistent with both the Seth and Michael entity models. These models were immensely helpful in filling in many details and creating and validating a more complete and consistent picture of reality. Books describing those models are easily available to anyone interested in further study, which I highly encourage.

Metaphysics is a story of hope, self-empowerment, and eternal growth. Metaphysical concepts are not hard to understand if taken in order as one builds upon another. They are about understanding ourselves. The entrances to the great learning centers of ancient Egypt were embossed with the phrase 'Man Know Thyself.' Metaphysical research is the process of understanding ourselves.

The Creator

The Universal Consciousness

There is a single transcendent intelligence in existence and each one of us is part of it. You might think of it as 'God' but I don't like the term because religion has created a distorted concept of 'God' and embedded it into our psyche. The Abrahamic religions are the biggest influencers as they describe God as: 1) a single entity apart from us; 2) our judge and punisher; 3) male; 4) in need of worship; and 5) offering special favors to those who do His bidding. None of this is true.

In *The Endless Journey* I used the term "Universal Consciousness" because I wanted the reader to think of It as an immense omnipotent mind, which we are part of. The Universal Consciousness shows Its love for us by providing an environment where we can evolve in our own way and without criticism or threat of punishment.

It allows us to create our own growth plan, and assists us with every aspect of the execution, and asks nothing from us in return. Understanding the Universal Consciousness is not easy because of the complexity of Its nature. However, it is important because It exemplifies the goals in which we need to strive. When we see the divine as different and apart from us, we misunderstand our true nature. We don't see the magnificent creatures we really are, and that someday far in the future we too will become equally awe-inspiring.

The Universal Consciousness is composed of every spirit in existence. All spirits are of equal importance but differentiated by their degree of wisdom. The Universal Consciousness can function as: 1) a single entity; 2) an infinite number of discrete entities; or 3) any combination between the two. For instance, It likely acts as larger combined entities when it creates more grand phenomena like universes, but It divides Itself into smaller individual entities, like us, when it chooses to incarnate into the universe. It does this in order to learn about itself and 'play.'[1]

The term "Universal Consciousness" does not truly describe Its real nature. So now I will use two other terms to describe this Entity.

All That Is

The Hermetic philosophers called the Universal Consciousness 'The All' because everything that exists is encompassed within It. An amazing aspect of this universe is that every object within it is enlivened by the spiritual sparks within 'All That Is.' Minerals, plants, animals, planets, stars and you and I all have a spiritual essence within us, which is part of The All. 'All is in The All, and The All is in all.' Think about it!

I like the term 'All That Is' because it suggests the magnitude and scope of the Universal Consciousness. Everything in existence is part of this immense mind and the term 'All That Is'

20

helps us understand the concept of unity. Even when the latest telescope looks out into the cosmos, everything it sees is just a tiny fraction of 'All That Is.' Everything in nature, every star, every galaxy, and every atom is part of 'All That Is.' Also the concept implies that 'All That Is' needs to be all that it can be, which is the ultimate motivation for everything.

Nothing would be more like hell than to exist for eternity and never change. Everything is evolving, which means 'All That Is' is never the same from one moment to the next. 'All That Is' wants to enjoy its existence and become greater. Our nature is no different. Infinite growth, excitement and joy are in our future.

The Tao

The final term I will use to describe the 'Universal Consciousness' or 'All That Is' is the 'Tao,' which is the term Lao Tse used over 2500 years ago. 'Tao' means 'Way' or 'Right Way' and it is meant to describe the nature of reality and the underlying order of things. It is the reality we are embedded in and are a part of. The term 'Tao' allows us to conceive of The Creator as more than just a huge mind. It is also the creator of processes, laws, and Universal Principles that guide us and aid us along our evolutionary journey.

Tao Te Ching was the book Lao Tse supposedly wrote some 2500 years ago, which explained the Tao's nature. It was written in ancient Chinese so it does not translate easily into English. The Michael entity describes the Tao as follows:[2] "The Tao is almost like a vacuum that is simultaneously a black hole and a white hole. You can align with the Tao in your deepest meditations and you can feel Its stillness. When you are as still as you can possibly be, you can sense the Tao in its fullness. It is the ultimate stillness, but yet it allows the ultimate power to exist. It is not only a power source, but it is the grid that holds all of the universes together. It is the nothingness that allows fullness at the same time, which in turn allows manifestation."

21

As one can imagine, it is impossible to fully describe what the Tao is like. The inner nature of the Tao is unknowable to man in his present state. The religions that have described aspects of God's nature as revengeful, angry, jealous or vain are wrong and demonstrate a limited understanding, as the Tao is all loving.

A key feature of the Tao and the universe It created is that nothing 'is' because everything 'is becoming.' Everything in existence is changing or transforming itself into something else. The seed is becoming a baby, the baby is becoming an adult, the adult is becoming an elder, the elder dies and returns as a more advanced seed. This cycle permeates every phenomenon: minerals, plants, animals, planets, stars, and galaxies. Everything is in a state of change and growth. Even the universe is following that cycle. Everything in existence is evolving into a higher and more advanced state of understanding.

The Tao is massive, and by our humble standards, it appears infinite. But the Tao is not infinite. Only the Tao's potential is truly infinite. In order to expand Its scope and obtain more of Its potential, It is forever exploring new aspects of Itself. The Tao is continuously growing and expanding and gaining wisdom. It is an amazing mind with unfathomable wisdom. But It will still spend eternity learning to further understand Itself.

The Tao learned to grow and reproduce, taught itself every piece of wisdom now in existence, and It continues on its journey towards perfection, ever evolving and always enjoying; and we are going with It.

I will use the terms Tao, Universal Consciousness, All That Is and even God interchangeably depending on the concept that seems to most aptly apply.

Vitality, Action and Identity

Permeating everything that exists both within and outside the Tao is an infinite source of dormant energy, which is the original substance of every creation the Tao has ever formed. This unlimited source of potential energy is of unknown origin. Until it is activated this energy remains in its dormant state.

The most amazing aspect of the source energy is that it has an innate ability to become conscious. This energy is dormant until it is activated, at which time it becomes what might best be thought of as a 'vitality,' which can be considered an identity. An identity can be the tiniest bit of energy, an atom, a galaxy or even the Tao. In other words it is something. The moment the energy is first activated it begins to have experiences and grow psychically.

The Seth entity says[3] that the nature of vitality, or what he calls 'action,' is continuous change, and what it changes is itself. This change comes from within and is a requirement for existence. If change were to stop, which the Seth entity says is impossible, the identity would return to dormancy. The identity has a desire to remain stable, which creates an imbalance between what it desires and its basic nature. This imbalance creates self-awareness or consciousness of self and at the same time it generates a creative desire that is inherent in all identities, including you and me. Therefore consciousness is not a 'thing' but rather a dimension of identity.

The initially activated vitality has had no experiences yet, so it is not conscious to the extent that you and I are, but it is conscious just the same. The more it learns the more it grows psychically. Because vitality is the only substance in existence, it forms all objects and beings. Since everything is formed from conscious energy, everything is conscious.

This is a difficult concept for most of us to accept but both the Michael entity and Seth entity agree that everything is conscious. It makes no difference if man created it or if nature did. Everything is conscious. It is not the configuration of matter that makes it conscious, but the energetic substance from which it was created. It is matter's innate nature that makes it conscious. We will expand on the nature of consciousness throughout the book.

Being pure energy, the nature of vitality is action. It has energized everything that we can conceive of: every shape, every thought, every spirit, every dream, everything. It is not only the fundamental building block of the universe, it is the only building block. Vitality is not only the internal force behind all creation, it is the creation itself. It is the energy from which we were created.

An identity that vitality forms can be as tiny as a subatomic particle, or as large as the Tao itself. An identity is anything that exists, including you and me, and is simply a unique 'form' that vitality has assumed.

Vitality forms identities by acting upon and transforming itself into them. This transformation is a continuous process. Its action is a self-enhancing process such that no action is ever completed and nothing ever ends. Everything just continues to change and evolve. One action simply leads into another, which means only a tiny amount of vitality could eventually seed a universe. It is through this process that the Tao and this universe evolved into what they are now.

Vitality can be created but it can never be exhausted or weakened, and it can never be destroyed. Once created it can only be transformed. It permeates all of life and gives rise to everything in existence.

The Eastern philosophers call vitality 'chi.' The energy work done in Reiki, acupuncture and other Eastern practices are using vitality to heal. Since everything is created from vitality, animals as well as plants are receptive to its healing capabilities.

We see energy in many different states like electrical, nuclear, chemical, wind, water, solar, and ultimately matter. These energies are the outward expressions that vitality takes in the physical universe. It is only due to our uniquely designed senses that we can detect it in the forms we do.

24

Spark versus Spirit

Spark

A spark is a term used by the Michael entity that describes any identity that has the capability that we would attribute to a being no matter how small or seemingly unimportant. The beings I am referring to might be plants, amoebas, or lower level animals, for instance. In other words it would have the sophistication to be an identity that could reproduce, and survive in an environment of some sort, as opposed to, say, an atom or molecule. The Michael entity uses the term spark to refer to you and me because if we think of the Tao as a huge star or even a galaxy, then we would be a mere spark within it. The term spark also implies a vitality or energy associated within it, and a spark certainly implies an unlimited amount of potential energy available to grow into a fire. Although it may be a tiny spark today, it has the capability to evolve into whatever it chooses, like a star or even a galaxy. Without all the individual sparks there would be no star, so each spark is of great importance. Of course, some sparks have evolved into much larger entities than the term 'spark' implies. We might do better calling those beings flames or even raging storms, but they all began as a tiny spark. As such, each spark plays an important role in the evolution of the Tao.

However, I like the term spirit better for the larger sparks because people are more familiar with the term. Spirit implies a nonphysical essence within our core being. As such, I will use 'spirit' to apply to identities that have reached the general level of a human. I will use the term 'spark' to refer to an identity that has not yet evolved to our human level. Identities that have evolved to levels that are much higher than mankind I will refer to as 'greater spirits' or the Tao.

A spark evolves by expanding its consciousness, which is done by having first-hand experiences. In order to make sparks unique, each spark evolves according to its own self-directed plan.

It receives advice from more advanced entities but it makes the ultimate decision in regards to the path it will take for its evolution. There is no timetable that it needs to follow or rules that force it in one direction or another. It is only limited and guided by the level of its wisdom and imagination. How it chooses to develop is totally its own decision.

Sparks have attributes like: creativity, intelligence, reason, memory, imagination, responsiveness, curiosity, and of course, consciousness. Even when a spark has minimal experience or wisdom, it still has these attributes, although their full potential is latent and awaiting development. Being part of the Tao they also have an attribute of immortality. Once a spark is created, it never ceases to exist.

A spark's whole existence and purpose is based on learning about itself, because when it learns about itself, it is learning about All That Is. When sparks become greater, the Tao becomes greater. Sparks change via evolution and one might not recognize the original spark because of its many transformations, but it never ceases to be, know itself, or remember its past experiences.

Also, sparks never lose their individuality. The Tao creates individual sparks and they join with other sparks to form larger identities but they always retain their individuality. Some Buddhist sects believe that in time the individual spark loses its identity and becomes part of the Tao in what they call Nirvana, but the Seth entity maintains that this is not correct. Every spark retains its individual identity.

Spirit

Eventually, all sparks evolve into spirits. Although I will occasionally refer to sparks, this book is about spirits. Unless I state otherwise, the characteristics and behavior I describe are in regard to spirits like you and me.

Our spirit is our real self. Spirits are not required to live difficult lives like we do. The Tao provides many other areas outside our reality where spirits choose to reside and experience life in a much easier environment. We are the intrepid crusading spirits who have chosen to break new ground and suffer the fears and discomforts of feeling separated from the Tao. Nobody forced us to be here. As hard as it might be to believe on our bad days, this was our idea. We wanted the excitement and the chance for rapid spiritual growth, so we chose this life.

Each spirit is a small but important part of the Tao. We are important because we are unique. There is no other identity exactly like us, so we provide a unique perspective to every experience we encounter. There are an unlimited number of individual spirits that exist within the Tao and they are all interconnected. Although we each have an individual identity, we can also function as part of a larger entity, or even the Tao. A spirit's true power is in its imagination, creativity, and consciousness.

Chapter 2

The Structure of the Universe

We cling to our own point of view, as though everything depended on it. Yet our opinions have no permanence; like autumn and winter, they gradually pass away.
Zhuangzi

Key Concept: There is an inner universe that controls the physical one that we experience.

We think of our universe as an immense ancient structure that is rapidly expanding and encompasses everything in existence. But what we experience is only the physical portion of a truly fantastic universe.

Science tells us the universe is a physical structure that miraculously produces psychological creations like us. The ancient hermetic philosophers saw it differently. They said reality is mental and the universe is a creation within the mind of the Tao. They saw the universe as an idea, an amazing and ever changing thought distributed throughout the Tao. If the Tao is a mind, as it surely is, then the only things that exist besides the mind itself are the mind's thoughts and emotions. As such, what we perceive as objects are the different patterns that thoughts and emotions cause vitality to assume in our reality. This seems impossible to us because we view ideas as nonexistent intangible concepts. But ideas are the force behind vitality, which is the force behind the universe. They have a reality of their own, each with unique forms and durations.

It is important to understand that the physical universe that we are familiar with is the exterior manifestation of an inner universe, which existed long before our physical universe came about. The original or inner universe still exists and functions as a source that feeds and sustains the visible universe that we know.

Structure of the Universe

When scientists use the term 'universe' or 'cosmos,' they are only referring to the physical portion, which consists of the external aspects of stars, galaxies and the other matter and energy we can detect with our present instruments. When I use the term 'universe' I will be including other spiritual realms, not just the physical realm that we can see.

The universe consists of seven 'Planes of Creation.' Although most everyone uses the term 'plane,' to include the Michael entity, I like the term 'field' rather than the more common description as a plane because it more accurately describes its nature. These are spatially collocated energy fields, separated into different frequency bands, each with its own material densities and structures. A field is a region in which each point within it is affected by a force, which is a good description of the universe. We can relate it to our own experience by comparing its structure to a radio tower transmitting its signal by radiating an electric field at a specific frequency and with a defined intensity. The tower's bandwidth or frequency spectrum is simply the range of its transmitted frequencies between the highest and lowest. The intensity of the field is determined by its power output. Multiple transmitters can successfully operate from the same tower and the resulting fields will overlap without causing interference provided their frequencies are far enough apart for the radios to differentiate them. The universe works in a similar way. The Tao creates energy fields that each cover a certain frequency spectrum or bandwidth along with different intensities. Our five outer senses perform the same function as a radio in our previous example in that we only detect the physical field, which has the lowest frequencies and highest material density of the seven fields.

Another reason I like the term 'field' rather than 'plane' is that it helps us realize that the world which we think of as solid, is not. The term 'plane' implies a false perception of something solid, whereas the earth only appears solid to our five senses. I cannot walk through a wall because my physical field cannot penetrate the wall's physical field. However, as far as my spirit is concerned, the wall is not a barrier at all. As such, I refer to the universe's 'planes' by using the term 'fields.'

Although we experience the physical universe through our five outer senses, we have another more subtle inner sense, which I will discuss later, that is capable of perceiving the other fields. However, generally we can only perceive the physical field because our brain is saturated with data from our outer senses. If we could quiet the outer senses and refocus the inner sense, as some psychics and mediums do, then we could experience the other fields because they are all around us. We have within us all the tools needed to experience the entire universe, but those tools are temporarily hidden from us as we are presently expected to focus on the physical field.

The entire universe, including all seven fields, is only a small part of the Tao. It could be viewed as the Tao's research and development arm. The Tao is using this universe to discover new aspects of itself.

The Inner Universe

If we could see the universe as it really is, we would think it was a very strange place. From our perspective, it consists of an outer portion that we perceive and an inner portion that we do not perceive. Every being that exists in the outer universe has its primary existence in the inner universe. We could not exist in the physical world if we did not have our major presence in the inner world. As amazing as the outer universe is, it pales in comparison to the inner universe.

Inner and Outer Universes[4]

As we discuss the workings of the universe we will be referring to the inner and outer universes. The outer universe is the enormous expanse we perceive here on earth, to include our solar system, our galaxy and all the galaxies and energy formations that our telescopes have detected. But even this is minuscule compared to what science has not detected, which is the inner universe. It is the intelligence within the inner universe that created our physical laws and meticulously selected the universal constants that make the physical universe possible. The workings of this unseen inner universe are what cause us to mistakenly attribute the synchronous events in our lives to chance, but nothing could be further from the truth.

Although the universe is a single psychological structure, our five outer senses only allow us to perceive a tiny portion of it. The inner universe is not only the source of the outer universe but influences its every action. To comprehend the nature of our reality, we need to understand the nature of the inner universe and some of its capabilities. The inner universe is true reality. It provides the resources and activities required for the outer universe to exist.

To get a sense of its magnitude and function, imagine yourselves wanting to experience a sporting event with your friend. First you both need to agree to go to a game, then you need to decide which game to go to, when, and how to get there. On the day of the event you decide that you will drive your car and pick up your friend on the way. You choose your clothes, gas up the car, drive to the stadium, park in the lot, pay the parking fee, and then buy a ticket. You find your seats, buy food and drinks at the game, cheer for your team, and then drive your car home, dropping off your friend on the way. Because you two are fairly sophisticated people, you have all the requisite capabilities to make this happen. At the end of the day you have experienced a sporting event.

But to be able to make this experience possible, many things needed to have already been accomplished. For example: 1) the sport needed to be created; 2) the league and teams needed to be organized; 3) the stadium needed to be built; 4) the players needed to be trained; 5) the uniforms needed to be designed, manufactured and purchased; 6) the car needed to be invented and built as did the roads and fuel; 7) the food and drinks needed to be sourced, processed, bought and shipped to the stadium; and 8) you and your friend needed to meet and create a relationship. I could go on and on but I am sure you see the enormity of the background effort required compared to the relatively trivial effort needed to attend the event. The activity that takes place behind the scenes that allows you to attend this single game greatly exceeds the effort required to actually attend the game.

Now if we think of going to the game as being proportionate in scale to the outer universe, then the inner universe would be proportionate to the activity that takes place behind the scenes to make your experience of going to the game possible. In short, our lives are full of experiences that on the surface seem pretty straightforward. What we don't see are forces behind these experiences that not only allow them to happen, but also make them happen.

The Fields

Seven
The Tao has created a number of universes before it created ours. Our universe is based on the number seven. The Michael entity said they were aware of twelve other universes based on different numbers. It is not clear why one number has an advantage over another, but as we discover the characteristics of our universe the number seven continually reoccurs. We get a glimpse of how seven works when we look at the musical scale where there are seven notes between each octave in the

acoustical range. Also we can perceive seven colors in the rainbow: indigo, violet, blue, green, yellow, orange and red. As we go through the various aspects of this book, you will notice that the number seven continually reoccurs.

Aspects of the Fields of Creation
There are seven fields of creation in our universe: physical, astral, causal, akashic, mental, messianic and buddhaic. Each field provides a unique energy experience. We exist for a certain duration in each field except for the akashic field, which has a different purpose.

The physical field that we live in is one of the seven primary fields of creation. As mentioned earlier, a field is a frequency band and the fields of creation are the primary frequency bands in this universe. The physical field is the lowest frequency band and the most dense of all the fields, and our body is composed of energy in the physical field. Because our consciousness identifies with our physical body, we think of ourselves as being part of the physical field. In fact, we are so tied to the concept of the physical field that we believe if our body dies, we will no longer exist, but this is a well-orchestrated illusion.

In order to have the experiences we want, identifying with our body is critical for the physical field to be effective. For example, fear and negative energy do not exist in the other six fields. A key reason to incarnate is to study the characteristics of the negative energy, which we do by experiencing it. We can only feel those emotions if we see our world as real and we identify with our body. Knowing that nothing could harm us would obscure the emotions.

After we are done incarnating onto earth, we will experience five of the six other primary fields, which we do one at a time. To accomplish this task our spirit has created multiple bodies for us. As such, we now exist in six fields simultaneously, but our physical consciousness only perceives one at a time.

The astral field is the frequency band closest to ours and is by far the easiest for us to interface with. All living things on earth have their primary or spiritual existence in the astral field when they are between earthly experiences. Its focus, like the physical field, is on emotional energy. One difference from the physical field is that negative energy can only be supported at the very lowest levels of the astral field. This is unlike the physical field, which can support negative energy on all levels.

We are able to experience the astral field between lives because we have an astral body, which perceives it. When we are in the astral field we are no longer limited by our physical body's five outer senses. For example, sight in the physical field is a limited version of seeing in the astral field. Not only are there colors that we cannot detect in the physical field but our astral vision is spherical and much clearer. In the higher frequency fields our perception is even more refined.

The Michael entity said:[5]

> When we die, at first the astral field will appear like a heightened and more beautiful version of the physical field. This will be created for us and with us to make us more comfortable in our transition. Some people see idealized and exaggerated versions of Greek and Roman temples, which many consider to be the height of human accomplishment. Those who like modern architecture may see their environment with brilliant skyscrapers and the types of architecture that could only be accomplished through the most modern engineering technologies. We will see heightened versions of gardens, lakes and forests. This gives us a chance to see how beautiful our lives in the physical field really were. Whereas dealing with the problems of life we may not have noticed it.

We have this experience for a while but when we are acclimated to the astral plane and don't need that experience anymore, we start to see the pure energy that the astral field is actually composed of. Because the astral field is also about emotional experiences, it is more fluid looking. There are vibrant colors, including colors that we are not capable of seeing in the physical field. It is awash in the deliciousness of beautiful emotion only a portion of which most human beings are able to feel when physical. It is all the good feelings of the physical field heightened and purified and uplifted and more. This is our medium, we are living in these feelings, and it is, especially when we first cross over, potentially quite euphoric. Then we get used to it but it is still a blessed thing.

The Michael entity went on to say that the astral field is where we plan future lives, which I will go into in depth later on. But even after we are done with our physical lives, we remain in the astral field until we are ready to move to the causal field.

The next higher frequency field is the causal field. This is where the Michael entity and the Seth entity presently reside. The spirits retain all their individuality but they join with the other individual spirits in their larger Entity. The causal environment is very formal, meaning that it has shapes and forms as opposed to the soft emotions of the astral field.

Seeing in an astral way is greatly expanded from seeing in a physical way but it is a reduced form of seeing compared to causal seeing. What we see is at a level of complexity that humans could not fathom unless they were an accomplished out-of-body traveler like Robert Monroe.[6] Apparently, he was able to temporarily raise his vibration to allow him to visit other fields. In the causal field everything is patterning. It is literally viewing thought forms in their natural state. It is a little bit like looking through a kaleidoscope in four or five dimensions. The Michael entity says that it is unfathomably beautiful. It is also huge as it takes up more space because it does not need to be condensed into solid form. One can go from perceiving the microcosm to the macrocosm instantly and see the connections between the two extremes.

In every field we have a dedicated body, which allows us to perceive that energy in a special way. Again, the causal field is collocated with the physical and astral fields. Spirits in each field perceive themselves as being solid, and they would perceive those in lower fields as being denser and those in higher fields as being less dense.

Life in the causal and higher fields is very different than in the physical field. For example, we don't need shelter, or clothes, or food to protect our body so we don't need a house like on earth. That said, we have a place amongst other beings where we gather, discuss, and deal with our responsibilities. This would be akin to our home on earth. We might say that our home is with the group we identify ourselves with as that is where we rest energetically. We raise our consciousness as we move through the levels of the different fields, which allows us to identify with higher levels of self. As such, where we reside in the spiritual world is not so much at our individual home but within our greater group.

Our spirit always remains individualized. But at the same time it is part of a much larger entity, which is composed of other like-minded spirits. This is a foreign concept that takes a bit of thought to even begin to digest. As we evolve, we slowly come to realize that our greater self is much more important than our individual self. As our spirit evolves this becomes clearer. The spirit starts to identify with this higher self because it learns that being part of a more advanced being with a greater purpose provides it with much more meaning and value.

The physical world is concerned with learning about emotions, which we experience individually. The Tao is about evolving as a united, massively capable entity where all information is shared for the sake of the whole. Our spirit understands this but after experimenting for thousands of years with discrete aspects of our individualized nature here on earth, we need to transform back to being an integrated member of the Tao. This takes place slowly as we rotate through the higher fields.

It is hard to get good information on the mental, messianic and buddhaic fields because the entities that are available for us to communicate with have not been there yet. By the time an entity reaches these higher fields they no longer have a focus on the physical field. They have moved too far away for it to concern them.

However, the Michael entity does offer some insights. He says that the mental field is an inside out version of the causal field. In the causal field we are observing a kaleidoscopic shape-shifting of thought forms around us. In the mental field we experience it more as being within us rather than around us. This is a difficult concept to understand on a human level. The messianic field looks like the reverse of the astral field as it becomes more internal. The buddhaic field is apparently the most interesting because it is the reverse of the physical field experienced in a purely energetic way. You might say that it is like being in the middle of a nuclear fission reaction. Our cycle eventually leads us back to the Tao where all the individual experiences unite with our spirit.

Akashic Field

The strangest and maybe the most talked about primary field of creation is the akashic field. Although it has been written about by thousands of people down through the ages, there is a lot of confusion with its nature and purpose. It is known as the place where the records of all mankind's history are recorded. This is true but the story is more complicated. The purpose of the akashic field is to record the wisdom that the Tao has discovered from its activities in the universe. It has no interest in what went wrong or the mistakes that were made along the way. It is only searching for Truth. Since truth is elusive and ever changing, so are the akashic records. They are living records and require a great deal of skill to access and understand.

Although all seven fields are collocated, the frequency and density of the akashic field's energy is between the causal and mental fields. This makes it much easier for beings existing in those two neighboring fields to access the records. The Seth entity says that all energy has an electric nature and the akashic field's electrical nature is such that it interpenetrates with every spark and spirit in all the above-mentioned fields throughout the entire universe. It does it in such a way that it records every thought, emotion and action experienced by everything. During our life, our akashic records are retained within the akashic's electrical elements that reside in our cells. There is also a corresponding akashic memory associated with every aspect of our consciousnesses. Effectively this amounts to every being in the universe having a parallel energy field.

The accumulated information creates a complete record of our existence in each life. When we die it is correlated with previous experiences in a refinement process. Eventually the data is sent to the akashic field for further refinement, integration and storage.

The refinement process in the akashic field is extremely complex because it requires an in-depth understanding of each experience. It is not just a matter of recording the raw data. Experience can be thought of as the raw material of the universe. The challenge is to integrate the information with similar experiences gathered from beings in diverse situations. As new information arrives, more clarity is achieved. Experiences are not single isolated events, as they appear to us. They are highly coordinated events between multiple spirits, entities, and even larger groups of beings. These experiences are continuations of multi-life investigations that spirits from points throughout the universe are investigating.

We do not see the correlation between events in our life and those in past or future lives. We do not see how issues are examined from many perspectives. It is the job of the higher-level identities and, ultimately, the akashic record keepers to refine the experiences and determine the best truth available to date.

Some of the more sophisticated investigations can stretch out over millions of years and with millions of spirits participating. Inputs arrive from a multitude of realities. The present status of any problem is what is in the records. As our lessons are assimilated and refined and we get better insight into the data, the records are updated. The errors and mistakes along the way are not retained. The akashic records only retain the refined portion of the lessons we have learned. The Tao does not care about the mistakes that occurred along the way.

The planning that is required for this level of pursuit of knowledge is unfathomable to us. We might think that our prelife plan is fairly complex, but it pales in comparison to the Tao's efforts. But our plan has meaning and is important because it is a subset of the Tao's search for truth. Our piece may be small in comparison to the bigger picture, but we are doing our part. We are important!

The records are detailed to a degree of noting when a tiny animal might have died a million years ago or when a flower bloomed in the Middle Ages. Everything is recorded but it is not all kept. Only the significant events are retained. But what you and I consider meaningful might be very different than what the Tao decides.

When a psychic looks into our akashic records they are simply looking into the records that we carry within us, which are not yet refined. Many of the things they find in our records and report back to us are not necessarily significant. The records that we carry with us are only a small piece of the story. However, when an entity like Michael looks into our records, he is looking into the akashic field.

The information in the akashic field is available to anyone able to understand it. The records are accessed by viewing them through a 'window.' When retrieving information, one does not actually go into the field, they just perceive it from the outside.

The akashic filing system is amazing. For example, in searching the records, one's thoughts determine the records that are retrieved. If we are standing on a piece of property, the records are biased towards that spot unless we direct them elsewhere. Our thoughts about that property would separate the focus of the records from the thousands, millions or even billions of years that property may have been in existence. One's thoughts are what determine which records are retrieved.

Events and issues can be viewed from multiple perspectives if desired. For example, if we wanted to review the creation of the United States Constitution, we could review it from each signer's perspective, and indeed, from the perspective of every person that influenced the event. As new information becomes available, records are altered and the non-relevant data is discarded.

If one was to research the records in an effort to find the truth about a particular issue, there is no guarantee the records contain the ultimate truth one might be seeking. The records are simply the latest refinement of 'truth' as it is known by the Tao. The Tao is using the universe to seek the ultimate truth, but there is no reason to believe that it has been found yet or that it is even possible to find it.

The records are very hard to understand so there is a great deal of training required. This is one of the primary activities of the entities existing in the causal and mental fields. However, it is fairly easy for a psychic to review the akashic records that are still in the physical field, which include those from our past lives. But after we cross over for the final time and our spirit sends the records of our experiences to the akashic field, it becomes more challenging to retrieve them. Identities existing in the causal and mental fields can most easily access the records because their frequencies are closest to them.

Metaphysical studies have revealed that we can look back at any point in history and watch it happen like it was a movie, which is a tough concept to understand. However, we are not necessarily looking at precisely how things actually happened, like an uncut homemade movie. Instead it is more like a professional documentary that only highlights the important information. We are simply looking at the present status of a compilation of events that may be still evolving. In the process of viewing we can see the important events that led to the present understanding.

Our society is struggling with issues like prejudice, slavery, biases, social fairness, hate, etc. These are age-old issues that the Tao has been studying since long before mankind or even the solar system came into existence. All we are doing is adding subtle insight to the issues, but if they were already resolved then we would not be dealing with them.

Perceiving the Fields

We describe the universe as divided into separate 'planes' or 'fields' to make it easier to understand. How we perceive the energy in those fields creates an illusion. There are many other material objects around us that are just as 'real' as our matter, but our senses are designed to not respond to them, so we simply do not perceive them. Arranging the perceived matter such that it makes sense to us is critical. If we are to perceive a tree or an ocean, the necessary matter needs to be organized in such a way that we perceive the objects in a meaningful way.

People who can tap into the astral field are considered to be psychic. Some people have more developed psychic abilities than others, such as mediums, channels, clairvoyants, and clairsentients, and are more sensitive to the frequencies of the astral field. These people will actually see, feel or somehow perceive spirits that exist in the astral field and even communicate with them. The spirits they sense may not appear to be as solid as we are because their bodies are not as dense, but they can be detected and often seen. Of course, we can occasionally see spirits when they materialize in our dreams, where they appear solid. But in our dreams we are in another reality, and the dream images that we create make them appear to be solid like us.

Late in my mother's life I was surprised to learn that she was clairsentient. In her case she was able to communicate with her spirit guides by posing a yes or no question. If the answer was yes she would immediately receive a tingling sensation beginning at the top of her head and going down to her feet. If the answer was no she would feel nothing. When I learned of this capability I decided to test her abilities. I would create questions for her to propose that I knew to be true and I knew my mother was convinced they were wrong. Time after time my mother was astonished at the answers she received. After I was convinced her capability was dependable, I had her create some questions. Although most of the answers came out the way I suspected, there was one that did not. My mother was an extremely devout born-again Christian so we had different views of the church's doctrines. Throughout her questioning, all her answers supported my expectations until she asked if Jesus was more important than I thought, and the answer was yes. At the time I felt that Jesus was very important, although the church had grossly distorted his message, so the answer took me by surprise. Years later I came across a discussion by the Seth entity that explained the difference. I have not added it in *Our Eternal Existence*, but if you are interested in Jesus's purpose and how it actually played out, it is documented in various places in the Seth literature, including *Seth Speaks* and *The Seth Material*.

Sub-level Fields

The seven primary fields of creation are spatially collocated. All seven fields surround us. This is why psychics are able to communicate with spirits in other fields so easily. They don't have to go anywhere. They just change their focus.

Each primary field is divided into seven sub-levels. The earth's field supports all seven sub-levels in the physical field simultaneously, but mankind only experiences the 4th level. The higher the level the less dense or more ephemeral it is. Apparently, some past human civilizations have lived on this earth in the fifth level, but they are no longer here. The Michael entity says it is possible for our civilization to move into the 5th level, but that will not happen for thousands of years, if ever. In order to move to a higher level the humanity's frequency of vibration would need to rise considerably. If it did, we would have a lighter and less dense body, which would be less likely to have diseases or be injured. It is highly unlikely we would ever move to the 6th or 7th level because we would not be able to have the physical experiences that we desire.

There are many metaphysical discussions proclaiming our immanent ascension into earth's higher sub-level fields. Mankind is indeed in the process of raising its vibrational level but this is not a short-term effort and the Seth entity says that this is unlikely to occur in our lifetime.

Cycles and Grand Cycles

Our spirit's permanent home is in the Tao. When a spirit is ready for a new experience in this universe, it is cast from the Tao simultaneously with many other spirits that have the same general maturity and interests. Each spirit has a plan for its evolution so before a spirit is cast from the Tao it decides what it wants to study and the experiences that will best further that quest. Existence is a series of adventures. We can be tentative and evolve more slowly or we can be daring and evolve more rapidly. It does not matter what challenges we choose, but if we chose a series of human lives on earth, we can be considered highly adventurous.

There are an unlimited number of areas into which a spirit can journey. The more experienced the spirit, the more sophisticated the opportunities it will have to choose from. For the most part, these experiences are first defined in broad terms and in general areas of exploration. They become more specific when we have had previous similar experiences and the spirit has a better understanding of what it is trying to achieve. For example, do we want to just be exposed to the concept of prejudice or do we want to have a more advanced experience like others being prejudiced against us?

Each field the spirit enters is considered a cycle. In other words, we cycle through the physical field, with many lives in each cycle. The Michael entity says that the physical field is the first cycle we are exposed to and it can take as little as 3-4000 years to complete or as long as >100,000 years. The more experienced the spirit the longer it is likely to stay in each field because the wiser spirits remain here to teach the younger ones, who often hurry off after they complete their minimum requirements.

Mankind has evolved to a point where our journey away from the Tao involves extended periods of time in six of the seven fields in the universe. Eventually this particular journey will end and the spirit will return to the Tao. The Michael entity refers to the journey between the time a spirit is initially cast from the Tao, travels through the six fields in the universe, and then returns to the Tao as a Grand Cycle. For humans these might last for over a half million earth years. It is probable that a spirit will have 5, 10 or even 20 Grand Cycles as a sentient soul before deciding to pursue other endeavors. In order to expand its experiences, it is unlikely that a spirit would have multiple Grand Cycles on a single planet. Spirits are looking for diverse experiences so the more diverse the cultures and life forms it is exposed to, the more it would learn.

Creation of the Universe

Many of these concepts are very different from what mainstream science teaches. Science is in its infancy. It is, at best, only a few hundred years old. What science says in a million years will be very different than what it says today. It is important to keep this in mind as we search for a better understanding of reality.

Science has based its core assumptions on the concept that our space-time reality, which we see around us, remains uniform to the farthest extent of the universe. So when our telescopes look at distant galaxies, we assume that our space-time reality extends all the way to that galaxy. If this is not accurate, as the Seth entity contends, then the core assumptions of science are creating serious errors in their theories.

Although scientists working within their field realize that their theories are just that, theories, the media has a tendency to portray them to the public as proven facts. I think it might help some of the less technical readers if they realized just how unsubstantiated some of the scientific theories really are. Because this book is based on a spiritual reality that is so different than what we have been exposed to by science, it is worth taking a quick look at a commonly accepted scientific theory that contradicts this material to see what it is based on.

Big Bang Theory

The Big Bang Theory supposedly describes the creation of the universe. Until the early 20th century scientists generally believed the universe was static and all the stars were in fixed positions. The Big Bang Theory is based on astronomer Edwin Hubble's observation in 1929 that all the galaxies in the universe are moving away from each other. The obvious assumption, looking back in time, is that all the galaxies must have had a common starting point. This implies that a single explosion caused our universe. Unfortunately for this theory, in 1998 scientists Saul Perlmutter, Nick Suntzeff and Brian Schmidt discovered that not only was the universe expanding, but that expansion was accelerating. The simple explosion of the mythical "Big Bang" is not enough to explain why the universe's expansion is accelerating. In response, scientists' only hope of salvaging this theory was to propose that another force, in this case they assumed it is gravity, is causing this acceleration by pulling the universe apart. To add some level of credence to this proposition scientists needed to identify enough mass and energy to make their algorithms comply with their observations. Unfortunately their calculations showed that in order to make their theory work, 95% of the mass and energy of the universe is missing. That is a lot! In a clever recovery mode, they are now saying 95% of the universe is 'dark' so we cannot see it. Thus, science is hunting for all this dark energy and dark matter. Normally a discovery like this would be a death blow to any theory, but because scientists insist on a physical cause for the universe, they have no other explanation for its creation. Instead of saying they simply do not know, they created dark energy and dark matter.

There are numerous other issues with the Big Bang Theory. The magnitude of the energy required to create and maintain the universe is virtually infinite, so how all this matter/energy became condensed into a tiny spot, called a singularity, is totally unexplainable, and I maintain it always will be because it did not happen. But science ignores this problem, and because it has no rationale as to how it could have happened, it implicitly assumes a miracle took place. The fact that science is willing to simply overlook this problem should make one highly skeptical of the Big Bang Theory in the first place.

However, from my perspective the most improbable concept embedded in the Big Bang Theory is that inanimate matter, which by science's definition has no intelligence in and of itself, was able to come together and create the universe and everything in it in the first place. Yet when these inanimate or 'dumb' particles get together and form brains and neural networks, consciousness arises. The concept of 'dumb matter' is a paradigm that is so fundamental to science that they cannot see the absurdity in it. If dumb matter can create intelligence that would surely be a miracle, and this miracle would need to reoccur in every human birth. However, I am not siding with the Abrahamic religions, which assert that God creates a new spirit at every birth, which makes no sense either. The answers lie elsewhere.

For those who have not worked in the field or questioned the validity of some of the 'scientific facts,' it might surprise you how much of science is driven by the politics within the halls of our prominent educational institutions rather than the cold hard facts it professes to be based on.

Chapter 3

Consciousness

You are what you think about.
Buddha

Key Concept: Conscious energy is the source of everything in the universe.

Science tells us that everything in existence is physical, and all physical objects are composed of atoms. Metaphysics goes a step further and says that the building blocks of atoms are self-aware energy, which is the vitality mentioned in Chapter 1. Whether it is a tiny spark or a skyscraper, every identity is made of the same conscious energy. The fact that spiritual energy is self-aware is a difficult concept to get our minds around. An atom, a leaf, a car, and the Tao Itself are all made from the same energy. Vitality is the only substance in existence, so spirits are a sophisticated form of vitality.

Trying to understand the amazing nature of spirits is a challenge. Since consciousness is a spirit's most important and critical attribute, the Seth entity often refers to a spirit as a consciousness. I follow that approach because I think it is easier to understand some of our more subtle and startling characteristics when we talk about them in terms of consciousness. However, to be completely accurate, we are not a consciousness. We are a spirit that is conscious.

Nature Is Conscious

Most people will agree that animals are conscious, at least the higher-level ones. But consciousness does not stop with the animal kingdom. Plants are conscious as well.

48

Pamela Montgomery, who was a guest on my radio show, wrote a book titled *Plant Spirit Healing* in which she documented her many experiences working and communicating with plants. She found that plants have the following characteristics: individual personalities; feelings; an ability to heal us; an ability to actively forage for scarce resources; use of sophisticated cost benefit analysis; the ability to take defined actions; a perception of themselves; use of intricate signaling systems; and the ability to analyze light, gravity, water, vibrations, chemicals, temperature, sound, and predators. They can do these things because they are spirits just like us. They are not quite as aware as animals but they are not far behind.

Numerous studies have shown that plants respond to human emotions. Love causes them to be healthier and more vibrant, and hate and poor treatment causes them to recoil and shrivel up and die. Meditative and classical music has been shown to enhance plant growth, while loud hard rock retards it. We say some people have a 'green thumb' while other people cannot grow grass. The difference is that some people simply care more about their plants than other people do. It has been shown that prayer and meditation focused on specific plants can help them thrive. Not only are plants conscious but they can communicate with each other, feel pain, search for water, and can do about everything else an animal can do except uproot themselves and walk away. There have been literally hundreds of studies that show the responsiveness of plants to human and other animal actions and emotions. If you want to investigate the phenomena the Internet is full of such examples so I will not repeat them here.

However, consciousness does not stop at the plant level. Minerals, cells, the wind, and oceans are conscious as well. As I mentioned earlier, everything in existence is conscious, at least to some extent. It is hard enough to conceive that minerals and plants are conscious, but it is a real stretch for us to believe that our cars and our furniture and our houses are conscious.

But everything in existence originates from a single source of vitality. If one thing is conscious then everything must be conscious. There is no dividing line. Unconscious matter could never form conscious identities. The neurons in our brain do not create consciousness. If vitality was not conscious then nothing would be conscious.

You and I, single celled animals, plants, and rocks are all just various forms of vitality. Unconscious objects do not exist. If vitality was inanimate, all the forms it created would be inanimate as well. Of course, if the vitality was not conscious, it could not create any of these forms in the first place. Consciousness is the amazing attribute of vitality that allows everything to exist.

Consciousness Units

The smallest form of vitality that can be activated is what the Seth entity calls a consciousness unit or "CU." They are so tiny that it would take millions of them to form an object the size of an atom. These are the building blocks of the Tao. Since they are self-aware and everything in existence is comprised of CUs, then everything in existence is self-aware or conscious. CUs are not mini spirits, however, they are spirit 'stuff.'

One of the most important aspect of CUs is their immortality. Once they are activated, they never go out of existence. They will transform themselves an unlimited number of times, but they never cease to exist.

Another key aspect of a CU is its unpredictability. It can do anything it desires, which is the source of our free will. This also gives it the ability to form an infinite variety of configurations.

We could never see a CU but if we could it would rarely be found in isolation. It is difficult for a tiny CU to individually create a significant experience for itself because its abilities are so limited. Therefore, it has a propensity to join other CUs to form larger and more capable identities. As the CU evolves it will always have more sophisticated experiences when working as a part of a larger creation. Even though a CU views itself as part of a larger group, it always retains its original identity.

No matter what experiences it has and what organizations it joins, it always remembers its previous experiences. It grows as it gains knowledge, but no matter how large it becomes, it can never be broken into smaller parts.

Gestalt

Consciousness is a very strange substance. Individual CUs are amazing in their own right, but the real magic is in their ability to form larger identities.

A gestalt is an organization whose whole is greater than the sum of its parts. The nature of consciousness is such that when CUs combine, they form gestalts. When two CUs join together their combined consciousnesses form a new consciousness that is greater than the sum of the original two. However, the original conscious units never lose their individual self-awareness. They each learn from the combined identity and they always retain the individual knowledge they learn from their experiences.

The combination of each resulting consciousness is a more capable gestalt. The combined consciousness actually has an awareness of its gestalt nature. It sees itself as the larger entity it has become. The consequences of this phenomenon change the entire concept of who and what we are.

When two CUs combine, they do not merge together and become a single larger CU. They simply function as a larger identity, each providing their own unique capability to the union, but still retaining their individuality. They both gain wisdom from their joint experiences, and when they separate, they retain the first-hand knowledge they gained from their combined experiences. Also, they always retain a communication with the other CUs in any gestalt that they previously were a part of.

When a new CU or gestalt replaces an existing one, it attains the memories of the previous identity in regards to the history of that organization. For example, if an original identity was a cell that was injured in a mishap, the replacing cell will gain the memory of that injury. However, it does not gain the depth of knowledge or understanding that the previous identity learned from that injury. The identity that first had the experience will always have a deeper knowledge than the newly arriving identity, which only has vicarious knowledge. Whereas the replacement cell might know the incident occurred and the result of the injury, but it will not have all the detailed knowledge that was gained by the original cell while the injury was occurring.

Like us, all CUs only gain true wisdom from first-hand experiences. We have access to other knowledge but our understanding is on a more superficial basis. The difference would be akin to reading about an event versus actually experiencing it.

Using a physical object as an example, the combining process begins at the subatomic level and grows into the molecular and cellular levels. It continues forming objects at higher and more sophisticated levels like an organ and a body. A new consciousness is created at every combination and that consciousness is an independent identity in its own right. It has its own attitudes, expectations, desires and creativities. For example, an organ like a heart has its own consciousness. It knows its role in the body and guides all the smaller gestalts within the heart. It works with the other organ gestalts in the body as well as the overall body gestalt. Although it is dependent on the other identities of the body for its experiences, the other identities are also dependent on it. All gestalts work together for the good of the whole because cooperation gives them the best chance to have significant experiences. Of course, each gestalt within a body will have different experiences because they have different roles.

The Web of Consciousness

No spirit is a single highly developed CU. It is a hierarchy of gestalts consisting of limitless numbers of CUs. Each CU has a propensity to be part of an identity that can have more significant and complex experiences than it could on its own. By the time an identity reaches a spirit's level of evolution, the gestalts within it will have formed a level of 'permanency.' CUs form alliances with other CUs creating gestalts whose components have similar interests. This forms identities that stay together for longer periods. Initially they move around and try different combinations, but eventually they establish a relationship with similar-minded gestalts that creates an organization that stays together and forms a somewhat permanent structure. These gestalts are inclined to remain with the spirit for long durations and multiple experiences. Individual CUs and gestalts are free to leave the identity, but: 1) there are enough CUs in a spiritual identity that if one or more did depart, which over time is inevitable, it has accumulated enough energy that any departure would have a minimal impact on its nature or capability; and 2) gestalts are seeking relevance, and the more advanced the spirit, the more likely the gestalts will want to remain with it.

Therefore, a spirit can be thought of as a combination of a great number of gestalts, each performing specialized tasks, with a single gestalt managing the overall activity of the identity. CUs are generalized in that they are capable of performing many tasks. They are only temporarily specialized when they are focused on a specific task for the benefit of the greater organization.

Gestalts don't stop at the spirit level. A spirit is part of what we can call a greater spirit. Even though the spirit is independent of its greater spirit, it provides a particular function for the greater spirit that it is uniquely capable of doing. No matter where they each go and what reality they experience, there will always be a link between them.

The concept that there is always a greater spirit continues up the evolutionary ladder until it reaches the Tao itself. Every spirit is connected to a higher-level spirit, as well as spirits it has worked closely with in the past. This creates a web of consciousness where everything is tied together.

It helps to visualize this web as if it existed in our three-dimensional space and formed a pyramid. The highest levels of the pyramid contain the most advanced spirits, with the Tao being at the pinnacle. Within this pyramid, every spirit is connected to a multitude of other spirits, some at higher levels, some lower and some lateral. The communication between these spirits is via telepathy, so the result is effectively a web of consciousness.

In our example, the nodes within the web are the spirits and the connecting threads are the communication links. The lower we go in the pyramid, the less complex the spiritual nodes become, but the format remains the same. If we peered far enough into the web, eventually we would find our individual spirits. We could then go into our spirit where we would find the multitude of gestalts comprising our spirit. We could continue this process until every spirit, spark and CU is identified, as every identity is included in the web. The Tao is distributed amongst all beings and over all universes, and yet it is a single consciousness.

It is the web's all-inclusiveness that ties us together within the Tao and makes us part of a single giant gestalt entity. What affects one of us affects us all, even if only in some minute way. It is said that any great disturbance here on earth is felt to some extent everywhere in the universe. Wars, famines, nuclear bombs and other great psychological disturbances are felt far beyond our solar system. Is it any wonder that the more highly developed civilizations within our galaxy want to see what we are doing? They have come here in the past, they are here now, they will be with us in the future, and they are surely not looking for trouble. If anything, they may be trying to prevent it.

The creation of spirits and their inner nature is highly complex so I will deal with it in more detail in later chapters.

Duality in Nature

Quantum physics has detected the dual nature of both matter and light where they function simultaneously as a particle and a wave. The discrete particles of matter are called electrons, protons, etc. As matter moves it displays dual wave-particle properties, which have been demonstrated in numerous electron beam laboratory diffraction experiments. Light acts the same way. The wave nature of light is obvious but we are less familiar with the discrete nature of light, packets which are known as photons. Since matter and light are made of conscious energy, it stands to reason that consciousness would also have a dual nature, and it does. In fact, matter and light have dual natures because consciousness does, not the other way around.

Consciousness can function as an individual entity, like you and I seem to do, or as a wave where it is distributed over a wide area. It is hard for us to understand the wave nature of particles, and it is even harder for us to understand the wave nature of consciousness. It is the nature of our reality and how we experience the universe that makes both these concepts so difficult. However, even when a consciousness or a particle functions as a wave, it never loses its individuality.

A way to look at our wave-like nature is that our consciousness is not a single highly developed CU, as we might suspect, but a gestalt of immense proportions. Consciousness is not located just in our brain, as we usually think of it, but distributed throughout our body. However, it is actually far greater than this. Our consciousness is also distributed throughout our mind, which is in the psychological realm or inner universe. When we realize that our consciousness is also part of our spirit and the many greater spirits we are part of, plus all the various gestalts our CUs have been associated with during the eons that they have been in existence, we can see how our consciousness is ubiquitous. It is hard to tell where one consciousness or spirit ends and another begins. There are no actual divisions of identities or consciousnesses.

Science tells us that everything in existence is energy, but they do not tell us that the true nature of energy is spiritual 'stuff.' It forms both the physical objects we are familiar with and the spiritual entities we are not as familiar with. Energy and consciousness are inseparable.

Aspects of Consciousness

Vitality or consciousness is a difficult concept to visualize. A spirit's consciousness has a number of inherent attributes that are not obvious. However, these characteristics impact our lives in significant and often subtle ways. Here are a few aspects of consciousness that are counterintuitive.

Self-Aware Structures

As mentioned earlier, everything in existence is conscious. Believing this at first seems like an outrageous concept because we think of consciousness as such a human characteristic. It is just hard to believe the desk I am sitting at has its own awareness. We are used to only identifying consciousness when it reaches a more developed state. We don't recognize it in its early stages. Consciousness evolves from a very basic state, and in its early stages it has a propensity to manifest as objects, which in our physical field are physical structures. However, just because a desk is a conscious psychological structure does not mean that it is a 'personalized' psychological structure. My desk is not a miniature person. It does not have free will. It is simply self-aware. It is an aware object, but not an enduring spiritual entity. The individual CUs in my desk are immortal and will someday join spirits of their own, but the objects they form are temporal. They are not spirits nor will they ever be. The desk gestalt and its smaller gestalts like the drawers and pull handles are not ready to accept responsibility for their decisions yet. They are still just learning what it is like to have different experiences. Eventually pattern that forms the desk will dissipate and the desk will only remain a memory of those that interfaced with it.

Infinite Mobility

Infinite mobility means that our consciousness or spirit can instantaneously go anywhere at any time. By simply thinking that we want to go someplace makes it happen instantly. It is our body and the physical field we are in that restricts our mobility. Although this is not apparent in our reality, people who are adept at having out-of-body experiences can travel around the world, around the solar system, or even around the galaxy virtually instantaneously.

Cooperation

Spirits are motivated to assist each other at all times. They have no competitive desire to outshine others because they realize that they are part of a whole. What is good for others is good for them.

Our culture has created a competitive world and we have assumed those characteristics also apply to nature. The evolutionist's "Survival of the Fittest" theory seems to be the order of the day, and the animal kingdom seems to reinforce this concept. But if this were really true, the universe could never exist. We see animals using each other for food, and we think 'dog-eat-dog,' but it is only the bodies of the animals that are sacrificed and die. We don't see the victim's spark hopping out of the body at the moment of death and scampering off to find another body. All we see are the hunter and prey at work, yet both the predator and victim learn from the experience.

If it were not for the innate desire of individual CUs to cooperate with each other, then gestalts could never be formed. Without gestalts, even the Tao would not exist. Our body is a gestalt made of CUs working together for a common good. Spirits could not exist if all the elements were not cooperating to support the whole. A spirit is in an endless cycle of forming symbiotic relationships, having experiences with other like-minded spirits, and then dispersing. It is an endless evolutionary cycle of birth, learning, and death only to be 'reborn' again, all the wiser.

Our culture has created this false sense of competition. We train our children to compete from an early age so they can succeed in our materialistic society, but it is not their inherent nature.

Creativity

Consciousness is endlessly creative and it is on display wherever we look. Nature has created an endless array of patterns for our curiosity and entertainment. We in turn have done the same in our culture.

Vitality's continuous process of transforming itself into something new and different is apparent even within ourselves. Every experience and every thought changes us in a real way. Our busy lives cause us to overlook these changes but they are readily apparent if we stop and look back on our life. We constantly change our surroundings, our ideas, our goals, and our relationships. In fact, if we are not creating something new in our lives we get bored.

Every organism's consciousness plays a key role in forming its own structure. From the smallest CU to the Tao Itself, new things are continuously being formed. Consciousness manifests endless patterns while simultaneously embedding itself into them. The purpose of spirit is to gain wisdom and become more significant. It uses its innate unlimited creativity to advance the process.

Distribution of Intelligence

We are used to believing that intelligence is localized in the human brain. But with our body consisting of intelligent gestalt organs, and those organs consisting of intelligent gestalt cells, we see that our intelligence is distributed throughout our body. It is also distributed in all elements of nature. With everything being conscious, it becomes apparent that intelligence is distributed throughout the universe. It is this distribution of consciousness that allows the universe to exist and function. Each plant, each leaf, each cell is aware of itself and its immediate purpose. Everything knows what it is doing, at least to some degree.

Specialization

The quantity of information available to us is astounding. As consciousness evolves, it is exposed to many new ideas. Some it finds more interesting than others. Because it has free will, it is able to follow its desires. Over time a continual emphasis in specific areas creates an expertise in that field of knowledge. Every spirit has special expertise that it has cultivated.

When higher-level gestalts are created, larger and more sophisticated tasks are planned, which require more specialization. These identities are created by handpicking specific skills and assembling them in purposefully-created gestalts. We think of ourselves as being born, which implies a 'potluck' creation of capabilities. It is more accurate to think of ourselves as creations for particular purposes. Gestalts are created with a purpose, and you and I are not exceptions. That makes us special.

Focus

Probably the easiest way to think about consciousness is by where it focuses its attention. We are used to only focusing on one thing at a time, but that is because our thoughts go through our brain, which views the world serially. However, our consciousness consists of numberless CUs and gestalts. Each is capable of focusing on different tasks. We are 'aware of' or 'conscious of' something when we focus on it. For example, we cycle through the fields of the universe by changing our focus. When we do this we don't necessarily go anywhere, we just raise our vibration, which allows us to focus in other areas.

In later chapters we will use the capability of multiple focuses to help explain the workings of our consciousness.

Awareness and Aliveness

In order to better understand our nature we need to start viewing the world differently. Understanding the difference between awareness and aliveness is a good place to begin.

Awareness

The level of awareness is a critical measure of a spirit's stage of evolution. Being aware of one's surroundings in an atom or tree is one thing but being aware of everything in the universe and how it operates is something completely different. One of the key measures of evolution is the magnitude and completeness of an identity's awareness. Throughout the Tao there are an infinite number of spiritual levels as no two consciousnesses are the same. Obviously, the consciousness of an atom is not as aware as the consciousness of a person, and the consciousness of a person is not as aware as the consciousness of an entity that oversees a galaxy. But they are all aware of their surroundings and their function in the realm in which they reside.

Aliveness

Everything that exists is self-aware and therefore alive. We think of aliveness as a trait of animals and maybe plants, but certainly not rocks or planets or man-made objects like houses and cars. Since everything is conscious, consciousness and aliveness go hand in hand. As we expand our consciousness, we become more aware of ourselves and our role in the universe. As we have more experiences, the capabilities of our spiritual attributes like creativity, curiosity, and intelligence expand and we could say we become more 'alive.'

All identities are alive but when a CU is first created its abilities are mostly dormant. Its capabilities are 'potentials' rather than 'actuals' because it has no experiences to expand its understanding. After traveling throughout the universe experiencing different realities, it becomes more conscious and more 'alive.' Both a mineral and a person are alive, but the degree of aliveness is very different. It helps to stop thinking of aliveness as something that either is or isn't and think of it as something we are all growing into. 'Aliveness' increases as our awareness expands. Consciousness is always becoming more alive.

Science sees space as the next and last frontier, but the true frontier is consciousness. We will never learn to conquer the challenges of space if we don't first learn to conquer the challenges of our mind. Our civilization will need to look within itself and learn about our own reality before the Tao will allow us to interface with its other creations.

Spiritual Structure
The structure of consciousness is confusing so let me try to lay out a highly simplified explanation using a vertical sequence. The Tao is the ultimate single entity or what we consider All That Is or Unity. Immediately below it in regards to evolutionary achievement are what we can consider Greater Spirit A. There are a huge number of these entities and their wisdom is staggering. Each Greater Spirit A is unique but we will categorize them by where they stand in relationship with the Tao. Within each Greater Spirit A there are a huge number of also extremely wise entities that we will call a Greater Spirit B. Each is a subset and the creation of a Greater Spirit A. They are each a small part of a Greater Spirit A. The sum of the Greater Spirit Bs make up a Greater Spirit A, but because they are gestalts, Greater Spirit A is actually greater than the sum of all the Greater Spirit Bs within it.

This process continues down to Greater Spirit C, D, etc. until it reaches our spirit as shown in Figure 1.

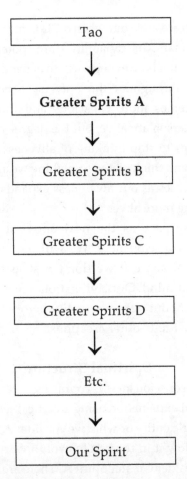

Figure 1: Spiritual Hierarchy

The Greater Spirits only differ from each other and our spirit by their level of evolution. As each entity evolves, it makes its greater entity greater as well.

If We Are a Gestalt, What Are We?

We are used to thinking of ourself as our well-defined body. But a spirit has very different characteristics, capabilities, and desires than a body. Our misconceived perception is no accident and is a subject we will be dealing with throughout the book.

But the initial process of seeing ourselves differently can be very disconcerting until we get a broader appreciation of our fantastic nature.

Understanding consciousness and the implications of being a spiritual gestalt requires a reevaluation of the concept of 'I.' We are used to perceiving ourselves as an individual identity comprised of 'solid' physical matter separate from everything else. Science contradicts that image when it tells us our body is mostly empty space and what is not empty is energy of some sort, but the implication of this description doesn't really sink in. We see ourselves as separate from nature and the objects around us. This contributes to why death is such a challenging concept for us. It appears that when the body goes away, we do as well. But spirit does not function that way. At death all we lose is the CUs that made up our body, not the higher-level consciousness that forms our personality. We even retain a memory of the knowledge those departing CUs gained during our life.

Consciousness has three characteristics that shape its behavior. 1) It has a propensity to combine with other consciousnesses to form more sophisticated structures than its own. 2) It occasionally moves from one identity to another. 3) It always retains its original identity and individual memories of its past experiences, even when it is identifying as part of another structure.

One way to look at our gestalt nature is to compare ourselves to the Boston Pops Orchestra, where each musician would be like a CU. Musicians come and go but the organization still considers itself the Boston Pops. Now let's assume that some of the same musicians also play in the Boston Philharmonic Orchestra when they are not participating with the Boston Pops. The Boston Philharmonic organization considers itself the Boston Philharmonic even though some of its musicians also belong to the Boston Pops and vice versa. But where does one start and the other stop? They simply have overlapping parts that they agree to loan each other when the need arises. The spiritual world interchanges its energy just like orchestras might borrow musicians.

The web-like nature of consciousness is not apparent in our lives because our individuality takes precedent in this life. Yet we consider it natural to wear many hats in life and participate in many experiences and belong to many organizations. When we are participating in family life, we might consider ourselves a parent or child. When we are playing on a team, we consider ourselves a member of it. Our spiritual energies are similar. When they are part of myself, they call themself by my name. When they are part of another identity, they use that identity's name. This is a natural outcome of our web-like nature.

We will go through the various aspects of being a spirit in a human form throughout the book. It is not surprising that our eternal nature is very different from our apparent mortal nature. However, it is surprising that who and what we are is even more amazing than the universe we exist in.

Section II

The Human Condition

Chapter 4

Essence, Soul and Personality

Knowing others is intelligence; knowing yourself is true wisdom.
Lao Tse

Key Concept: We are each a highly capable spirit investigating a small portion of our being.

Our true self is an incredibly capable spirit, of which we know and understand very little. Conscious energy has some pretty strange characteristics, but they become really bizarre when we see how they apply to us. What we experience and feel is only a tiny portion of our true self. Understanding who we are requires a completely different view of what it means to be human. It is a great story. We are amazing beings, but our true nature is so different than what we understand that it requires a whole new perspective.

Spirit
The process in which a spirit enters the universe and creates a human being is explained in great detail by Shepherd Hoodwin in his book *Journey of Your Soul*, so I will only describe it briefly here.

In order to experience the universe, a spirit leaves its permanent home in the Tao and slowly travels through the various fields of creation. The spirit gains experiences along the way and eventually returns to the Tao, which completes the Grand Cycle that we discussed earlier. This is a lengthy, intricate and highly coordinated adventure that varies greatly in detail depending on the desires and evolution of the spirit. Even though every step of the way is well planned, it allows for great freedom of choice.

The universe is composed of seven 'fields of creation,' which are all illusions of some sort. The spirit cannot experience a field directly because its inner sense would see through the illusion and it would be unable to have the intended experiences. It needs a way to 'sense' or feel the illusion. So a spirit creates an appropriate 'vehicle' or body for each field it plans to experience. For example, our physical body is the vehicle that our spirit creates that allows it to perceive or sense the physical field. This is just one of several vehicles that will be required for the entire Grand Cycle. Several steps need to be taken in order to create the various vehicles.

Essence

When a spirit is cast from the Tao, it creates what the Michael entity calls an 'essence,' which is the vehicle the spirit uses to resonate with the mental, messianic and buddhaic fields. These energies 'bias'[7] or focus how the essence perceives its experiences. The biasing process begins when the essence first leaves the Tao and is grouped into a 'cadence' of seven essences. Each position in the cadence provides the essence with specific energies that will give it the traits or biases the spirit has chosen.

Each cadence is then formed into a 'greater cadence,' with seven cadences per greater cadence. These 49 essences within a 'greater cadence become part of an 'entity' with ~1000 essences per entity. Seven entities make up a 'cadre,' which has ~7000 essences, and it continues on up from there. Each position within each grouping provides the essence with certain biases. In other words, the position of the essence in the cadence, the position of the cadence in the greater cadence, the position of the greater cadence in the entity, and the position of the entity in the cadre, all cause different biases or energies to be added to the essence. As a result, any identity the essence creates will have similar energies to those within itself. The effect is that the identities that the essence creates will view their experiences in a similar way.

The importance of this cannot be overstated because it focuses the spirit's future creations in a particular way. Each consciousness is free to evolve as it chooses, but by biasing the identity in a specific way, it gives the spirit influence, although not control, over the experiences it will have.

The essence is biased through the casting process in several ways. For example, each position in the cadence provides the essence with one of seven 'roles': king, warrior, priest, servant, sage, artisan or scholar. These roles are not equivalent to the vocations we normally think of, but are more like an archetypical perspective in which the essence will view the world. For example, an essence with a king bias would not necessarily be a king, but instead would view the world from a big picture perspective. He/she would want to create mastery over whatever issues were encountered. Likewise, a sage would search for insight; an artisan would seek originality; a priest would find the higher good; a server would assist others; a warrior would look for a challenge; and a scholar would want knowledge. The roles are meant to allow the spirit's 'vehicles,' like us, to view its experiences from different perspectives during each Grand Cycle.

The essence also selects a male/female ratio, which will influence how it addresses problems. It selects a frequency ratio of vibration, which will determine the rate of action it will use when addressing problems. It chooses task companions and essence twins, which will assist in dealing with issues.

Since the essence biases remain constant throughout the entire Grand Cycle, the spirit needs to carefully plan the essence biasing process before it leaves the Tao. The essence can be thought of as the lower or more limited part of the spirit. The biases intentionally focus the essence, which limits their perspective. The essence then creates a vehicle with astral and causal bodies, which we think of as our soul, and it can be viewed as the lower or more limited part of the essence.

Soul

The soul has the responsibility of executing the spirit's desired experiences in the physical field. It develops the detailed plans for the physical experiences, creates the physical beings, which for humans are known as personalities, monitors the physical experiences, and manages the entire incarnation process.

The soul continues to create personalities until it decides it has accomplished everything it can incarnating on earth. It then joins the other souls in the entity and they jointly wait for all the souls in the entity to complete their earth experiences.

After every soul in the entity has finished reincarnating, they gather together in the astral field and transfer as a group to the causal field. As they continue to transition through the higher fields they are reformed into ever larger groups. During the Grand Cycle the soul rejoins the essence and eventually the essence rejoins the spirit. After the spirit travels through the upper fields of creation, it returns to the Tao. The acquired experiences are integrated back into the spirit when it returns to the Tao, making the spirit more knowledgeable. However, the souls and their creations, like you and me, always retain their individuality. No consciousness ever goes out of existence or is ever absorbed by another consciousness. They just join together in a gestalt.

Human (Sentient) Souls

To recap, the soul is the spirit's vehicle that allows it to interface with the reality that it wants to experience. Since each reality can be experienced in multiple ways, the spirit needs to decide: 1) which reality it wants to experience; and 2) how it wants to experience it. These two factors are the main considerations for the characteristics of the vehicles the soul creates. The more evolved the spirit, the more advanced its soul will be and the more advanced the resulting personalities will be.

Each type of soul has a particular purpose. Humans have what the Michael entity calls sentient souls, which are highly complex compared to animal and other lower level souls. The human spirit has reached a level where it can reason logically and can accept responsibility for its own decisions. In our case, this allows us to have a wide range of complicated experiences and helps us investigate the subtle emotional nuances of our nature.

Sentient souls do not need to be mammals like us, let alone bipeds. Even on earth the cetaceans (whales and dolphins) have sentient souls, but we don't reincarnate back and forth between species. Once we choose a species we generally remain with it for the complete Grand Cycle. The universe has many different types of beings inhabiting sentient souls. This includes reptilian, plantlike, fishlike, and many we would not even recognize. Similarities to the many creatures in the original *Star Wars* bar scene probably exist somewhere in the universe, although maybe they are not quite as hostile. Some planets have only one type of sentient life while others have many types that usually interface intelligently and generally get along with each other.

Sentient Incarnation Process
The soul manages the incarnation process here on earth. It uses portions of its own gestalt energies to form its many vehicles. Energies focused on the physical field require an immense amount of support so the soul only incarnates a very small portion of its energies into the physical field. It decides which of its energies will be focused on the physical field and which will remain in the inner universe and support the physically focused energy.

The sentient soul's creations are known as personalities. A soul's energies that it uses to create these identities come from either the spirit/essence or energy that it has gathered from its other incarnations in this Grand Cycle. A sentient soul is capable of creating personalities that are logical, creative, emotional and attuned to the specific frequencies of the reality in which it will exist.

A sentient life is focused on feelings or emotions, so it is particularly appropriate for a human life on earth. Emotions are a challenging area to understand both for their complexity and variety. Experiences can be very intense, yet at the same time very rewarding. They encompass a wide range of feelings and trigger endless reactions, both within us and in others.

Because sentient life is so complicated, spirits require multiple Grand Cycles through the universe to have all the experiences they desire. Once our spirit decides to follow a sentient path, for all practical purposes we are committing ourselves to a set of 5 or 10 or even 20 or maybe even many more Grand Cycles. Sentient lives are interesting but very difficult so many spirits avoid them for that reason. But for the ones who dare, the growth is very rapid and rewarding. Eventually our spirit will finish creating sentient souls and try something even more challenging.

Personalities

A personality is the creation of a soul that can directly experience the illusion of the physical field. The soul is a gestalt, which means it is made up of many discrete energy packets. Because of this, the soul is able to use a portion of its own energy to create the personality. Personalities are what we consider to be 'us' because they contain the only portion of the soul that our conscious self is aware of during our life. But the soul could also be considered the real us as could the spirit.

The soul manifests a three-dimensional projection of its multidimensional self into the physical field. We can think of the personality as a partial representation of the soul in this reality. The portion of the soul manifested in the physical field consists of the physical body and the portions or 'compartments' of our soul that we think of as our 'conscious mind.' The 'conscious mind' is a newly formed assembly of energies that we will discuss in more detail in Chapter 5, The Human Psyche.

The soul can only give the new personality energies it has already obtained. A more developed spirit will create a more capable soul, which in turn creates a more capable personality. For example, the Michael entity said that it is fairly easy to tell the difference between two souls with equivalent experience in this Grand Cycle. One created from a spirit that has had three previous Grand Cycles as opposed to one that has had ten previous Grand Cycles.

The personality is an extension of the soul. But the personality that we perceive is only a small portion of the energy dedicated to our physical existence. A soul would never incarnate its entire consciousness into the physical field because an incarnated consciousness needs so much assistance managing its physical life. We are generally unaware of the support we get from the inner self, but if it was not for the consciousness remaining in the inner universe, the personality could not survive on earth.

The soul is the driving force behind the creation of the personality. The type of experiences the soul wants to have is the determining factor in the energy that it selects and the nature of the personality it forms.

Latent Energies or Nuclei
Gestalt energy is subdivided into groups of energy with similar interests known as nuclei. Each nucleus has its own desires, creativity, interests and aptitudes, but with somewhat limited and focused capabilities compared to the overall entity. Each identity is controlled by a single nucleus at a time. A nucleus capable of controlling a soul or spirit would have a great deal more capability than one controlling a personality. A spirit, soul, or personality will consist of multiple nuclei capable of controlling it, however, only one nuclei can control an identity at any given time.

The particular energies the soul chooses to focus on the physical field will influence the type of experiences the personality will have. The capabilities that the soul provides the personality have been developed to a given level and in a certain way by previous personalities. If the soul wants to have new experiences or perceive old issues in a different way, the soul will not provide the new personality with all of the previously developed energies. It will only provide the personality with a portion of the energy. These can be thought of as latent capabilities. The new personality will develop these latent capabilities differently than the previous personalities, which create new perspectives. Since the soul combines the energies from the various personalities, over the span of multiple lifetimes the soul cultivates a more complete set of capabilities, which further enriches it.

Even though these new energies are latent, the personality can develop them more easily than if it needed to acquire the energy from scratch. It would be akin to creating a new house built over an existing foundation. The foundation would guide the builder into the type of house to be created, but still leave plenty of room for personal expression. Similarly, having latent energy available does not restrict how the personality develops that energy or even which energies it develops. Although the latent energy encourages activity towards certain types of experiences, a wide selection of options is available.

We can think of our conscious personality as a carefully selected collection of energy in the form of discrete nuclei. Each nucleus is capable of controlling the personality during a portion of the life experience. The nucleus displaying the most dominant characteristics at the time of the personality's birth is chosen to be the initial core nucleus. The personality is then left to develop as it chooses without direction from the soul. Therefore, who we become is left up to our personality.

The personality determines which capabilities it will develop, and when and how it will develop them. The undeveloped nuclei will remain latent or have minimal growth during our present life, but will develop later. The more developed the soul, the more capabilities the personality will have been given.

Objectives

Sometimes it appears that we just stumble through life having one unintentional experience after the other with no real focus, but it does not work that way. Although we have free will to do as we please, our inner self provides us opportunities that guide us through life.

Our spirit has an evolutionary plan for its growth. It includes many areas of exploration and is coordinated with many other spirits. This Grand Cycle is only one of many Grand Cycles our spirit has included in its plan. In each Grand Cycle the spirit selects a portion of its larger plan for the soul to carry out. The soul then creates its own multi-life plan that is consistent with the spirit's plan.

The soul has principal issues that it wants the personality to deal with. Principal issues are usually highly complex situations that require many experiences over multiple lifetimes.

The issues that are described in our prelife plan are the primary concerns that we are supposed to investigate in this life. Our soul has probably been working on these same issues for many lifetimes. Our experiences contribute to our soul's understanding of those issues, but it would be rare that our experiences in one lifetime brought them to closure. For example, it would be unlikely that we could understand a complex issue like abuse in a single life. In one set of lives we might be abused, in another set we might be the abuser, and in yet another, we might have a third person's perspective. Of course, this is a huge simplification and the actual issues may have tens or hundreds of subtle perspectives, giving the spirit a chance to experience and view the subject of abuse from every possible vantage point.

Reincarnation

Each personality has only one life in the physical field. When we refer to reincarnation, we are saying that the same soul, the greater 'us,' continually creates new personalities. Since the personality is a subset of the soul, it is another portion of the soul that returns in different forms. The personalities are configured to have different perspectives in order to have different experiences. Since the soul and personality are part of the same being, a reincarnated personality is still 'us,' but with different goals, interests, etc.

The soul provides the personalities with a psychological continuity from life to life that creates a reservoir of skills and knowledge that we can each draw on. We are working on issues that are derived from experiences that had their roots in our soul's personalities thousands of years ago.

One might expect psychological issues to carry over from life to life but it is surprising that physical traits can also carry over from one personality to the next. Dr. Ian Stevenson was the Carlson Professor and Chair of the Department of Psychiatry at the University of Virginia, where he worked for some 50 years. He did a great deal of work on reincarnation and some of it focused on how biological events in past lives are tied to physical traits in this life. Among many other findings, he discovered numerous people who had birthmarks, physical weaknesses, or even deformities that he was able to trace back to previous lifetimes with what he believed to be a high degree of correlation. These traits may have resulted from a highly stressful death in a recent past life. For example, someone who dies of a knife wound in a traumatic incident may be reborn with an associated birthmark. The Seth entity confirmed Stevenson's findings that physical traits will occur in subsequent personalities when the intensity of an experience is so great and so traumatic that it cannot be resolved before the next reincarnation.

It is possible to determine when our soul began incarnating in this Grand Cycle and how many personalities our soul has created. The Michael entity, via Shepherd Hoodwin, can provide that information by checking the akashic records. He can even tell us how many sentient Grand Cycles our spirit has had, which is a standard part of the Michael Reading chart.[8]

But it is far more difficult to determine the nature of the problems our soul has been working on and how long we have been at it. One issue leads to another and reincarnated lives become a continuous stream of interrelated issues.

Reincarnation is a critical issue and very misunderstood even in the Eastern religions. In order to fully understand metaphysics, it is extremely important to grasp the concept of reincarnation so we will discuss it in much greater detail in Chapter 7.

Child Prodigies

Although generally the personality needs to develop each particular capability on its own, the soul is able to give the personality additional energies in certain areas if it wants to stress specific behavior. When certain energies are slightly more developed than others they show up as what we think of as natural talents. Examples of this would be an 'ear for music,' or unusual athleticism, or a very high intellect.

Occasionally people are born with highly developed abilities. History is full of stories of child prodigies like Mozart, who could write beautiful music at five years old. If the soul imparts an unusual amount of fully developed energies into the personality, then the experiences it chooses will focus them in a specific direction. It is not that child prodigies cannot develop other aspects of their personality, for they certainly have all the latent energy needed. They are just less likely to do it because they are so focused on their primary expertise.

Spiritual Creation Process

The physical field is an extremely difficult place for a spirit to exist. This surely does not surprise anyone, but it is far more difficult than even we suspect because we do not realize how much help we get. The body and conscious mind require a huge amount of support in order to have the experiences described in the prelife plan.

The gestalt nature of consciousness is what allows the soul to create personalities. Gestalts can be configured and reconfigured by moving nuclei in and out of an identity, which in our case is our personality. Even during a life, the personality can be provided additional energy by the soul if it is required to execute the prelife plan.

Creating a personality is like building a company. We create a business plan and then we hire the people with the skills to operate and grow the company. Likewise our soul creates a prelife plan and then selects nuclei that will be able to implement the plan. The energy that forms the personality is chosen with great care, and with the anticipation of being able to deal with the many circumstances that will arise.

As such, we are a unique blend of energies selected to achieve specific goals. Our energy configuration will give us a unique viewpoint in regards to our experiences. This is necessary to help round out and deepen the spirit's perspectives on certain issues. We think of ourselves as being the random consequence of our parents' DNA, but that is not the case. What we consider to be our 'I' was intentionally created in a certain way. Our personality is a purposeful creation.

Body Blueprint

Every personality has a blueprint detailing how its energies will manifest in the physical body. It defines how it will grow and even how it will appear at each stage of life. It first takes effect when the embryo starts growing in the womb and defines the creation and purpose of every cell in our body. It is part of the prelife plan and is retained in the personality throughout our life.

Our soul, working with our personality's nuclei, creates the physical body by implementing the blueprint, which is a physical replica of our psychic self. Science assumes that the DNA somehow does this, but it is the consciousness that continuously feeds its specific blueprint information into the DNA that actually constructs our body.

There are such things as mental genes, which all beings have. These generic capabilities can create any physical form depending on the guidance they are given. The data from our blueprint is used by the mental genes. The body's chromosomes translate the coded data from the mental genes and use them for specific cell guidance. The combination of the genes that we inherit from our parents and the mental genes determines what our body will look like and how we will behave.

What this means is that we grow in accordance with our blueprint. We think of aging as an open loop process whereby we grow randomly over time. But in actuality our cells follow the blueprint.

Dominant Nuclei

The soul selects one of the many nuclei that it has put into the ego to be the core nucleus that is the decision maker for the personality in the beginning of life. Each nucleus has a propensity to form specific personality traits so the personality's dominant attributes will be determined by the controlling nucleus. As we grow through childhood the dominant nucleus will shape our likes, attitudes, desires, and abilities. If the soul wants the personality to have musical or athletic ability, then it will include that energy in its gestalt. The other nuclei in the ego provide secondary capabilities that we may or may not take advantage of.

Later in life, our controlling nucleus or energy center changes as we mature. What was important for us as a child or teenager is not able to sustain our early adult years. The business world or parenthood requires different focuses. One nucleus gets stronger in relation to the others in an ebb and flow relationship. Our life often changes direction when this happens. The dominant nucleus at any given time chooses which traits to actualize. As our life evolves and we go through our mature adult and then senior years, different aspects of our life become more or less important. We can look back over several decades and see where these changes occurred and how they affected us. For example, a major career change would probably be the result of a change in the controlling nucleus. A change could be detected as simply as having a sudden change in food preferences from one period of your life to another, which has probably happened to everyone.

The changes in our lives as we age are part of the soul's plan. It tries to lead us to the experiences it wants us to have. The soul does not care exactly which experience we choose as long as it meets its requirement. For example, if it wanted to have a competitive experience, it would not care which sport we chose or if it was not a sport but a business opportunity or a game. It is the mental or psychological aspect of the activity that is important.

The soul knows what we are inclined to do and which nuclei will likely be in control at each point in our life. We have free will so we can change the script, but it is more probable that we will follow the plan.

Fragments

Fragments are good examples of how the gestalt nature of consciousness gives the evolutionary process incredible flexibility. Sometimes the soul does not need to create a full personality in order to have a particular experience. In this case the soul may choose to put a small part of its energy into what we could call a fragment.

The definition of a fragment is a bit arbitrary. One could say that every being is a fragment of a larger being. Personalities are all fragments of their soul just like the soul is a fragment of its spirit, and the spirit is a fragment of a greater spirit, and on up to the Tao. However, the way I use fragments is when I refer to an identity that has a limited set of energies compared to ourselves and therefore is restricted to a specific set of probable experiences. Fragments are much more limited than a personality in the types of experiences they can have. Their energy focuses them on a very limited range of options.

As an example, the Seth entity noted that he had recently put some of his energy into a dog because he wanted a particular experience, and that was the best way to get it. This does not mean that Seth reincarnated as a dog. But it does indicate the huge flexibility that a spirit has in using portions of its energy to investigate specific issues. Remember that it is the mental response created from an experience, not the physical activity that is sought. All objects are props, to include your and my bodies and even the dog's body. The object's only purpose is to elicit mental responses.

It is worth noting that our energy can be given to another identity and we will gain the experience it has while in that identity. The energy needs to follow the limitations of that form while in that reality.

Our soul creates many full personalities and numerous fragments, both on this earth and elsewhere to include other realities. Since the fragments are created by our soul, our personality would not be aware of their existence during our lifetime.

The concept of fragments demonstrates another strange aspect of consciousness. It reminds me of the Mr. Potato Head toy. By changing its facial features one can change its entire appearance, but it is still Mr. Potato Head. As a gestalt, the soul too has interchangeable parts, and by changing the personality's energies, it can change the nature of the personalities and fragments, but they are still part of the soul.

Free Will
When the soul creates a personality it gives it complete freedom to do as it wishes. The soul is unable to change the decisions of the personality, even if it disagrees with its actions. Once created,

the personality will always control its activities. Every CU, fragment or full gestalt personality is an independent identity with the ability to make its own decisions.

Our free will is limited by two things: 1) our capabilities; and 2) the laws of the reality we incarnate into, i.e. on earth our bodies cannot fly without mechanical assistance. As such, each identity controls its own evolution. It has free will and can do what it likes within the bounds of its environment and capability. It is impossible for the soul to control the personality. In fact, it is impossible for any consciousness to control any other consciousness. This is why no one is responsible for the actions of another. We can and should assist others whenever possible. But inevitably we are each only responsible for our own actions. When the personality is born in the physical field, it will have an independent evolution of its own choosing.

Mineral, Plant and Animal Souls

We have been focusing on human souls but these are only a small percentage of the souls, not just in this universe, but also here on earth. Each of us has had many other incarnations before we were able to live this sophisticated sentient life.

Consciousness starts entering the physical field very early on as parts of atoms, molecules and cells where it gains an understanding of the workings of the universe. Eventually a young consciousness reaches a level of maturity where it chooses to have a more advanced experience in the physical field. It may start out being a mineral, which allows it to experience conditions in the physical field like weathering, planet dynamics, temperature and pressure changes, winds, erosion, etc. The mineral consciousness feels the camaraderie of other minerals and feels attached to and part of a group. The mineral soul is a group soul so many sparks will simultaneously join together to form a composite soul. Each spark that would like to experience the mineral world would participate in creating the group soul that it will join. There is no ego involved in group souls so there is no concern about rival relationships.

Eventually after thousands of cycles as a mineral, a spark might feel it is ready for a plant experience. Here the spark will be able to experience growth and a more sophisticated level of life. A plant is a system, much like an animal that needs nourishment, water and sunlight, defenses against predators, and the ability to withstand weather, fire, disease, etc. Plants have sophisticated communication systems so they learn to be reliant on and supportive of others. Plant souls are also group souls like minerals. Plant souls will start out at the low end of the evolutionary ladder as grasses, and over time and after many reincarnations they work their way to the top of the plant food chain as more sophisticated trees.

In time, plant sparks will feel they are ready to experience animal life, where movement is more important. They might begin as lower animal group souls like amoebas. It is only when they get to the higher animal life forms that they have individual souls or 'hive' souls, which are dedicated to a single animal.

Hive souls are different than human souls in their simplicity and limited responsibility. However, the biggest difference between mankind's consciousness and other beings on earth is our thinking ability. Our imagination and ability to reason logically and deduce conclusions is unique to sentient beings on this planet. However, reasoning is an option not a requirement, but we do not see it that way. We have a tendency to judge intelligence by its ability to reason. We are so prejudiced in extolling the value of reason and logic that we underestimate the value of the life other beings have chosen to experience. We treat them as second class citizens although they have the same basic structure and value as we do. But reason and logic are only one type of conscious experience and one is not better than another.

Direct cognition through the inner sense is an equally valid source of knowledge and far more efficient form of communication.

What we consider 'lower level identities' communicate through telepathy. We wonder how schools of fish, large flocks of birds and large herds of animals can all choose to change direction simultaneously. Telepathy allows all members to get the information simultaneously. In fact, some of mankind's greatest achievers have been given information via telepathy but this form of communication remains a mystery to mainstream science. Since the universe is a mind, it should not be a surprise that everything communicates via telepathy.

Consciousness does not have to follow a sequence of mineral, plant, animal and then human existences for its evolution. There are many different types of experiences available to a spirit and there are no prescribed paths. Everything is choice!

Non-Corporeal Experiences

Angels and Archangels

Angels are a good case in point where a spark might not go from an animal soul directly into a sentient soul. Angels have evolved to about the same level as humans, but they have chosen not to incarnate into the physical field as they consider human life more stressful than what they want to experience. Because they will not be incarnating onto earth, they do not need a sentient soul. They have an angel soul that creates their astral body because their work is primarily in the astral field. Instead of incarnating, they slowly get used to living life as a human on earth by working in the background and assisting us in executing our prelife plan.

Our culture is full of stories about people being assisted by angels. It is unlikely that all those stories are true because it is very difficult for an angel to physically interfere with our life. They work with us during our sleep and assist our guides. At some point angels will probably end up incarnating into an earth-like environment on some planet, but in a different cycle. The angel experience allows them to be exposed to the rigors of life on earth more slowly. Angels consider humans very daring beings who have agreed to deal with the realities of human life in the physical field.

Archangels, on the other hand, have most likely already incarnated into human bodies in previous Grand Cycles and are now assisting mankind in other ways. These would be the leaders of the angels. Archangels rarely interfere with human lives and would only do so in an emergency, such as if something was going to prevent us from executing our life plan. If someone has a physical encounter with an angel it is most likely an archangel as they are more skilled in manifesting in the physical field. Angels often appear as larger than humans because they use their astral bodies, which are significantly larger and less dense than a human body.

The type of soul we choose is based on what lessons we want to experience, rather than how evolved we are.

Chapter 5

The Human Psyche

Man, know thyself, then thou shalt know the universe and God.
Pythagoras

Key Concept: Consciousness controls matter.

The Human Experience

In *The Endless Journey* I said that we are a spirit having a life experience, which is true, but now we are going more deeply into our nature. Our understanding of ourselves is so misconstrued that it requires a whole new concept of who and what we are.

As discussed earlier, consciousness has both a web-like or group nature and an individual nature. This dual nature makes understanding who and what we are very different than how we are accustomed to seeing ourselves. There is an underlying connectedness in all things, but we don't see it. It is the individual aspect of consciousness that we are learning to understand in this life, which is why we see everything as separate and apart from each other. In order to understand ourselves, we need to appreciate both aspects of our nature.

Inner Conscious vs the Soul

Before we get into the various aspects of our consciousness it is important to understand the distinction I am making between the inner conscious and the soul. The inner conscious is the portion of the soul that is focused on supporting the personality during a lifetime. However, the soul is greater than that and it may be supporting multiple personalities or performing other functions simultaneously. The best way to think of the inner conscious is as being a dedicated portion of the soul.

The Psyche

Our psyche is a small but important node in the Tao's web of consciousness, and at the same time it functions as an individual entity. As such, it sees itself as both an independent identity following its own evolutionary path, and as a valuable part of the greater web of consciousness. It has its own emotions, desires, intellect, reason, curiosity, and all the characteristics that we think makes us human. Probably its most important aspect is its eternal, unlimited expansiveness.

I define our psyche as including the inner conscious, and the personality, which includes the ego and the subconscious. I like the term psyche because it ties the three main parts of our consciousness together and makes us realize that we are much greater than the conscious portion of the personality, which is how we normally see ourselves. Although the psyche is a creation of the soul, it includes portions of the soul. The soul separates itself in order to create the personality, another independent identity. This seems a bit confusing but remember that the soul is a gestalt made up of independent conscious units, each with their own free will. Essentially, all the soul is doing is selecting certain aspects of itself to focus on the physical field.

Since the psyche is created by taking nuclei from the soul, the personality becomes a permanent subset of the soul. Because this was the process in which all identities were created, one can begin to see why everything in existence is tied together and can be considered one. The easiest way to understand a psyche is to look at where its energy is focused.

Our psyche has three discrete dedicated focuses: 1) the ego, which we think of as our conscious self, is focused on the daily activities in the physical field; 2) the subconscious, which is primarily focused on controlling the physical body; and 3) the inner conscious, which is focused on guiding the ego throughout its physical life. We could view each compartment as if it were in a trance and focused on its specific objectives during a single lifetime.

Our psyche is a very real and tangible identity that exists both in the physical field and in the inner universe. It does not include the physical portion of the personality like our brain or other physical parts of the body. We cannot see it or touch it or sense it in any physical way because our outer senses are attuned to physical reality, but inherently we know it exists and it continues to exist after we die.

Ego

During life, the ego is the part of the psyche that is focused on the physical field. We think of it as our 'conscious mind' or 'I,' even though it is a very small part of our psyche. The ego receives most of its inputs from the five outer senses and the subconscious. The ego and the subconscious control the body's actions through the brain.

The physical environment is a complicated place for a spirit to operate. As physical identities, we have a body that needs to eat, be sheltered from the elements, avoid harm from numerous external sources, deal with diseases and injury, and manage other physically unique issues. There are not many other places where an identity needs to worry about its body more than it does in the physical field. It is the dedicated focus of the ego that does this for us.

Our inner conscious has access to the wisdom of the universe, so it is a much wiser and more capable decision maker in regards to nonphysical activities. But it needs to take its direction from the ego during our life. When we are about to step in front of a moving bus, it is the ego that immediately decides to jump back. Since it is the ego's responsibility to protect the body, it stands to reason that it is the ego that chooses all of our experiences.

The ego has no memory of the prelife plan, the soul, the soul's past lives, the spirit or even the Tao. It begins life with a completely fresh outlook towards the physical field and grows with us during our life. It does not know which experiences the soul wants to have so it needs the inner conscious's guidance throughout life.

The ego has numerous latent energies that it can develop over time, but the energies it chooses to develop depends on its interests, needs, and attitudes. If we are shy and timid we might not feel comfortable in developing our aggressive skills, and if we are very athletic we might not develop our musical or art talents. We are inclined to develop the skills that come easiest to us so our latent energies guide us towards certain types of lives. When the soul creates a personality, it has a pretty good idea what the likely outcome will be.

The ego consists of various energy nuclei, each with a particular set of interests and capabilities. But only one nucleus can be in charge of the ego at a time. Numerous nuclei are potentially capable of being the dominant energy within the ego, and they will change positions over a life. The soul initially selects the nucleus it thinks can best carry out the initial portion of the prelife plan, but that is the last time the soul is able to directly affect the personality. As our life evolves and our interests change, different nuclei will likely take over the control of the ego. The ego's controlling nucleus during our teenage years is probably not suitable to guide our entire adult career. Even in our adult life, the dominant portion of the ego will change. For example, if we began our career as a technical specialist and then moved into lower, middle and upper management, the ego's dominant nucleus would likely change several times.

The Experiencer

The rhetorical metaphysical questions: "When we see, who sees?" and "When we feel, who feels?" can be answered: "The ego." Our spirit chose a sentient life because it likes to have physical experiences, but it is the ego that actually has those experiences. Our ego is the part of us that deals with all the emotions of life. It feels our pain and suffering along with our joys. It is confused by the illusion, feels the loss from its security in the spiritual world, and takes on all the hardships this world throws at us. The ego is the valiant crusader that faces this difficult life with all its perils. It fights depression, deals with disease, and wanders unsuspectingly through the challenges of life. The ego is where our beliefs, attitudes and expectations reside. It chooses our experiences and feels their intensities.

However, the soul has a psychic connection with the ego. Everything that the ego experiences, the soul feels. Although the ego interprets its experiences as physical events, it is the mental aspect of the experience that is real and lasting and it is the mental portion of the experience that the soul senses.

Ego's Responsibilities
There are several key requirements that the ego must have in order for us to be successful on earth:

First, it must buy into the illusion of the physical field. It accomplishes this by interfacing with the physical field through the five outer senses. The massive amount of data received from the outer senses dominates the ego's attention, which ensures that the illusion is the center of its focus. The ego's inability to directly interface with the inner sense conceals the knowledge of the inner universe.

Secondly, the ego needs to deal with and prioritize the many short-term challenges of the physical field. This is far more complicated than we might think and is the main capability that separates us from the other animals. Keeping a budget, driving a car, and reading a paper require a sophisticated psyche far beyond the capabilities of the rest of the animal kingdom. Even our most mundane tasks, like shopping for food, are more complex than we realize.

Thirdly, the ego needs to have the experiences the soul outlined in the prelife plan, even though it does not consciously know what they are. Since the ego has free will and is unaware of the prelife plan, it has to be guided in the direction of those experiences. Therefore, the ego must be able to receive guidance, but not direction, from the inner conscious. It receives these inputs through intuition, hunches and gut feelings.

Fourthly, the ego needs to live a sophisticated-enough life to have the experiences prescribed in the prelife plan. The ego is guided towards these experiences by developing its latent talents. If a personality wants to be a successful artist, it needs to have the skills to do so. In this regard it is assisted by being endowed with specific latent artistic energies that the soul provided. It is given a smorgasbord of inherent related abilities and free will to develop any capability it wants. This gives the ego a propensity to develop skills that will lead it towards occupations and vocations compatible with the prelife plan.

Finally, when the ego does have a prelife plan experience, it needs to view the experience from a specific perspective. The soul is very particular how an experience is perceived. The ego is able to accomplish this by being endowed with the personality traits and capabilities that will be described in Chapter 9, Creating a Life.

Influences on the Ego
The ego matures and evolves along with the body. It begins life with a multitude of latent energies that it will choose from to develop. Its interests will determine which energies are selected. As we mature, our ego is continually influenced by our family, friends, social and cultural environments. Although there are many outside influences impacting our life, under normal development, cultural effects are overrated. Most of our core characteristics showed up at birth. We see children from the same household and even identical twins grow up to lead very different adult lives. We attribute this behavior to different attitudes from parents or schools or various outside influences,

which is true to a minor extent. But the biases and latent energies we are born with are the major contributors to our personality's characteristics. Even identical twins have their own unique set of biases.

However, an unstable family life at an early age can cause the personality to mature in ways that are counterproductive to its prelife plan. Growing up in broken homes, living in high crime rate areas, and being exposed to societies in upheaval can cause a child to ignore certain capabilities and substitute destructive behavior. No one has a prelife plan to be a criminal or terrorist. This is learned behavior that reacts defensively to its environment.

Multiple Personalities (Dissociative Identity Disorder)

There have been a number of books written about people who have multiple personalities. They switch from one to another and each personality is unaware of the others. This occurs when multiple nuclei vie for dominancy of the ego.

The ego contains multiple potential nuclei that are energetic enough to control it. Usually one is much stronger than the others at each period of life. Normally the process of two egos changing dominancy is a slow controlled process taking place over time. However, at any given time in our life, only one ego should be dominant.

If a second nucleus becomes as dominant as the original ego before its allotted time, control of the conscious mind can alternate between them. Normally the original ego would cede control to the new ego but sometimes the old ego does not want to give up control. When this occurs, the individual will be at the mercy of the alternating egos. In extreme cases, it is possible to have three, four or more egos vying for control. Each ego will have very different personalities, characteristics, likes and dislikes, and even things like allergies and other ailments because it will have different energies that it manifests.

Subconscious

The subconscious is an area of the mind dedicated to controlling the body. It interfaces directly with the ego and the brain, but unlike the ego, it also interfaces directly with the inner conscious. Its primary responsibility is assuring that the body responds to the ego's wishes, and in addition acts as a buffer between the ego and the inner conscious.

In order to allow the ego to concentrate on our experiences, we need an automated process to control our body functions. But the extent of that control is surprising. Our subconscious controls all aspects of the the physical body, and for simplification I divided the subconscious into two functions: Operations Manager and Body Blueprint Manager.

Operations Manager
In daily life we exercise, sweat, shiver, sleep, get sick, change temperature, vary our attitude, etc. and they all require the body to make different physical adaptions. Our body uses bacteria, viruses, secretions, enzymes, etc. in order to keep it healthy. We take it for granted that our body will automatically adjust to our environmental changes, which it does but it is not automatic in the sense we think it is.

Each internal process is actively managed, which is only possible because each function is a subsystem with its own dedicated consciousness. A multitude of subsystems continuously monitor the body's operation and coordinate their activities. None of these systems work independently, which is how we perceive them. Each system, down to the cell, is a dedicated identity. The operations manager monitors the actions of the body, and using precognition, it anticipates its needs. The operations manager then instructs every cell in the body what to do and when to do it. Each organ and each cell will then prepare for the event in a defensive and supportive manner before the event occurs. For example, if we are doing a vigorous exercise, the body's system will anticipate the need for cooling before the body overheats and starts the sweating process. The body uses precognition to respond to the environment, it does not do it reactively.

We also need our body to respond to our desires to move, which are learned responses. We start learning muscle movements in the womb and that continues through life. The operations manager works closely with the ego, and provides instruction on when to move, where to go, and what to do. If the ego decides to stand up, the operations manager determines which muscles to use and how and when to move them. Athletic events like hitting a golf ball or skating would be impossible if we needed to think about the movement of every muscle.

Body Blueprint Manager

The subconscious effectively contains the 'body blueprint' that was discussed earlier. It is an image of how the body should appear at every stage of our life. It is coded in electrical pulses with the detail going down to the cell level. It was a creation of our soul and is documented in our prelife plan. Constant tweaking of our body is required to ensure we 'grow into' the person the soul planned for us to be. Of course, our personality has free will so we can change from the originally planned image, but whatever we develop into needs to be monitored and controlled to ensure it happens. For example, if we were supposed to be fit and slim at 50 but the ego decided to be out of shape and fat, it would be our choice and the body blueprint manager would need to adapt.

Atoms and molecules are continuously entering and leaving our body as cells die and are replaced. The body blueprint manager replacement process is an amazing function. Atoms, molecules and cells join together to form new identities. Each identity has its own level of consciousness so it understands its purpose and functions appropriately.

When particles enter the physical field they know where to go and what to do. Every object in existence has a continuous stream of lower-level identities entering and leaving its borders. The atoms, molecules and even the cells within our body are constantly being replaced, yet the functions they perform miraculously remain unchanged.

Science recognizes this phenomenon but assumes it happens automatically and without intelligent assistance. If this were the case it would truly be a miracle. This process is closely controlled via communication between the body blueprint manager and each participating identity. Each new identity needs to learn what its new role is. If it were not for the inherent consciousness within all matter, objects could not form in the first place, let alone retain their function for the duration of a life. This is a highly complex activity that does not happen by chance.

Cell Memory

Memory is an interesting phenomenon. Our overall personality has a high-level memory of all our experiences, but the lower-level identities, like cells and atoms, that make up our body also have memory of their experiences.

Each identity remembers every experience that happens to it from the moment it becomes part of any physical structure until it departs. The CUs that make up an atom or molecule have a memory of their experiences. In order for our body to retain the memory of its experiences, whenever an identity departs our body its memories are shared with its replacement. For example, if we burned our hand as a child, the replacement cells for the ones that had been injured would have been given the memory of that event. So the memory of the event stays with all our replacement cells for the rest of our life, even though the original cells are replaced multiple times. This occurs because elements of the subconscious manage the process.

Past Life Memories

The subconscious also contains the memories of our soul's past lives. We do not contain the actual energy of those past lives, just a set of their memories. The skills and knowledge developed in past lives allow us to learn skills much more rapidly than if we needed to start from the beginning. We can draw on those resources to help focus and support our life. In addition, every personality dies with unresolved issues, both karmic and otherwise. Before a soul's task is considered complete and it is able to move on to the causal field, all its issues need to be resolved. Our psyche participates in the resolution of these past life personalities' issues whenever possible. This process might literally take thousands of years and many subsequent personalities to complete. Some issues can be resolved in the astral field, but some need to be worked out in the physical field.

In *Many Lives, Many Masters*, Brian Weiss, MD, spent two years with a patient whose past life issues were interfering with her present life. These were memories that had been passed down to her from previous personalities. This was an example of issues being brought forward for the present ego to deal with. However, in most cases, if the issues are to be resolved in this life this is usually done by our dreams, which we will discuss later.

The Inner Conscious

The inner conscious is by far the most interesting part of us. It is the core of the personality and as we previously mentioned is part of the soul. Unlike the ego, the inner conscious remembers who it is, the nature of its spirit, its previous personalities, the prelife plan, and its existence between lives in the astral field.

The soul only incarnates a small portion of the psyche's total energy into the ego and subconscious because the ego requires so much support from the inner universe in order to operate in the physical field. Most of the psyche's energies are in the inner conscious.

Despite being wiser and knowing what the personality is supposed to experience in life, the inner conscious cannot control the ego. In fact, no consciousness can control another. The three elements of the psyche are independent identities and have free will to do as they wish. One of the main functions of the inner conscious is to guide the personality towards the desired experiences by creating opportunities for the ego to take advantage of during life. It does this by following the prelife plan.

Prelife Plan

The prelife plan, which I discuss in detail in Chapter 9, Creating a Life, is the basis for creating the new personality. The prelife plan is a set of experiences that the soul wants the new personality to investigate. The nature of the desired experiences determine the configuration of the personality's energy. The attributes of the personality are aligned with the expectations set forth in the prelife plan by choosing nuclei that are inclined to participate in the desired experiences.

From the beginning of life, the inner conscious steers the ego towards experiences described in the prelife plan. The detail and patience of the inner conscious is astounding. For example, if our prelife plan had us becoming involved with creating a company in later life, the preparation would need to begin in childhood. At a minimum we would need to: 1) have the proper education, which requires guiding us through our childhood; 2) select appropriate employment and/or vocational activities; 3) expose the personality to the new company's potential importance; 4) meet the right people to advance the opportunity; and 5) develop the proper personality traits to accept the challenge. The inner conscious needs to enlist the assistance of others to create these opportunities for the personality. The inner conscious searches through millions of potential people to find ones with compatible interests and that will be in a position and place to assist us when needed. It then coordinates their lives, and 'chance' meetings are often set up decades in advance. Untold actions need to take place to overcome obstacles, create backup plans, and to shift priorities as the ego matures and changes its goals. All this needs to happen for every experience the inner conscious wants us to have; and an equivalent effort happens simultaneously for all eight billion people on this planet. This sounds unbelievably complicated because it is. But it gives us an idea of the amazing capability of the inner conscious.

Creating the Personality
The different elements of the psyche work together during the creation of the body. The experiences the soul selects in the prelife plan will have an impact on all aspects of the personality even to include the type of body it will need. At conception, the inner conscious immediately starts molding the personality. This process continues throughout life as the inner conscious continually compares the expected adult image with the prelife plan blueprint and adjusts the body as needed to meet the blueprint's requirements.

Despite the inner conscious's long-term focus on executing the prelife plan, it is focused on supporting the ego's short-term desires. But the ego does not remember the prelife plan so it chooses the experiences it wants to have without awareness of the plan. The inner conscious will do whatever the ego decides so it is continuously taking what it believes to be inputs from the ego. In other words, the ego decides what it wants to do and the inner conscious makes it happen. However, since there is no direct communication between the ego and the inner conscious, as we will see more clearly later, this is the cause of many of our problems. This is an extremely important point.

Synchronicity
Everyone has experienced 'apparent' coincidences that have changed their life. We might have met someone at a party who

had just the right skills or knew the right person to lead our life in a new direction. I remember thinking about trying to find a certain person for several months. All of a sudden I met him crossing a street in Cambridge, Massachusetts where neither one of us normally went. That relationship has lasted all my life. These phenomena are referred to as synchronicity, but they are not coincidental. Synchronous events that appear so fortuitous and spontaneous are sometimes planned for decades in advance. Although the circumstances requiring the parties to come together appear to be unrelated, the souls of the affected parties actually cause it to happen.

There is nothing spontaneous about the key happenings in our life. Like-minded intentions are coordinated, meetings planned, and experiences set up by the inner conscious. Ultimately, the ego is guided, but not directed, to actualize the events created by the inner conscious. However, the ego has choices and many intermediate events can alter the ego's desires so nothing is certain until it happens. Synchronous events are simply the results of the detailed planning and execution by the inner conscious.

Brain

Science considers our brain to be our mind or psyche, but it isn't. Our brain interfaces with our psyche, but in comparison, the brain is extremely slow and cumbersome. The brain is physical and dies after death. The mind is a psychological structure, and continues to exist after death.

The brain is the physical mechanism that translates the subconscious's thoughts into information that the body can act on. We think with our mind but act with our brain.

Our inner conscious and our ego do not communicate directly with each other. The brain communicates with the ego and the subconscious. The inner conscious only communicates with the subconscious. The inner conscious filters and then processes an immense amount of information that it receives from the communication channels in the inner universe before it sends anything to the subconscious, and the subconscious filters it even further before forwarding it to the brain. Unlike the subconscious and the inner conscious, the brain can only process one item at a time. People who think they can multitask are actually rapidly changing their focus. This is an intentional part of how our reality is presented to us and why we experience the world serially, which is a concept that we will expand on later.

Psychic Currents

One might wonder what the motivation would be for a soul to give up part of itself, which will become independent of it. The key is that even though the personality is an independent identity and is able to do as it pleases, it is always a part of the soul. When a personality is created, it provides the soul with a new path in which it can expand its consciousness. Each personality pursues a direction that no other soul has traveled, which opens up a new perspective that expands the soul's consciousness.

We see our experiences through the outer senses, which are impacted by the physical elements like cold, color, weight, shape, etc. The physical objects that we encounter are props that enable the events to occur but at the same time distort the experience from an ego's perspective. But the soul is a mind and true experiences are mental not physical. The soul is connected to its personalities via psychic currents so it has direct access to the mental experiences and is not affected by the physical illusion. Of course, at death the undistorted experiences are also available to the personality.

The process of creating a new personality is taken very seriously. Because the soul is not only giving up part of itself, it is creating an eternal entity that will provide it knowledge forever. The soul has long-range goals that each personality needs to support. The energy it chooses and the experiences it selects in the prelife plan are chosen with a great deal of thought and consultation with others. But the prelife plan is only the beginning of the personality's independent journey.

Usually the personality returns to the soul and remains with it and they evolve in tandem, at least for awhile. But even when a personality becomes strong enough to evolve separately from the soul and is able to create its own personalities, the psychic currents always keep the soul and the personality connected. Because the future information gained by the personality is always available to the soul, in the end nothing is ever lost. It is all part of the strange nature of consciousness.

Extrasensory Perception

We are all aware of our five outer senses (sight, sound, smell, taste and touch), which create our reality. How our senses are designed determines our perceived reality. Although most species use some variation of these five senses, the parameters vary widely across the animal kingdom. We all know dogs have a much better sense of smell and hearing than we do, and many birds have much better eyesight. Some species even have additional senses like bats have radar and dolphins have sonar. Each sense is finely tuned to perceive a particular aspect of our reality in a specific way. Although each outer sense acts independently, in combination these senses give us a unique composite view of our world. This composite view uses the energy around us to create our reality. We are so dependent on our outer senses that it is hard to understand that none of these senses have any use outside the physical field.

When we die, we no longer have access to the outer senses, but we must have other ways to detect our environment. Literally tens of thousands of near-death experiencers tell us they could see the 'death scene,' hear voices after the incident, and communicate with spiritual entities. Obviously if there is life after death, which there is, we cannot be blind, deaf and mute.

We have another sense popularly known as extrasensory perception (ESP), which science likes to ignore. Unlike our outer senses, ESP operates in all realities. Although aspects of it are available to us here on earth, we are so focused on the physical field that we rarely use it, and generally do not even know it exists.

Telepathy is probably the most common characteristic of ESP that we experience on earth, although we often don't realize it is happening. For example, occasionally we have all experienced a situation where we are silently thinking of something while in a car or room with others present who are also silently thinking. Then one person says something that we were thinking about but had nothing to do with any prior conversation. This phenomenon is caused by telepathy. When our outer senses are quieted, our mind can sometimes perceive other people's thoughts directly without going through the outer senses. If atoms, molecules, cells, etc. are conscious, it stands to reason that they need some way to communicate. The Seth entity tells us that telepathy is the fundamental communication mechanism between all consciousnesses and is the only one available to lower-level life forms.

Intuition is another case of ESP as are clairvoyant and precognition capabilities. It is not an accident that our hunches and gut feelings can 'guess' the future. We will discuss the mechanisms for how this works in Chapter 10, Our Unique Reality. However, even in the most highly developed individuals, ESP skills barely offer a hint of its true capabilities.

ESP capabilities differ from our outer senses in that they expand as our consciousness expands. The more our consciousness evolves the more we will be able to take advantage of this sense. Although ESP is actually a single sense, it is so sophisticated that it helps to view its various functions individually. In some cases the differences between these characteristics are so subtle that our simplified model of reality makes it hard to distinguish their differences. The Seth entity referred to these ESP capabilities as our inner sense.[9] He briefly discussed the following characteristics of the inner sense that we do not normally experience:

Inner Vibrational Touch gives us a cognition of the world around us. This is an amazing capability that allows us to sense the consciousnesses in our vicinity. If we could use this sense while standing in the woods it would allow us to sense our surrounding environment like the trees, grass, insects and anything else we chose to focus our attention on. If this sense is highly developed, one would be able to sense what it was like to actually be that tree or grass or insect. If we were talking to someone, we would get an intuitive understanding of what they were trying to tell us. Of course, in our present state we could not fully feel them due to the limitations of our neural system, but we could get a sense of them. Our soul can do this now but in our present state our ego actually cancels the sense of the inner emotional feelings of others. We can only feel a somewhat shadowy sense of them. It comes to us through our inner conscious as a hunch or feeling like when a psychic holds someone's ring or other object. Our ego cannot perceive it directly but if it could this would be a great aid for our society by helping people better understand each other.

Perception of Past, Present and Future allows us to experience reality as it really is. This is an expansion of Inner Vibrational Touch where we can experience the past and future feelings of the other identities we sense.

The Conceptual Sense involves the instantaneous and complete cognition of a concept as opposed to knowing the identity of the source, which is Inner Vibrational Touch. This principle allows us to actually become part of the thought itself. Thoughts are energy, which produce unique electrical and chemical effects. The inner sense allows us to go inside the thought and experience it. We actually think that thought for ourselves and directly experience the concept. It is like being in the mind of the other person or entity who wants to communicate it to us.

Cognition of Knowledgeable Essence is like entering into another being and feeling their essence. It is not about knowing a concept as much as it is about knowing that being.

Innate Knowledge of Basic Reality is a sense that our soul uses all the time. It is understanding how the world works and how we can work within it. It allows man to walk, a bird to fly and an animal to hunt. This is what we call instinct. For instance, a beaver uses this sense to construct a dam and a spider uses it to create a web. They sense the universal concept behind what they are doing and they apply it in their own way to make it their own. They have no ego that would allow them to imagine the process, so they just sense it.

Expansion or Contraction of the Spiritual Body is a manipulation of our astral and other spiritual bodies. Unlike consciousness, a body has a well-defined boundary or limit, which prevents the energy from slipping away. Our physical body is pretty rigid and we cannot change it significantly without gaining or losing weight. But our many other bodies are not like that. For example, this is an ability to expand our astral body's boundary in order to increase our comprehension or reduce our body so we can fit into another reality.

Disentanglement from a Reality allows us to pull back from our physical senses and either dispense with our reality or enter another one altogether. We do this temporarily when we are in the dream world and finally at death.

Diffusion by the Energy Personality is a process where the various gestalt energies of an identity are divided up and then reassembled in another field. Our soul uses this process when birthing a new personality into the physical field. Our innate spirit does not break up, just the gestalt energies of things like our biases.

ESP or the inner sense can be considered an attribute of consciousness that applies to all areas of the Tao. Every spirit, no matter how insignificant, has these innate abilities. As we evolve, we will learn to better use and control them. Although they are accessible in all realities, they are camouflaged so well by the outer senses that they are hard to perceive in our physical reality.

The inner sense has other capabilities and we will spend eternity cultivating and expanding those powers as that is part of the evolutionary process. Even the Tao is still evolving and learning about all Its capability.

Memory

For most people the older we get the harder it is to remember things. We know the information is 'in there,' we just cannot recall it. It will probably surprise most people to know that every experience, every thought, and every emotion we have ever had is stored in permanent memory, which we will have access to when we die. The problem is that under normal circumstances, our ego can only access information via the brain. Over time some of the physical paths to the data within the brain become severed. This seems like a mixed blessing as we have all done things we would like to forget, but these negative experiences provide the best learning opportunities. If we actually forgot them, we would probably repeat those mistakes in future lives.

Within our being we have various levels of memory. Our brain stores a generalized memory of the important events from this life, which is what we remember. But the brain is the least reliable storage device we have. Being a physical object, it has a tendency to be unreliable. As we age it actually breaks down and we lose the passageways to where the information is stored.

All the information in the brain is remembered forever by our inner conscious. All the experiences we have, including all our dreams, are remembered and can be instantly recalled. The ego is normally unable to reach into these storage areas.

However, while under hypnosis it is possible to recover those hidden memories.

Our permanent memory is recorded outside the brain. The consciousness within the cells in our body actually retain total memory of all their experiences. This is coded within them and they retain it forever. The information is also passed to the subconscious and the inner conscious so we also have access to it after death.

Hypnoses can reveal memories from our early life, which is known as age regression. This allows us to bypass the brain's memory and go into the subconscious where long-term and past life memories are stored. When we search farther back we are able to recall our activities in the astral field before this life. Continuing back, we are able to remember all aspects of our previous life; then going back even further, we will recall our previous in-between life followed by another incarnation. We will be able to continue back to our soul's very first life to include its initial planning phase. If we are interested in exploring true reality, the in-between periods in the astral field will give us a much clearer view than the camouflaged physical fields.

If we go back even further, we will find the initial memory of the period when mankind was first incarnating into the physical field. This is long before we started incarnating on earth. We even have access to the memory of when the first spirit entered into the physical field. All this is available to us after we die, but we can glimpse portions of it now via hypnotism. Our spirit has 100% recall for every thought and every experience it ever had. We also can access all the wisdom of the Tao once we are able to understand it. Nothing is kept from us.

Mass Consciousness

Just as we have individual consciousnesses, so does every organization and event. Anytime two or more conscious entities join together it creates a higher-level consciousness of its own. Every country, state, county, town and even a small committee has a unique consciousness made up of the combined psyches of its constituents. We see its effects in sports where some cities always seem to have good sports teams and other cities hardly ever win anything. This phenomenon is controlled by the group expectations of the personalities living in the area, combined with their support bases and the team itself. It can be overcome and changed, but it requires a like-minded group of people to get that started.

Events like storms, floods, earthquakes, and other natural disasters have a consciousness made up of all the participants that are involved with the activity, including humanity. The consciousnesses of those who have been affected by a mass event have agreed to subconsciously participate.

However, no one is forced to experience a catastrophe. It might seem hard to believe that our inner conscious would agree to having our house destroyed in a tornado, but that is exactly what happens. Of course, the inner conscious is following the prelife plan or is simply doing what it believes the ego wants. Often it is the ego's inner thoughts that are being manifested. There are many reasons why an entity might choose to have this type of experience. It could be karmic, or an area of the ego's focus, or simply misguided beliefs. Whatever the reason, consent was given. This is an important topic so we will discuss it further in Chapter 12, Expectations.

Every inner conscious whose personality could be affected by an event is aware of it well before it happens. If they do not want to participate then they ensure the personality is not involved in the devastation. There are endless stories of people who were supposed to be somewhere that was devastated, but for some strange set of circumstances they missed out. A good example is that in New York City and Boston on 9/11/2001 there were many stories of people who were late to work or missed their airplane because of unusual circumstances. This was not fate. It was the result of many carefully executed plans.

Natural disasters are a way to rebalance the earth's energy. Having a hurricane or earthquake devastate an area may release enough energy to prevent a war, or famine or pandemic. We watch the events but do not understand the bigger picture.

Our view of the world is through a highly distorted opaque lens, where most of the pertinent information is missing or misunderstood. What appears to be a world full of disasters and conflicts is no more than a 'relatively' small number of people who have chosen to experience war, tragedy, or grief. Occasionally a catastrophic event occurs that impacts much of the world such as World War II or the Pandemic of 2020. If our ego does not want to experience the ravages of the event, then we will not. War or disease may go on around us, but we will not be affected. The ego may witness it and its consequences, but the soul only creates what it thinks the ego wants to experience.

All humanity participates in planning world events. We can offer our opinion even when we are the only opposing voice. If we don't like the decision of the majority, we simply get out of the way. This also goes for the animal and plant kingdoms as well.

However, just because someone chooses their hardships does not mean we don't owe them our sympathy, empathy and support. A tragedy is still a tragedy, despite its originating circumstances. The participants have agreed to learn very difficult lessons that will benefit us all in the long run. The onus is on us to assist them on their journey.

Out-of-Body Experience (OBE)

All three elements of our psyche usually remain with the body during our waking hours, but occasionally people have learned to have their ego intentionally leave their body, which is known as an out-of-body experience (OBE).

An OBE is simply a projection of the ego outside the body. In an OBE the ego actually leaves the physical body and travels to its desired location. The destination will be the person or place the ego concentrates on. The key is to think about the destination and not the method or route of travel. If one wants to go into the next room or travel out the front door you can think of the travel route. But if you want to visit someone or some place, it is best to concentrate on the destination. During an OBE the ego stops using the outer senses and uses its inner sense to focus on what it wants, just like we do when we die.

Robert Monroe was an OBE pioneer in the 1970s when he published his groundbreaking book, *Journeys Out of the Body*. He recalled experiences where he had traveled around the planet, visiting friends and actually scheduling meetings that took place while he was out of his body. He was able to corroborate his experiences with others via locations, types of apparel, and activities that he witnessed and the others later confirmed. He was even able to travel through the astral plane and communicate with friends who had died. These travels began in the late 1950s and continued for 14 years before he published those accounts. Because this was such a new phenomenon in his society, he had to painstakingly teach himself the various techniques, which he explains in detail in the book.

Things have changed a lot since Monroe's first book. Out-of-body experiences became a fashionable topic in the metaphysical world ever since 1992 with the publication of a US Army research program that experimented in remote viewing, which is another term for out-of-body experiences. It was also acknowledged that the USSR was working on similar technologies, and I am sure many other countries were as well and surely still are. The results have been astounding as people with OBE abilities have been able to mentally project their conscious and view sites they never visited physically. During their projection they reported seeing things that were unknown when the experiment took place but were later verified to have been there at the time of the test.

Probably the most famous incident occurred as a result of when a Soviet Tu-22 bomber, outfitted as a spy plane, crashed somewhere in Africa and the Russians could not locate it. In 1972 the US learned of the crash and wanted to recover the plane and retrieve the Russian codes. President Jimmy Carter later acknowledged that the CIA had given psychic Rosemary Smith a map of Africa and she was able to pinpoint the wreckage in the Central African Republic, even though it was completely covered by the jungle canopy.

Another verified example of an OBE was an experiment done by Russell Targ and Harold Puthoff with Ingo Swann, a noted OBE expert, in 1973. In a 20-minute session Swann was able to visit Jupiter and identify unknown crystalline structures in its atmosphere that gave Jupiter an appearance of having rings like Saturn. This phenomenon was unknown to science until six years later when in 1979 the Voyager spacecraft flew close by Jupiter and confirmed their presence with actual photographs.

The Seth entity says the following about OBE bodies (I paraphrase): "The OBE consciousness needs to take the form of a body during OBE travel because having no body would be very disconcerting for the experiencer. There are three types of OBE bodies one can use, depending on the experiencer's choice and capability. The most limiting OBE body that our consciousness assumes allows us to observe our physical body from the perspective of being outside of it but our consciousness will not have a levitating capability. The second OBE body, which is derived from the first, does not let us see our body but it knows where it is and allows our consciousness to levitate and travel throughout the solar system. The third type of OBE body is basically our inner conscious and we can go anywhere. The danger with the third type is our consciousness can become disassociated with the body and not recognize it upon returning, which can be very disorienting. The latter should be left to highly experienced OBE travelers."

The out-of-body experience is not a new phenomenon to humanity as Buddhist monks and others have apparently been traveling around the universe like this for a long time. This is a subject that science needs to take more seriously. For example, in the near future as we find planets that are similar to earth, it would behoove the scientific community to use trained OBE experts to investigate those planets for the possibility of life. Time and distance have no meaning in OBE experiences because consciousness travels outside our space-time reality so it has no effect on it. There are no limits to the places in the universe that our consciousness can visit.

Becoming a Soul

A soul is able to give up some of its energy to create a personality because it has become so robust that losing a small portion of its energy has little effect on it. The soul is said to have so much energy that its identity is 'indestructible.'

Young personalities, like the ones that make up most of mankind, are continuously struggling to establish themselves as indestructible. Nuclei search for a gestalt relationship that is compatible with their interests. In less sophisticated entities, this can result in all the energy departing and the entity disappearing. The actual CUs don't disappear, just some of the gestalts they had created will separate and the CUs will find other entities to become part of. However, the memory of those gestalts never disappear. Becoming indestructible requires accumulating enough energy to ensure its future as the entity it identifies itself as.

Each personality evolves and changes over time. When a personality becomes robust enough it wants to create its own personalities and grow from their experiences. It is not that a less capable personality could not create another personality, but if it was not robust enough to give the new personality adequate energy, the resultant incarnation could create problems. The new personality would still be part of the old one and the new karma would need to be resolved.

When a personality's physical life is over, it continues to grow stronger by gaining energy through lessons in the afterlife. It also gains as other past and future personalities' issues are resolved, and of course, from further experiences with the soul. When we are part of a sophisticated entity, we have learning experiences that are not available to us as less capable entities. We have a tendency to remain with our soul for quite some time, but we always remain a separate entity with our own evolutionary path.

However, there will come a time in every personality's evolution when it will decide to be the lead consciousness in a spirit. When we grow strong enough our interests will likely change and we will want to pursue our own path.

Some souls are so robust that they continually create personalities that develop on their own immediately after the life experience is over. Yet some souls rarely produce new souls. It depends on the amount and type of energy they are able to provide the personality.

Because we were created from our spirit's energy, we will always be part of that spirit, even when we choose to develop separately. Spirits are interconnected in a web of consciousness and there are no well-defined boundaries where one spirit stops and another starts. All the energy in existence is connected together in a group structure. At a macro level, we are all one. The Seth entity, which we will call Seth (1), also had a Seth (2) that channeled through Jane Roberts. This was his original spirit from which Seth (1) was created and later separated. Seth (1) referred to him as his big brother. They were separate in that they went their own way but they were connected by a bond that will forever tie them together. The boundary that we think defines who we are is much more nebulous than it appears in this life.

Chapter 6

The 'Death' Experience

If you are not afraid of dying, there is nothing you cannot achieve.
Lao Tse

Key Concept: Death is a transition back to the astral field.

Death Is an Illusion

Death is probably mankind's most common fear, primarily because of its unknown nature. The idea that our consciousness ceases to exist is very unsettling for most people. But our consciousness is never extinguished and death is only a perception because we don't know who or what we are. No spirit ever dies, including animals and plants. The personality transitions into another reality and the only thing that ends is the physical form, and even those elements simply relocate into other objects. Life was never meant to be permanent nor would we want it to be if we understood the process. Death continues the cycle of life and is a well-earned rest from a very difficult existence.

Death's Timing Is a Choice!
Except for suicide no one dies unless their inner conscious agrees to it. Near-death experiences (NDEs) are good examples of this. In an NDE the ego leaves the body just like it does when it dies. The difference is that the NDE ego returns to the body and continues with its life. It is common that the ego is told that its time on earth is not over and it has more things to accomplish. Occasionally the ego has completed enough of its plan and it is given a choice to either stay in the astral field or return to its body. If the time is not right, the ego is encouraged to return to physical life.

People often wonder how life can be fair when they see babies and small children die. But we view life through a keyhole. Babies die for many reasons and it is always what they have chosen. Their inner self may choose to wait and return when conditions are better or it may be because they want to try life but are not quite ready for all that goes with it. Life is not easy and sometimes souls just want to sample it and then quickly leave and slowly absorb the experience. At the other end of the spectrum, some highly developed souls are studying the natal and/or early life processes. These souls might have hundreds or even thousands of very short lives and maybe never live a full life in this Grand Cycle. When babies die, their consciousness survives like everyone else's. They exist in the astral field and are as mature as the other spirits. They have their reasons for ending their life, just like everyone else.

Death is necessary for all species because it allows for the regeneration of its members. The beauty of death is that it provides a chance to rest, evaluate our experiences, and see how our various choices impacted others. During life it seems that others caused our problems, but in death we are shown that all our experiences were self-created.

However, after resting in the afterlife, the desire to continue the evolutionary process slowly draws us back to the physical field. We return to the world with renewed enthusiasm and energy. A personality reincarnates with a certain naivety and aggression, which allows it to forge ahead with the experiences it planned. Death is simply the process of our consciousness choosing to leave our body and disassociate from the physical field for a while.

Death's Timing

Both our birth and our death are sublimely timed by the universe. Every identity or object that manifests in the physical field establishes the duration of that manifestation before it is created. However, sophisticated personalities like ourselves can alter those decisions but only under certain guidelines.

There is nothing haphazard about when we are born or when we die. We choose to be born because we want to experience life. When we lose the desire to live, we die. We did not have to come here and we do not have to stay. All is choice and we do what we want to do when we want to do it. But it is not the ego's choice, it is the inner conscious that decides. The ego is unaware of its purpose and how well it is doing. The inner conscious knows when life should end. If the ego really wants to end its life, the inner conscious will accommodate it by creating an acceptable circumstance where it will happen. The ego never needs to take on that responsibility.

Options for the timing of our death are considered long before we are born. Each prelife plan identifies numerous potential 'exit points.' Depending on the decisions we make during life, we may decide to stay with a preplanned exit or change it. When we choose to leave life is a function of how well life is progressing. Unless our ego takes over and commits suicide, which is never a good idea, our inner conscious decides when we die. It knows what we are trying to accomplish and how well we are doing, and it knows what the ego is feeling.

There are many circumstances that might convince the inner conscious to terminate the personality's life. The following are a few common reasons:

First, when we are out of synchronization with our life plan, especially if we are accumulating large amounts of karma, we may choose to die so we do not make an even bigger mess for future personalities to deal with. It is very easy for the personalities of young souls to get off course during a stressful life, and death allows them to regroup. We see people who have turned to crime die violently and often at an early age. Their inner conscious has agreed to this in order to help them regroup and refocus for a future life. Death provides an opportunity to reset our priorities. A chance to have a new start under different circumstances is one of the most likely reasons an inner conscious might choose an early death.

Second, when we feel a lack of love, we may choose to return to the spiritual world. Few people are willing to be lonely for too long. It is not unusual to see older couples who have lived together for a very long time die within a short time of each other. Even animals will choose to die when they are living without love. Although sometimes living a life without love can be part of our prelife plan, it is often because we have made poor decisions and our life has gotten out of control. We have free will, and when we do not use it wisely, our life can become difficult to deal with. Of course, it is always fixable, but sometimes an ego does not see it that way.

Third, the body may have lost its usefulness as a learning and experiencing tool. This might happen after the body has had a bad accident or disease. The inner conscious simply decides it can no longer have the experiences it desires in that body.

Fourth, it may have completed its prelife plan and feel it does not have any more useful tasks to accomplish. This can happen at any age, including as a baby if our goals only involve infant experiences. This is one of the least likely causes of death, especially for a young or middle-aged person, because our prelife plans are extensive and there is more to experience.

Fifth, in some cases an inner conscious might use its death to protest conditions it feels are intolerable. This is especially common during epidemics, pandemics, famines, wars, plagues and other mass disasters. Mass events are always a joint agreement between the inner consciouses of all the affected entities, including the animals and plants. In a mass event it is likely that if one person died to protest some conditions, many of the other deaths would have been for the same reason.

Sixth, we might want to perceive our experiences from a different perspective. This happens when we become too extreme in our views and are unable to have the experiences our soul is seeking. Some personalities of advanced souls are able make this change during their life, but most personalities will die, start over again, and recreate a whole new prelife plan.

Seventh, eventually when our body is old and dysfunctional, we prefer to die. Life becomes more of a struggle than we are willing to accept. If we have accomplished all that is possible from our prelife plan, we might decide we can evolve faster in the astral field or in a new body on earth.

Eighth, once the body reaches a certain pain threshold it releases the consciousness. We hear about near-death experiences where the consciousness anticipates a painful accident and leaves the body an instant before it happens. This is likely what happens in wars and other major destructive events.

Ninth, some deaths are involved with karmic ribbons. We may need to experience a violent or sudden death in the middle of a productive life to show us the tragedy we caused someone else. Karma can go both ways, in that it might involve the people left behind who need to experience a loss. In karmic situations, the event will be agreed upon ahead of time by all parties and will be part of everyone's prelife plan. The exact event is not necessarily identified in our prelife plan because life takes so many twists and turns. In this case, the inner conscious of the involved individuals will choose the event in real time, so the experience might happen in one of many possible ways, but the result will be the same.

Tenth, there are very rare cases where a highly advanced spirit will change places with another highly advanced spirit. In this case there is a mutual agreement between the two souls in which one will leave the body and another will take its place. This is extremely rare and usually happens at the very end of the reincarnation cycle, after the soul is ready to stop creating new personalities.

Accidental Deaths

We read about natural disasters where people were 'accidentally' killed, apparently, against their will. But these disasters are not nearly as haphazard as they appear. In each case, the 'victim's' inner conscious will be aware of the pending disaster and purposely put the personality in a position to be killed. The victim's inner conscious would have previously decided to die, and so it finds a socially acceptable circumstance for its death. If the personality did not die in this tragedy, it would have died in another one soon thereafter. The media is often relaying stories of people who did not take an airplane flight and the plane went down and all passengers were killed. This is simply a situation where the inner conscious sets up circumstances to avoid being killed. It is equally as common in other types of disasters like mass killings and auto accidents, but the stories are not as likely to be publicized or even known by the unsuspecting non-victims. The spiritual world is fully aware of future disasters, even the ones that seem to be spontaneous events. It is worth remembering that fearing things like airplane travel, or drowning or other common fears are groundless. If our inner conscious wants something to happen to us, it will find a way. If it does not, then nothing will happen.

If we did not live relatively short lives, death would eventually be necessary anyway because at some point we would simply outgrow our body's limitations. Our wisdom would no longer fit into our body. I find it interesting when I read about near-death experiences and the experiencers say that when they first 'died' they felt a huge expanse of their wisdom, but when they returned to their old body, they thought they would not fit into it. It seemed as though they were being shoehorned into the body. These seem like cases where the experiencer has accumulated greater wisdom than their body could easily handle. It is probably the clearest example of why death is necessary. For us to continue to evolve as sentient beings, we need a body capable of giving us the experiences we want. A body that will suffice for a very young soul's personality may not meet the needs of a wise old sage. In fact, even lower life forms need to die and be born again in a form more adapted to the new experiences it wants.

Ultimately, we learn a great deal from dying. This is especially true if it is caused by violence or sickness. Our beliefs cause us to be born, live, and eventually die. Analyzing our death can be very instructive.

Suicide

Suicide is a complicated issue worth understanding because in a way it seems that all our deaths are a form of suicide since we not only agree to them but make them happen. Under normal circumstances our inner conscious decides when to die. It understands life's purpose and can judge when a death is prudent. When the ego decides to exit life without the inner conscious's consent, it is a very different circumstance.

The inner conscious knows the personality's plan and understands what can and cannot be accomplished by the present personality. When the inner conscious decides to leave, it does so for the good of the personality, and others around it. The ego does not have this knowledge. If the ego decides to die it is because it does not want to struggle through the living process. This is never a wise decision. The problems the ego tries to escape from through suicide will not go away at death. Those same problems will continue to return, life after life, until they are dealt with.

The other aspect of dying too soon is that we are not able to assist others in achieving their goals. Our responsibilities are far reaching. When we selfishly cut our life short, others may be unable to complete their life plans.

The Death Event

It is worth remembering that no one is ever born without a purpose and no one ever dies without a purpose. We plan the key events in our life, and death is no exception. Death is simply the demise of our physical body and the transition of our consciousness out of the physical field. Death should not be a scary or mysterious process. There is no pain or unpleasant experience involved with death. In fact, death is a much easier process than birth. Birth is a violent, aggressive action where energy transforms itself into the physical field. Death is simply our consciousness disassociating itself from the physical field. It is a passive activity that happens extremely rapidly.

However, there is no actual point of death that we can point to where all our parts suddenly 'die.' The consciousnesses of the cells and organs stay with the body for a while as it is only the psyche that suddenly departs. The cells in the body can remain 'alive' and in place for extended periods of time. Their future is different than ours. However, that does not mean we are still alive. When the psyche leaves the body, we are 'dead.'

Astral Body

Our spirit creates a separate vehicle for each field it plans on visiting and it does not shed that vehicle until it is completely done with it. Since death only involves the physical body, we still retain our astral, causal, and mental bodies after death. When consciousness leaves the physical body, the ego stops focusing on the physical field and starts focusing on the astral field. It is like stepping out of one reality and into another. Our ego suddenly finds itself in the astral body, which it had all along but never noticed. The astral body will seem as solid and natural to us as the physical body did even though it is not as dense. Whatever reality we are in seems as real and solid to us as our life here on earth. However, we will have far more freedoms in the astral field where disease and injury do not exist, and our thoughts can create objects at will. But like all our illusions, the astral environment is our creation in cooperation with others.

Immediately after death, especially if we have a great fear of it, we may not realize what happened and we might think we are still alive. However, once we begin to interface with the physical world, we will realize we cannot impact anything. We will immediately notice that we have a different way of sensing our environment and moving through it. Our thoughts will no longer be constrained by the physical field's time delay so our actions will instantaneously follow our thoughts. For example, if we just think about going somewhere, then we will be there.

During life, the astral field information is always available to us through our inner sense, but our outer senses overload our neural system so we do not normally detect this information. When we die, our five outer senses stop overriding our inner sense and we are able to perceive the astral field. After death we can still sense the physical field, but not as clearly as when we were 'alive' because we are not focused on it. We do it through our inner sense, which is not attuned to the physical environment like our outer senses were.

Telepathy

During life, the inner conscious is in continual communication with astral entities like our spirit guides and deceased loved ones. This normally occurs during sleep so we rarely remember it. Telepathy is the communication technique used in the astral and higher fields. In fact, the Seth entity says it is used by all of what we call nature in the physical field. Humans are the only ones on earth that use languages but we have telepathic capabilities as well. However, we are so focused on our verbal communications that we assume most of the telepathic information that we receive are our own thoughts. Mediums communicate telepathically with the astral field. Actually, anyone could do this if they were able to temporarily ignore their outer senses. This is often done during deep meditation, which opens up channels to the spiritual realms.

Mediums and psychics have developed ways to focus on the astral data by quieting the mind and lessening the impact of the physical senses. By subduing the physical data and focusing on the astral data, it becomes possible to communicate with those that have crossed over.

Everybody has a telepathic capability, but most of us do not use it during our lives. Once we die our brain is no longer a bottleneck and our senses are not consumed by physical data, so we can manage a great deal more information.

Death Scene

NDEs are a great source of information for understanding what happens at the moment of death. For all practical purposes the individual died but later returned. Tens of thousands of their stories are amazingly consistent across different cultures, around the world, over all ages, and with both genders.

Immediately after death the 'earth-focused' portion of our consciousness can and often does remain partially focused in the physical field, at least for a short while. Our consciousness may remain at the scene of death and watch the activities to see what happens next, especially if it is a sudden unexpected death. People who are recently deceased will often try to contact loved ones and let them know they are still okay. If the living person has psychic capabilities the deceased might try to contact them via telepathy, but it is more likely the deceased will appear to them in their dreams. The people most closely involved with the deceased are often suffering from such intense emotions that this type of communication is temporarily blocked. Sometimes a less emotionally involved person is more likely to be the recipient of the dream. This was the case when my wife died. Neither myself nor my children had a dream experience, but another closely related family member did experience such a dream.

In the case of extremely untimely deaths of people who feel a strong sense of responsibility for those left behind, it is not unusual to see ephemeral images of the person near their previous residence even several weeks after death. This is a phenomenon that can actually happen during life. If a consciousness focuses extremely hard on being in a certain location, their image can begin to manifest in that location. The consciousness does not go there, just the image.

Also, there have been many stories about someone who died and a person in another location thousands of miles away becomes aware of the death the moment it happens.

A person who dies of old age or a natural death is likely to leave the scene more quickly. They are less likely to have unfinished business to distract them so they spend less time departing. If there is a funeral within a few days after death the deceased will probably stay around for it but then leave and start its new existence. However, if the death was sudden and unexpected, a consciousness will often stay close to the people it was involved with for a while.

Transitioning

The actual process of death is best viewed as crossing over or transitioning from a physical experience to an astral experience. Nothing actually dies, it just changes form. Every object we experience in life is simply consciousness in a physical form. No consciousness ever dies. In fact nothing ever dies.

Our inner conscious and subconscious reside in the astral field throughout our life so they do not need a transition period. It is only the ego that experiences a transition. In fact, the field we experience at death is all around us now but we don't perceive it because we are literally hypnotized by the physical field.

Frequently, people who have had near-death experiences report seeing a small light at the end of a tunnel shortly after death. This is the cord that connects us to a location in the astral field.

Just thinking that we would like to travel through the tunnel towards the light causes it to happen. Near-death experiencers have reported numerous sensations during this trip. It is fairly common to feel a high speed or rushing experience as one goes through the tunnel. Sometimes we are met by a loved one who escorts us through the tunnel but often we simply do it alone.

Like all realities, the astral field is also an illusion. It allows us to have the experiences we want. Our inner conscious creates our reality in this life with the help of others, and it also creates our reality in the afterlife, also with the help of others. Thoughts create objects in both realities but in the physical field, matter has a sluggish response to thought. This is not the case in the astral field where our thoughts instantly create astral or pseudo matter. Astral matter is similar to physical matter except it is not as dense and it vibrates at a higher frequency.

The Adjustment Period

Our spirit guides make every possible effort to assure we have a smooth transition into the afterlife. Similar to our physical life, our beliefs at the time of death determine the initial experiences we have upon entering the astral field. Our beliefs create our reality. Our misconceptions about the afterlife at the moment of death will need to be corrected before we can seriously begin our work between lives. Neither heaven, hell, nor oblivion is an accurate description of the spiritual realm. If our spirit guides determine that it would be a huge shock for us to see the astral field as it really is, they will help us create the scenario we expect to see.

Our astral field illusions will seem as real to us as our physical life seemed. The Seth entity says our spirit guides play the parts of the key entities in our imagined drama. We will perceive a world that has depth, more colors, animated beings, etcetera, just as we would expect it to be. For example, if we expected to be greeted by a holy figure or even God, then a sequence of events will occur where we are immediately warmly welcomed into the afterlife and praised for all our fine deeds and loyal efforts. If we believe that evil exists and there is a heavenly battle waging between good and evil with demons and other evil forces vying for our soul, then our guides will help us create that scenario in the spiritual world. But those demons and angels will be our spirit guides in disguise playing out the scenario of our beliefs. Even if we believed that our consciousness ended at death we would go into a state of suspension. But this too does not last. It is simply a transition until we are able to slowly adapt to a new reality.

My daughter was an emergency room nurse at the beginning of her career and she related a story of a homeless man who came in and was truly down and out. He was lying down in the ER when he suddenly sat up, let out a terrified scream and died. This naturally upset the entire room. What had surely happened is that he saw what he expected to see when he died. Undoubtedly he was eventually brought back to reality by his spirit guides. We create our own reality, and then we live with it, at least for awhile. Understanding who we are and the nature of things can save us a good bit of suffering.

The goal is to gently alter our beliefs and ease us into the astral field. Like the illusions in the physical field, the death experiences will seem just as real as the physical experiences, and are just as valuable. Everyone who needs to reset their beliefs will be successful.

Life Review

After we emerge from the tunnel and deal with any misconceptions, our consciousness is then greeted by well-known loving spirits. We have a joyful reunion with our deceased friends and relatives and we are welcomed back home.

No feelings are hidden in the spiritual realm. Unlike on earth, in the spiritual realms spirits do not play social games and pretend to be something they are not. We might think that we would have universal love for everyone in the astral field but this is not always the case. People who treated us poorly, including close relatives, may not be our favorite people after death. Yet some of our adversaries in this life might be our dearly beloved in the afterlife. Their adversarial actions may have simply been planned at our request during the prelife planning process.

Eventually we will need to review our past life and understand and absorb our life's lessons. The life review is like seeing a movie of our life except now we experience the emotions that we caused other people. If we made someone feel happy then we will feel their positive emotions. If we made someone feel badly then we will feel their negative emotions. We feel the joy and sorrow that we brought to others at the same level of intensity that they felt. This allows us to see the impact our life had on others. What goes around comes around.

Life after Death

After death our consciousness no longer uses its five outer senses to perceive its surroundings because those senses no longer exist. Instead, our inner sense immediately takes over and our perceptions are greatly expanded. For example, because our consciousness in the astral field is not limited to seeing through the narrow cone-like vision created by our eyes, we have spherical vision. Also not being restricted by our brain, we can accommodate a great deal more data. The communication process is telepathic, which is faster and more accurate than speech.

After the initial period of adjustment discussed earlier, the astral field will at first appear to be very similar to life on earth. There is wonderful music, which is more complex than in this life. There are schools available to study new areas of knowledge, minus the often misleading cultural beliefs we learn on earth. There are places to visit for personal development and entertainment and even other realms and dimensions to visit and study. We can even travel around the galaxy and see the amazing creations other minds have produced. There is as much organization and structure in the astral field as here on earth. Like on earth, existence in the astral field has a purpose.

Life Analysis

We do not stop learning from our physical experiences after death. Our life has many more lessons to teach us. After an adjustment period, eventually we do an in-depth 'Life Analysis,' which is much more comprehensive than our initial life review. Instead of just seeing how we impacted others, we see how a different action on our part could have impacted others as well as ourselves.

During the life analysis we are able to test alternate approaches to our problems, change our decisions and see how they would have turned out. This requires our reviewer to create mental images of the events, to include simulating the other people who were involved. Of course, those actual people are not present. Thought figures are created that have the same tendencies as the actual participants so likely responses can be achieved. Without the constraint of physical time, each event can be reviewed quite rapidly.

By doing this, we can see and feel the impact of our decisions. As such, we view our recent life very differently than we did when we were alive. We come to recognize that we were responsible for what happened to us. When life seemed unfair while we were living it, we learn that our life was really just a reflection of our actions. Our beliefs created our experiences. Even though others may have encouraged us to act poorly, our actions were our own choice. We cannot control the circumstances life brings us, but we can control our response to them. Seeing our life from this perspective gives us a whole new understanding of how others felt about our relationships.

The political, religious and social issues that we felt so impassioned about at the time take on a new light. During our life we see what we believe to be reality through a distorted and limited perspective. What we believe to be truths about life are only our ideas about life. The life analysis helps us see ourselves as we really are. It is a learning tool not a punishment. If we were cruel or self-centered and always talking down to people, then this will likely be a long and difficult process. No matter how we lived our life, this is always very illuminating. Everyone makes mistakes because that is how we learn. Our life review simply gives us a clearer perspective on the choices we made.

One of the more surprising aspects of this analysis is realizing that the past can be changed. We think the experiences that we had during our life are cast in concrete but that is not the case. During life we see experiences as physical events. But we are psychic beings and it is only the mental and emotional aspects of an experience that have any meaning. The physical illusion makes it appear that our experiences are physical, but the physical world is only a mechanism to allow us to have psychic experiences. Life experiences are flexible even after they occur and we can change the mental and emotional outcome of any situation by reliving the experience and making different decisions. The revised decisions allow us to literally alter our emotional reaction to events that occurred in our past. If we suffered trauma, we can recreate that experience and by making different decisions relive the experience without undergoing the trauma. The revised event is just as valid as the original and our response can supplant our original memories. We are here to learn, not to suffer from bad choices. Death gives us an opportunity to change how events impacted us. Of course, this does not change the impact our actions had on others. Only they can change that and they do.

Establishing Communication with the Deceased
Most people have known someone who has died that they would like to talk to. Actually this can be done and is a simple process.

If you do not have psychic capabilities of your own, using a medium or channel is an excellent way to interface with a spirit. Even though the spirit is anxious to communicate with us, the living person usually activates the process. However, one time when I was communicating with my deceased wife through a medium my parents showed up because they had some things they wanted to discuss.

The most important thing to do is establish confidence in the medium, which is easy if you are contacting someone that you were very close to. One has to be careful as there are frauds who try to lead clients into telling them what they want to hear. They do this in a highly skilled manner by extracting information through questions, idle chatter, monitoring your responses, and/or your body language. I recommend a medium as opposed to a mentalist or psychic. Not that the latter two cannot be the real thing, but my experience is that they are more likely to be con artists rather than a medium or channel. While establishing the validity of the medium, be sure to provide the medium with as little information as possible about both you and the deceased person. Be cautious of mediums who ask you questions and try to find out your thoughts. A spirit will know that you want proof that you are actually communicating with them so the spirit will offer information that only you are familiar with but the medium could not know. This is relatively easy to do when contacting someone with which you had a very close relationship.

Once you are convinced you are communicating with the actual spirit you are seeking, then the deceased person will tell you what they want you to know. Very often the deceased will do most of the talking, especially if they have recently died and they have things they want to say. It is very helpful to record these sessions so you can transcribe them later. Specific terminology can be very insightful and it is difficult to absorb all the information in real time. Spirits can offer advice if you ask for it, but the spiritual world has restrictions on what information it can provide. Discussing your future, giving specific details about your agreements with other living people, and offering specific detailed direction is rarely done. However, spirits will often give general guidance. They can also discuss issues about your past relationship with them. This can be extremely helpful for handling diseases, planning future activities or just understanding life. It is also very comforting for the loved ones left behind to know that the deceased are still a part of their life.

There are a number of ways spirits can help those left behind. For example, if someone dies suddenly and their spouse is expected to live a long time, the deceased might assist in finding them another companion. The deceased would have a very good idea what qualities would be appropriate for a new companion. This information would then be coordinated with the inner conscious of both parties, and seemingly synchronous events would take place for the two parties to meet. Obviously, everyone has free will so it would be up to the two parties to decide if they wanted future contact. This system would be the envy of any personnel recruiting organization or dating service.

Activities in the Astral Field

Like earth, the astral field is an illusion so it has cities with houses and buildings. It has forests, lakes, gardens, etc. Any hobby or recreational activity available on earth is available in the astral field. As it is on earth, these things are joint creations of both other entities in the astral field and ourselves. The purpose of an illusion is to give us experiences and we do that in the astral field just like we do it here. Eventually we begin to see it as it really is. But initially we take advantage of the illusion.

We know and interact with a huge number of other spirits in the astral field so there is no shortage of companionship. But like here on earth, there are some entities we work more closely with than others. We have many choices of activities we can pursue from the frivolous to the serious. If we had a particularly difficult life we might choose to simply rest for a while. We might do this by sitting in a country retreat fishing or gardening or traveling around the universe and seeing different civilizations. Because we are not limited by our physical body, we can travel outside the physical field so travel is extremely rapid. What could be more interesting than playing *Star Trek*, traveling throughout the galaxies, and studying alien cultures?

No matter how stressed we were from the last life, eventually we will want to continue the task at hand, which is our evolution. We have learned much from our previous lives and we will want to address the issues we are still dealing with. We go to classes, communicate with experts, and try out our new ideas. This can be a long process or a relatively short one.

Astral Responsibilities

Spiritual life has a great deal of responsibility inherent in it. When our soul 'signs up' for a series of sentient lives, we do so with the understanding that we will complete the full cycle of lives through the reincarnating process. We are part of a group of entities who accepted the responsibility to assist each other life after life. No one is alone in this process. We work together as a team helping each other in many ways. We do this by assuming interrelated responsibilities as family members, friends, adversaries, work associates, etc.

If we choose to remain in contact with the physical world, it will be because we want to monitor the lives of the loved ones we left behind and assist them if possible. We will have a whole new appreciation for the problems and issues we left behind, both with our loved ones and adversaries, because of what we learned in our life review and life analysis. We will also have a much clearer understanding of what they need and how they can live a happier and more productive life.

We can provide them guidance through their spirit guides, interface with them during dreams, or communicate through mediums and channels if they are so inclined to use those sources. It is surprising how much assistance we can provide to those left behind. However, we may just want to participate with them in their physical activities, albeit as a spirit. If we decide to accompany a loved one on a trip, we might be with them on the airplane or just show up along the way. We can easily be fully aware of all aspects of the trip. Once all our loved ones pass over, our active participation with the physical field will greatly diminish until we reincarnate once again.

The afterlife is a busy place. We meet new people, help others, visit friends and plan our future. It is not a place to dawdle. If we are a fairly mature and experienced soul we may act as a spirit guide for a friend or in some cases a stranger. We can either be a full-time guide where we would stay with one person throughout their life or do it part time. We might even be a specialist if we have developed a competence in a specific area.

Eventually planning our next life becomes a major focus in the afterlife. Along with our new understanding of our most recent past life, we also have access to all our spiritual knowledge from our previous lives. This gives us great insight into the type of experiences we will want to have in the next life. We will discuss this process in detail in later chapters.

Apparitions

Everyone wonders if apparitions or ghosts exist and, if so, what they are. Most people have encountered events that they believe might be related to ghosts. Ghosts do exist but they are not what they are made out to be.

Ghosts are usually human personalities, although they could be animals who have died but have not come to grips with their death. When we die, two things happen: 1) our consciousness is released from our body; and 2) our ego's focus changes from the physical field to the astral field. Ghosts, of course, lose their bodies but their ego is so consumed with something in the physical field that they never change their focus.

All fields in this universe have seven levels and we exist on level four of the physical field. Ghosts exist on the 6th or 7th level, which is much more ethereal than our fourth level.

The ghost is only a partial psyche. The main portion of the psyche is in the astral field. Since they no longer have the ability to create a 'solid' physical body they usually cannot interfere with physical reality. It would take a great deal of effort and expertise for them to even make a noise, let alone cause something to happen. However, it is possible in certain situations.

Ghosts are consumed by some specific aspect of their physical life. Their interest consumed them when they were alive and they carry that focus with them in death. They simply cannot accept any other viewpoint than the one they are so committed to. In death, they are trying to change a circumstance that they were unable to accomplish during their life. They may even be trying to take revenge on someone, which they are no longer capable of doing. They become temporarily stuck between earth and the astral field. Generally, they perform repetitive tasks. It is kind of like the movie *Groundhog Day* except the tasks are much simpler and of shorter duration.

Apparitions are not necessarily connected with the deceased. Anyone who has a highly emotional thought and projects it can create an apparition that could appear in a specific location or even another reality. If the apparition is seen by others in another reality, then they will not know who it is, but if they are fairly advanced they will know what it is. The creation of apparitions is a natural phenomenon of consciousness and occurs when we have an out-of-body experience.

When we lived in New Jersey we had a close friend who lived next door die of cancer at the age of 43. He was a very responsible father and husband and his ego was not ready to 'desert' them. During the first week after his death my wife said she saw him twice. Once cutting the lawn and once coming around the corner of his house.

If a ghost is bothering you the best approach would be to say something like: "You have to leave now! Go in peace!" Ghosts know we are more powerful than they are because we do not have their fears, so they will obey. Problems can only occur if we let them. If we are afraid of them then they might take advantage of the situation and we might do something foolish as a result.

Eventually the ghost will realize that it needs to return to the astral field and it will do so. We cannot reach the ghost from our field but spirits will eventually be able to reach it and explain their predicament. When an ego is stuck between fields no growth can occur. This might take months or centuries of earth time. Because of the ghost's confusion, it will eventually need to work through its fears in the astral field before reincarnating again. Ghosts are a natural phenomenon and not to be feared. When you encounter one that you do not want to be around, be strong, act firm and simply take charge of the situation. As in every situation, fear is your biggest problem.

Psyche's Options after Death

The psyche does not disappear after death. It always maintains an existence as an independent identity with control over the talents and capabilities it cultivated during its life. But it has a number of options as to how it will evolve.

The psyche will never return to earth in the exact energy configuration that it was in at death. It will continue to evolve by supporting the soul's new creations and pursuing other interests not directly connected with the soul's present incarnations.

If the psyche is unusually strong and has had the requisite experiences, like being both a mother and father, and has had a full childhood, it may choose to become a soul of its own. In this case it would create its own personalities and develop them through the reincarnating process independent of its originating soul. This is how every soul began so it is not unexpected or discouraged. Of course there is a great deal of expertise and effort required to be a soul so not every psyche is ready for that responsibility. However, some souls are strong enough to continually produce psyches that choose this path.

On rare occasions a very strong and mature spirit chooses to return to earth and make a major 'cultural changing impact' on society. Apparently figures like Buddha, Christ, and Michelangelo followed this path. They specialize in a particular field and advance it in some significant way. Afterwards, this psyche will often choose to return to the soul, give up its ego, and evolve as a part of the soul. No matter what the circumstances, the psyche always maintains a close relationship with its soul.

All of our choices are excellent options. Eventually we all become strong enough to go out on our own as a spirit. There is no timetable or pressure to do anything. It is simply what we think we are ready for. No matter what we choose, our psyche always remains part of our soul's gestalt, even when the two are far away in different realities. What we learn and accomplish makes both us and our soul greater, which in turn makes the Tao greater.

Section III

Evolution

Chapter 7

Reincarnation

Life and death are one thread, the same line viewed from different sides.
Lao Tse

Key Concept: Reincarnation is a reality.

What Is Reincarnation?

One of the most misunderstood concepts in religion, science and metaphysics is reincarnation. We spend our lives hearing rumors and judging them to be true or false without ever investigating. If we want to understand who we are and how life works, we need to investigate certain key issues and reincarnation falls into that category for many people. First and foremost, to accept reincarnation we have to realize that we have an eternal element within us that survives death. This is more of a scientific issue as the major religions support this concept. Mainstream science and parts of philosophy are the only areas that struggle with this. However, anybody that disparages reincarnation needs to look objectively at paranormal activity like Near-Death Experiences, Out-of-Body Experiences, and other ESP phenomena, and they will soon realize that their core beliefs need to be reevaluated. The world is not as it seems to be.

Confusion concerning reincarnation arises because we do not realize who we are and what is reincarnating. If we think of ourselves as souls, then we absolutely return, and we do it many times. If we think of ourselves as just the personality, then we do not return. The soul would not want to create an identical personality. The soul creates new psyches with different biases, different prelife plans, different agreements, etc. A soul incarnates by creating new personalities.

Western Bias against Reincarnation

Evolution is the reason we are here and reincarnation is a key piece in the evolutionary process. Incarnation is the process that allows our soul to transition into an organic body and appear to be at one with it. It is a necessary deception that allows us to believe the body we join is truly who we are. The process of a soul incarnating over and over again is referred to as reincarnation. This is one of the most difficult concepts for many Westerners to accept, even though over 50% of the world's population accepts it and indeed takes it for granted.

Unfortunately, many of us have been so indoctrinated into the false belief that reincarnation does not exist that we are unable to evaluate the data on its merits, and I was not an exception. Being raised in the scientific and Christian communities, my negative views on reincarnation were so strong that it took me a full decade from the first time I saw supporting data that I could not refute until I was convinced it was the only practical answer. For those that do not accept it, you might want to ask yourselves why. Have you thoroughly investigated the data or just rejected the concept for religious, scientific or social reasons?

There are three primary reasons that reincarnation is rejected: 1) the 'exoteric' dogma of the Abrahamic religions discounts it; 2) the Eastern religions that support it have incorporated misinformation into their doctrine that is false and challenges its believability; and 3) mainstream science does not support it. But when we examine the rationale behind these reasons, they show that ulterior motives have impacted the data.

Western Religions

Western religions and associated governments have been vocal critics of reincarnation for the last 1500 years. These have not been impartial bystanders. Certain clergy and many monarchs opposed reincarnation because it was believed it would weaken their power over the people. They thought that if the people believed that this is just one of many lives, then they would not be as awed by their oppressors. The elites knew that it would be much more difficult to sell their omnipotence and grandeur to the people when the fleeting nature of the hierarchy's power was understood. It should be noted that until some 500 years after the time of Jesus, virtually everyone accepted reincarnation as a fundamental principle.

Christianity, Judaism and Islam all taught reincarnation at their onset. Let's take them one at a time starting with Christianity.

Christianity

When Jesus lived, Hinduism had been around for thousands of years and Buddhism was 600 years old, both religions having reincarnation as a major tenet. The concept of reincarnation was well-known in the Middle East when Jesus was a young man. It is inconceivable in his travels to Egypt and in other areas where He preached that He was unaware of the concept. Of course, if one believes He was God, He obviously would have known about it. If Jesus did not support reincarnation, then He would have taken great pains to renounce it, but He did not. The following three segments are from *The Endless Journey*:[10]

> Christians believed in reincarnation for the first five hundred years after Jesus, and it was not until the Holy Roman Emperor Justinian, who may not have even been a Christian, forced the Christian Church Bishops to ban reincarnation at the Fifth Ecumenical Council circa AD 545. At the time it was a highly controversial decision and supposedly only passed by a single vote even though Justinian dictated the result. As the doctrine was slowly canonized some 500-1000 years after the death of Jesus, the Church leaders followed Justinian's

edict because it helped support the story that they wanted to tell. Slowly but surely during Christianity's evolution, Jesus's message and attempt to revise Judaism took a back seat to the personal ambitions of the Church and State and much of what Jesus taught was lost.

In *The Case For Reincarnation*, Joe Fisher notes that: "... the fact remains that before Christianity became the vehicle for the imperial ambitions of Roman Emperors, rebirth was widely accepted amongst the persecuted faithful."[11]

Fisher goes on to say: "Believers in reincarnation were neither to be induced by promises of heavenly bliss nor intimidated by threats of hellfire; they didn't need priests and ritual devices such as the confessional to guide them along the straight and narrow path to God."[12]

Many people do not realize that the four gospels in the Bible were chosen by the clergy from a much larger number of gospels available at the time. The others were banned because they did not corroborate the Church's story. Between 1947 and 1956 a set of documents were found in Egypt known as the Dead Sea Scrolls. The documents are believed to have been written between 400 BC and 200 AD. Many of the texts were copies of known Jewish and Christian documents, some of which are in the Bible and Torah. But also amongst these texts were documents known as the Gnostic Gospels. These writings expand on the four Gospels (Matthew, Mark, Luke and John) canonized by the Church and included in the New Testament. Gnostic Gospels like Origen and Thomas expanded on the many sayings attributed to Jesus to include clear passages showing Jesus believed in and taught reincarnation.

Unfortunately, the early Church Fathers decided not only to disagree with these teachings but to ban them as heretical, and they destroyed or confiscated all copies that they could find, until all of a sudden they turned up as part of the Dead Sea Scrolls. It seemed clear to me that any organization driven to ban and destroy certain books and beliefs must have a hidden agenda, and I was sure it was based on self-interest.

Although much of Jesus's support for reincarnation was kept out of the Bible during its creation and many revisions, they did not succeed in obliterating it all.

John 3:3: "Jesus answered and said to him, 'Truly, truly, I say to you, unless one is born again he cannot see the kingdom of God.'" This 'born again' has nothing to do with the modern day practice of rededicating one's life to Christ as is taught in many fundamentalist sects. This 'born again' really means to be 'born again' *just* like it says.

John 3:8: "The wind blows where it wishes and you hear the sound of it, but do not know where it comes from and where it is going; so is everyone born of the spirit." John clearly believed the spirit is alive before it is born.

The Christian doctrine is based on a number of false premises and reincarnation is a major one. The Church knew the people would not follow the Church's teachings if God was guiding their spiritual growth through reincarnation. In fact, the Pope, who arrogated himself to the position of being between God and man, would lose all his self-proclaimed Godly authority. It became clear that reincarnation did not work within the confines of the way the Church implemented Christianity so it was intentionally excluded from the doctrine.

I soon began to realize that my misgivings about reincarnation had no foundation in Christianity but I thought it would be interesting to see how reincarnation was addressed in the other two main Abrahamic religions, Judaism and Islam. Since all three religions had a similar origin, I surmised that traces of a belief in reincarnation would be present in them.

Judaism

The fact that reincarnation is part of the Jewish tradition will come as a surprise to many people but it made sense to me after what I discovered with Christianity. All religions have a strong mystical element, which is purported to be the real teachings of the religion that are only known to the 'initiates' or those special individuals that have achieved higher metaphysical understanding. As one would expect, Judaism has a very strong mystical element, which is known as 'Kabbalah.' The key concepts of Kabbalah are written in the *Zohar*, which was 'revealed' more than 2000 years ago. The *Zohar* is a spiritual text that supposedly explains the secrets of the Jewish Bible, the universe, and every aspect of life. The *Zohar* clearly states that the concept of reincarnation is an accepted aspect of Jewish belief as can be seen below:

> As long as a person is unsuccessful in his purpose in this world, the Holy One, blessed be He, uproots him and replants him over and over again.
>
> *Zohar* I, 186b

> All souls are subject to reincarnation; and people do not know the ways of the Holy One, blessed be He! They do not know that they are brought before the tribunal both before they enter into this world and after they leave it; they are ignorant of the many reincarnations and secret works

which they have to undergo, and of the number
of naked souls, and how many naked spirits roam
about in the other world without being able to
enter within the veil of the King's Palace. Men do
not know how the souls revolve like a stone that is
thrown from a sling. But the time is at hand when
these mysteries will be disclosed.
Zohar II, 99b

Somewhere along the way mainstream Judaism dropped the
concept of reincarnation. It was probably an attempt to placate
the political powers of the time as Christianity had done.
Unfortunately, this made it much more difficult for Jews to
understand the nature of the universe and how they fit into it.

Islam
Islam also builds the case for reincarnation as stated in the Koran:

And Allah has caused you to spring forth from
the earth like a plant; hereafter he will turn you
back into it and will bring you forth anew.
Quran, Sura 71:17-18

How can you make denial of Allah, who made
you live again when you died, will make you
dead again, and then alive again, until you
finally return to him?
Quran, Sura 2, The Cow, Verse 28

God is the one who created you all, then
provided you sustenance, then will cause you to
die, then will bring you to life.
Quran, Sura 11, Verse 38

> Surely it is God who splits the seed and the
> stone, bringing the living from the dead; and it
> is God who brings the dead from living.
> Quran, Sura 6, Cattle, Verse 95

Clearly the Abrahamic religions have a long history in support of the belief in reincarnation.

The fact that it is supported in the Bible, Torah and Quran and was a firm tenet during the early centuries of all the Western religions make the present doctrines highly suspect.

Eastern Religious Myths

The Eastern religions have professed reincarnation since their origin. But over time and through the addition of certain political considerations, reincarnation has morphed into a concept that is hard for Westerners to accept. But these concepts are myths and do not have any real validity.

In fact, Eastern religious myths regarding reincarnation have made it easier for the Abrahamic religions to convince their members to renounce reincarnation as well. For example, the Hindus claim that if we are bad we will return in the next life in a lower class or even as an animal. This is a fallacy and is only a method used by the clergy and higher caste members to control the masses. One is not reborn at a higher or lower social status because of one's actions in a previous life. We are reborn with a purpose and that is what determines our next life. In fact, most Hindus will not even be reborn as a Hindu. The Hindu caste system is a political creation not a spiritual one.

As far as returning as an animal, we never return to life at a lower evolutionary point than we have achieved. As such, without exception, a human will never return as an animal. The sacred Hindu cows are not anyone's ancestors. They have animal souls and they were never incarnated into a human body.

146

Evolution is a one-way street and there is no going back. Once our soul has reached a certain level, that is the lowest it will ever be. It might take several additional lives to move our evolution significantly forward, but we will never go backward.

Also another false Hindu belief is that when we die our soul goes into a state of suspended consciousness and whatever was on our mind at the moment of death determines what we become in the next life. This is not how reincarnation works. Our consciousness never leaves us. In death we are fully aware of all our past lives and indeed continue to evolve between death and our next incarnation.

Science

Science is another source of thought that rejects reincarnation. Those of us brought up in the scientific community are taught to believe life is just an accident and we only get one chance. But science is not the fountain of all knowledge as it proclaims to be. As stated previously, we should keep in mind that science is in its infancy and what it preaches today it will revise again and again in the future.

One reason Western science does not like the concept of reincarnation is because science is so focused on the material world it does not recognize the spiritual nature of reality. It is hard to accept reincarnation if one does not believe in a soul. No matter how much data points to a transcendent spiritual force or an eternal soul within each person, science clings to its old ways. The problem is that science is focused on understanding the physical universe. Thus, they call their study of natural phenomena 'physics,' implying everything is physical, and that is what they study. Science restricts its definition of the physical world to the field of existence that we can perceive either with our five senses or our instruments. So far our instruments are not much more than an extension of the physical senses. Great progress in this area will not occur until science is able to understand the inner sense. Their view is a highly restrictive requirement when we realize that all we can perceive, even with our instruments, is the camouflaged world. Not only doesn't the soul consist of physical material, it does not even exist in the physical field.

The focus on materialism has left science with an untenable position as it tries to explain life and creation. Since science has not found the soul yet, it is left explaining life as simply a well-organized (by whom, one might ask) material body with a fantastic nervous system that somehow has become self-aware. A viable explanation for consciousness has not been put forward by science, even in quantum physics.

Science believes that when the body dies there is nothing left to go on living. Even though science is finding amazing new discoveries supporting the independence of consciousness and the body, old ideas are hard to alter. Science will never come to grips with a true description of reality until it recognizes that the physical universe is the result of consciousness and not the cause of it.

Medical and Scientific Evidence Supporting Reincarnation

It seems most people who have seriously investigated the scientific data supporting reincarnation, and have done so with an open mind, inevitably convince themselves that reincarnation is either a fact of life or, at a minimum, realize the supporting data is too difficult to ignore. This is especially true in the last 50 years because the exponential increase in communications has helped bring new information to the populace. Probably the biggest handicap to the wider acceptance of reincarnation is the stigma that is still attached to it. Many people in the academic and scientific fields are concerned that their reputation and employment will be negatively impacted if they publicly support reincarnation. However, if we are looking for truth, then ignoring the available data and submitting to peer pressures are not going to help us find it.

Before we can believe in reincarnation, we need to believe that there is an eternal inner spiritual essence within each of us. If we cannot get past that, then believing in reincarnation is hopeless.

Medical and Psychiatric Data

Near-Death Experience (NDE)

NDE is an area where there is a huge amount of data supporting an eternal inner spiritual essence. Although there is a long list of authors that have written about their experiences, Dr. Jeffrey Long is one of the most knowledgeable. Dr. Long is a physician and radiation oncologist; and the founder of the Near-Death Experience Research Foundation. He is the author of: *Evidence of the Afterlife: The Science of Near-Death Experiences*; and *God and the Afterlife: The Groundbreaking New Evidence for God and Near-Death Experiences*.

I had the pleasure of having Jeffrey Long, MD as a guest on *The Common Sense Spirituality Show* several times and he has done more to further the research of the NDE phenomena than anyone I am aware of. The Near-Death Experience Research Foundation has a database of over 3500 NDE investigations. Although no two NDEs are identical, there are common characteristics that appear across large numbers of NDEs. The following is what Dr. Long had to say about those common characteristics:

1) **Crystal Clear Consciousness.** The level of consciousness and alertness during near-death experiences is usually even greater than that experienced in everyday life, even though NDEs generally occur when a person is unconscious or clinically dead. This high level of consciousness while physically unconscious is medically inexplicable. Additionally, the elements in NDEs generally follow the

same consistent and logical order in all age groups and around the world, which refutes the possibility that NDEs have any relation to dreams or hallucinations.

2) **Realistic Out-of-Body Experiences.** Out-of-body experiences (OBEs) are one of the most common elements of NDEs. What near-death experiencers see and hear of earthly events in the out-of-body state is almost always realistic. When they or others later seek to verify what was observed or heard during the NDE, the OBE observations are almost always confirmed as completely accurate. Even if the OBE observations during the NDE included events far from the physical body, and far from any possible sensory awareness of the experiencer, the OBE observations are still almost always confirmed as completely accurate. This fact alone rules out the possibility that near-death experiences are related to any known brain functioning or sensory awareness. This also refutes the possibility that NDEs are unrealistic fragments of memory from the brain.

3) **Heightened Senses.** Not only are heightened senses reported by most who have experienced NDEs, normal or supernormal vision has occurred in those with significantly impaired vision, and even legal blindness. Several people who have been totally blind since birth have reported highly visual near-death experiences. This is medically inexplicable.

4) **Consciousness During Anesthesia.** Many NDEs occur while under general anesthesia, which is at a time when any conscious experience should be impossible. While some skeptics claim that these NDEs may be the result of too little anesthesia, this ignores the fact that some NDEs result from anesthesia overdose. Additionally, the description of an NDE differs greatly from that of one who experiences "anesthetic awareness." The content of NDEs that occur under general anesthesia is essentially

indistinguishable from NDEs that did not occur under general anesthesia. This is further strong evidence that NDEs are occurring completely independently from the functioning of the physical brain.

5) **Perfect Playback.** Life reviews in near-death experiences include real events that previously took place in the lives of those having the experience, even if the events were forgotten or happened before they were old enough to remember.

6) **Family Reunions.** During an NDE, the people encountered are virtually always deceased, and are usually relatives of the person having the experience and sometimes they are even relatives who died before the experiencer was born. Were the NDE only a product of memory fragments, they would almost certainly include far more living people, including those with whom they had more recently interacted.

7) **Children's Experiences.** The near-death experiences of children, including very young children who are too young to have developed concepts of death, religion, or near-death experiences, are essentially identical to those of older children and adults. This refutes the possibility that the content of NDEs is produced by preexisting beliefs or cultural conditioning.

8) **Worldwide Consistencies.** Near-death experiences appear remarkably consistent around the world, and across many different religions and cultures. NDEs from non-Western countries are incredibly similar to those that occur in people in Western countries.

9) **Aftereffects.** It is common for people to experience major life changes after having near-death experiences. These aftereffects are often powerful, lasting, life-enhancing, and the changes generally follow a consistent pattern. As the experiencers themselves almost always believe that near-death experiences are, in a word, real.

If you are seriously trying to determine if there is life after death, I would highly recommend that you include Jeffrey Long, MD in your investigations.

Hypnotic Regression (HR)
Hypnotic regression is another area that has received a great deal of attention recently. When under hypnoses, tens of thousands of people in different cultures from around the world and in all age groups have reported vivid memories of past lives that have a consistent theme. If you have had no experience with Hypnotic Regression and you are seriously searching for evidence, Dr. Brian Weiss's book titled *Many Lives, Many Masters* is a good place to begin. Dr. Weiss graduated summa cum laude from Columbia University in 1966 and received a medical degree from Yale University in 1970. He worked in the Department of Psychiatry at Yale University and then at the University of Pittsburgh; and later became the chairman of the Department of Psychiatry at Mount Sinai Medical Center and Associate Professor at the University of Miami's School of Medicine. In his book Dr. Weiss recounts an experience he had in 1980 when he met a patient named Catherine who suffered from anxiety attacks and a broad range of fears to include water, airplanes, choking, etc. After not responding to 18 months of traditional therapy, Dr. Weiss decided to try hypnotic regression to see if some trauma occurred in her childhood that may have caused her fears. They were both surprised that while under hypnosis Catherine was able to regress to previous lives. She was able to move through those lives at will and stop at important circumstances and relate them in incredible detail. Over a several year period and many sessions, Catherine was able to recall a dozen previous lives as well as the time between her previous lives. She was able to remember specific incidences that corresponded to each of her fears. As time progressed and she was able to bring these instances into her conscious mind

her fears began to rapidly disappear, and eventually she was no longer plagued by these symptoms and was able to live a confident and happy life. Since that time, Dr. Weiss has explored the past lives of more than 4000 patients with similar results. It turned out to be a common occurrence for anyone hypnotized by Dr. Weiss to remember past lives.

When I first began researching reincarnation, I found Dr. Weiss's story nothing short of astonishing. I was curious how common this phenomenon was so I searched for other books on hypnotic regression, which were easy to find. Although there were a few questionable authors who seemed to continually run into famous historical figures, which I discounted, there were many very good authors, like Dr. Michael Newton, who have found similar results with literally tens of thousands of patients around the world. One of the most startling findings for me was that under hypnosis some of his patients became fluent in languages with which they had no familiarity in this life. This is known as xenoglossy. The sessions were recorded and language experts were able to interpret and verify the recordings.

In another book *Unlearned Language: New Studies in Xenoglossy*, Ian Stevenson, a medical doctor at the University of Virginia who I mentioned in Chapter 4, related his experience with two of the most interesting and well-documented xenoglossy cases on record:

1. Dolores Jay, who under hypnosis manifested as 'Gretchen,' a German-speaking personality, was fluent in German when under hypnosis, a language that she was never exposed to.

2. Uttara Haddur, a native of Maharashtra in western India, who over a fifteen-year period of her life was repeatedly taken over by the personality of 'Sharada,' a young 19th century Bengali-speaking woman. 'Sharada' was able to speak Bengali, a foreign language for Haddur, and to

identify many accurate details of Bengali life in the 1800s such as various kinds of foodstuff that she would have had no knowledge of in her present life.

Dr. Stevenson thoroughly researched these two accounts and was convinced they were credible. When a hypnotized person is fluent in a language that they are unfamiliar with in their conscious state, hallucination is an irrational cause. When this is coupled with a detailed description of that culture, which is verifiable by other means, reincarnation needs to be seriously considered.

I eventually sought out psychiatrists who had not written a book or tried to make money on hypnotic regression but performed similar therapy, and I found their experiences were indeed very similar. Hypnotic regression critics' main argument is that hypnosis causes patients to hallucinate, but the stories are too consistent and the occurrences are too great to accept that rationale.

Although it is impossible to explain these phenomena as illusions, they continue to be ignored by modern science as evidence for the concept of reincarnation. Many people would rather stick to the comfort of their core beliefs than look at the evidence.

Remembered Experiences

One of the key reasons people struggle with reincarnation is because they do not have a memory of any past life. However, there are many people who do remember past lives.

Ian Stevenson's book *Where Reincarnation and Biology Intersect* is one of the best scientifically argued accounts in support of reincarnation that I have found. The book is an abbreviated version of Stevenson's impressive multivolume work, *Reincarnation and Biology*. He had many scholarly papers to his credit before he began his long career in paranormal research. Dr. Stevenson devoted forty years to the scientific documentation of past life memories of children and adults from various cultures and had over 3000 cases in his files when he died.

Stevenson often investigated stories of children with past life memories. Typically if past life memories occurred it was first noticed in children between 2-4 years old who would begin to tell their parents that he or she had lived before. They would often remember their previous family and eventually, after months or years of nagging, the parents were often willing to take the children to find their remembered family. The children would often be able to guide them to their old house once they were in the neighborhood. Usually the children recognized some if not all of the people in the home, knew their way around the house, and offered personal information about a deceased family member that was corroborated by the family. Inevitably the remembered family member had died a year or so before the child was born. The deceased usually died suddenly and sometimes violently but often at a fairly young adult age. Occasionally Stevenson was able to find detailed mortuary records describing the deceased's death and a description of their fatal wounds. Often the wounds would correspond with birthmarks on the child. Usually the child lost their memory of the past life by the time they were seven or eight, and always lost it by the end of their teens. However, the relationship between the child and the remembered family would often last a lifetime if the remembered family considered the child to be a reincarnated relative. By the time Stevenson found out about the incident, months or even years had gone by after the families had met so Stevenson was not present at the initial meeting and needed the child and members of the two families to corroborate the events. However, Stevenson independently retrieved the mortuary records and compared them to marks or deformities on the child. Stevenson's data seemed to imply that the deceased died before it had accomplished what it wanted in its earlier life and had a driving need to return.

Stevenson was a conscientious and meticulous researcher who tried to find evidence to refute reincarnation, however, he was no more successful than anyone else in suggesting a credible mechanism for the transfer of memories in apparent reincarnations, or in explaining how physical characteristics of a dead person could become imprinted on an unborn fetus.

Stevenson was extremely well thought of by his peers in the academic and scientific fields, and I never found an instance where his character was impugned. Critics argued that he did his research in cultures that tended to accept reincarnation. But how else could he do it? If parents reject the concept from the beginning, the child would never have an opportunity to reconnect with their old family before the memories disappear. His detractors based their reasoning on speculation and said things like he was probably misled by the people that he talked to or the interpreters, but none of his actual findings were ever disproved. It is easy to sit on the sideline with your own prejudices and criticize, but it is much more difficult to do the research to try and prove Stevenson wrong. In fact his critics seemed to have other motivations such as religious biases or a predisposition against all or part of paranormal experiences. I found Stevenson's research far more convincing than the detractors' arguments and I consider his research an essential piece of the puzzle for anyone wondering if reincarnation is true.

Medical Data Summary

I have only provided an extremely brief description of the tremendous amount of available medical data supporting reincarnation. Here is a short summary of the results:

1. Medical therapy has discovered many cases of prior life memory recollections among young children. These

memories were studied, categorized and confirmed through rigorous research.

2. Details that subjects recalled about their prior lives correspond to historical records. Furthermore, there was great consistency among prior life recollections of the same time periods of cultural and geographical areas that the subjects were not exposed to.

3. Some subjects were fluent in foreign or ancient languages that they did not learn or have any exposure to during this lifetime. If hypnosis was involved then after the session ended the person no longer could speak or understand those languages.

4. Some subjects among relatives, friends, or even strangers recalled the same people, events and details independently.

5. Recalling past life agonies and events were instrumental in addressing and often alleviating today's ills and problems, such as panic attacks and long-time pain.

I found that the critics of reincarnation had very little evidence to put forth. They either had a bias against it or were not motivated to investigate the evidence.

Psychics

Science has discredited psychics for years because they look beyond the physical world for answers; but when some psychics, time and again, are able to accurately explain and predict future events, then in good conscience they should not be summarily dismissed. Edgar Cayce is a case in point. He was probably the most famous psychic in the 20th century. He was born on a Kentucky farm in 1877 and was an average unassuming man. He worked as, amongst other things, an insurance salesman, photographer, and store owner. His hobbies were gardening and teaching Sunday school and he was a devout Christian all his life. He and members of his family developed several serious afflictions, and even though he had no medical training he was able to cure them by going into a self-induced meditation or trance at which time he spoke of a remedy. His fame soon spread and he began giving 'readings' for strangers that resulted in an amazing number of cures. In the beginning, almost all of his 'remedies' were by way of holistic medicine, which resulted from questions asked of him during his meditative sessions. After a few years he was asked to give broader readings that included topics such as astrology, ancient civilizations, financial reports and about anything else the populace could think to ask him. Between 1901 and 1945 Cayce gave 14,306 readings, all easily available on the Internet. Besides his massive number of healings, he accurately predicted such things as the 1929 Stock Market Crash, World War II, and finding the Dead Sea Scrolls in 1945. Cayce believed that he received his information primarily from his subconscious mind but occasionally he was able to obtain information from other spiritual sources. He spoke of reincarnation as factual while in his trances, but he struggled with it for years during his waking hours until he was able to reconcile it with his deep Christian faith. He never accepted money for his readings and consequently was a poor man all his life. How Cayce was able to cure hundreds of people, speak foreign languages, and predict future events with no previous exposure to this knowledge is an unanswered question. As it turned out, Cayce along with other well-regarded psychics such as Emanuel Swedenborg consistently insisted upon the reality of reincarnation.

Multi-Life Themes

Understanding the concept behind reincarnation is more important than one might think. We have a tendency to think of this life as 'one and done,' but our soul takes a very different view. Our present life is setting the stage for our next life. Its multi-life perspective sees our issues as a continuing research project. We can think of a life as being a single day in the life of a soul. The issues that we are wrestling with today will not go away at death unless they are adequately resolved. Our emotions in this life can act as a baseline for a future life. This can cause problems for us to deal with if we are not careful. For example, if we hate someone, then we need to resolve that hate in this life or it will put into motion a situation where we will hate someone else in a future life. When we die our health issues go away and our mundane earthly problems go away, but our emotional problems do not go away. We take them with us because eventually they need to be resolved. This is the fallacy of suicide. People think they are escaping their problems but those same issues will need to be addressed in future lives. Evolution is a continuum and all our misconceptions need to be resolved.

Every life we have is in some way impacted by our previous lives. These impacts are very difficult to identify because they are a continuation of our soul's multi-life examination of particular phenomena. For example, if we have a life in which we are not happy with some of our decisions, we might want to return to a similar life and try it again. We would spend our time between lives in the astral field studying our past life in an attempt to fully understand what went wrong and why. Then we would plan a life in which we would address those same issues because all our issues need resolution.

The soul learns a great deal from each life and it uses those experiences as the baseline for future lives.

Desire to Return

Our soul is on an endless journey and after death we rest, evaluate our past life, visit friends, travel around the universe and do many interesting things. But we are eventually drawn back to the physical field. It generally takes decades to reincarnate but there are exceptions. Some souls who feel they have urgent unfinished business might reincarnate in a matter of hours, but this is both very unusual and difficult as the lack of adequate prelife planning can lead to serious problems.

When we do return most likely we will continue our journey on earth as opposed to another planet because we are acclimated to it and we will not need an adjustment period. It is possible to incarnate on a new planet or in a nonhuman albeit sentient form, but it would take us several lives to adjust to our new surroundings before much progress is made. It would be very unlikely that we would do this on our own. If we changed planets, it would be because sentient life on earth would have changed such that we could not have the experiences we want. This would surely impact a very large number of beings so we would change planets en masse. This might occur after a nuclear war or some cosmic event that significantly reduced the quality and quantity of lives available to incarnate into. Fortunately, there are literally billions of planets available for sentient life in humanoid form so there would never be a situation where we could not continue our evolution in about the same way as we do now. That said, there are humans now incarnating on earth who began their reincarnation cycle on another planet.

We stop reincarnating when our soul thinks it has done as well as it can in this Grand Cycle. Every soul has its own criteria of what it wants to accomplish. There are no minimum or maximum requirements that we all need to accomplish. Everything is choice.

The universe is a highly complex system and the Tao has put forth great efforts to create it. It would be difficult to support a theory that we only experience it a single time. We are provided with the opportunity to experience the universe as many times as we want and in as many ways as we want. Everything is choice! The universe is simultaneously a playground and a school. We can choose to experience it or we can choose to stay in the Tao and do something else. But once we choose to experience it, we commit ourselves to many lives and many experiences.

If reincarnation is not only possible but true, then the question arises: what returns? By looking at the process of incarnation, this tricky little question becomes much clearer.

Chapter 8

Evolution of Consciousness

What the Caterpillar calls the end, the world calls a butterfly.
Lao Tse

Key Concept: Consciousness evolves, not matter.

Maybe the best way to appreciate the importance of our life is to understand the amount of effort that has gone into creating it. Both religion and science imply that we are an accident of nature, but there is literally nothing accidental about us or the life we are living. We live in a world where our life is preplanned by us, but then we are given the free will to execute that plan any way we please. Our purpose is to evolve, but how we do that is up to us. Science recognizes that all the species on earth are evolving, but it trivializes it by making it appear to be a random process driven by mutation.

Expansion of Consciousness

We cannot understand evolution until we understand what is evolving. It is not the myriad of physical forms that are evolving, but the awareness of the consciousness within these forms. The consciousness of the Tao, which includes us, is evolving.

As discussed earlier, the Tao is a web of consciousness that objectifies itself in order to help it learn. It turns its own energy into a form that we recognize as a tree, or rock, or you and me. It then interacts with those objects in ways that help it see itself differently. It is this consciousness that is evolving. Every spirit is striving to become more aware of itself and its capabilities. The spirits within the Tao are driving evolution, not the bodies they incarnate into. Every spirit is seeking to expand its consciousness through the process of experiences. Evolution could better be defined as the continuous process of the expansion of consciousness.

Lives Have Great Value

Although we are all trying to evolve, spirits choose how fast and how stressful their evolution will be in any given duration. If you are a human on earth, then you have chosen a high speed and high stress period. We did not have to come here. We did it because we wanted to try the fast lane for awhile. Like everything, this has its pros and cons.

Experiencing the earth offers us an opportunity for great growth, but we don't have much time to spend here. On average, we probably only have about 60 physical lives on earth in any Grand Cycle. If we assume an average of 75 years/life, which is probably high, that means we are only incarnated for about 4500 years. Subtracting our childhood, teenage and old age years, that leaves us about 50 adult years in each life or a total of about 3000 years to experience adult life here on earth. If a Grand Cycle lasts for say 500,000 years, then we are human adults less than one percent of the time. With such a short time on earth, clearly, we want to make the most of it, so careful planning is needed.

The universe and everything in it is highly organized and very efficient. Nature is a finely tuned and highly-meshed network with every part critical to its well-being. This is easy to see on a small scale when mankind decides to relocate a plant or animal species for some particular purpose. Inevitably it immediately throws some other aspect of its new environment out of balance.

Everything that was ever created has a purpose and our lives are no exception. Nothing is left to chance and nothing is wasted. Every experience we have is a highly focused and valuable opportunity to learn. Spirits incarnate into the physical field with specific agendas to research and experience. A sentient life is a valuable investment. A spirit would never gamble its efforts by leaving them to chance and hoping some interesting experiences would come its way. Life is a precious gift.

Value Fulfillment

Because evolution is so important, the Tao has created a Universal Principle known as Value Fulfillment, which is the cornerstone of the evolutionary process. It says that spirits evaluate the value of a potential experience before they agree to undertake it. This means that we agree to all of our planned experiences in advance. Because of the limited time that we are in the physical field, every life, every experience, and every opportunity needs to be pre-evaluated by the soul to determine how much it hopes to gain.

It is the nature of consciousness to choose tasks that it expects to be the most personally 'significant.' Beings at every level, from an atom to the Tao Itself, have a desire to continually accomplish something of value, which contributes to their evolution in a meaningful way.

We don't need to have grand and glorious accomplishments like winning the Olympics or a Nobel Prize. We just need to be gaining wisdom, which we can do very humbly by caring for a pet or being responsible in school or on a job. The spirit gains value from learning and enjoying. We know that we are dependent on others for this and we also know that others are dependent on us.

There is a corresponding Universal Principle of Cooperation that I mentioned earlier. When incorporated into Value Fulfillment, this states that not only do we maximize the value of the potential experience for ourselves, but we also maximize its benefit for all the other entities that will be involved. This is a critical feature because it implies that not only are we looking out for the good of others, they are looking out for us.

When we see a world that appears to be driven by greed, it is hard to believe that everyone's inner conscious is based on helping others. Some people seem like they are 'bad to the core,' but this is impossible. People become confused, frustrated, irrational and vengeful out of ignorance and self-limiting decisions. They create a habit of seeing the world from a negative perspective. Eventually, these people will see the light and change their ways, although maybe not in this lifetime. They will have some difficult lessons in the process but they are not fundamentally bad, just confused. If cooperation did not exist and every identity or species was out for itself, like Darwinism postulated, then nothing could ever exist. Our gestalt would be torn apart by conflicting motives. Even the Tao could not exist!

To optimize a spirit's precious time here on earth, the personality goes through an extremely rigorous planning process, which is done before birth.

Initial Planning Process

Life is far more sophisticated and organized than we could ever conceive. We are not just having a life; we are in the process of spiritual evolution. Our spirit has created a Master Evolutionary Plan for its own growth, which is a subset of an even higher-level master plan created by higher-level spirits. Although our spirit's plan has been in existence for eons, it evolves as our spirit evolves. The more we learn the better able we are to decide what we want to study next. I compare the process to a scientist's progression through his career. He starts by taking technical courses in high school, then focuses on a specific curriculum in college, fine-tunes his studies in graduate school, and then truly specializes in one or more areas during his career. He knows roughly where he is going but not exactly how he will get there, or even exactly where 'there' is. Our evolution is no different. Of course, a spirit's evolution is eternal so we will eventually end up specializing in many of the areas, but we need to organize and prioritize the process. This life is an important piece of that plan and the more we accomplish the more valuable it will become. There is nothing haphazard about life. We are on this earth because we chose to be and we are having the experiences that we selected. Our soul knows what it wants to experience, and our life contributes to attaining those goals.

Revising Our Views
Evolutionary progress occurs as we broaden our psychological and spiritual perspective. We are trying to expand our awareness of who we are and the nature of reality. We can hone our mental and emotional attributes in many ways, but inevitably it requires changing our beliefs. Simply experiencing life contributes to this process, but if we do not change our thinking in some way, we will not have learned anything. Practices like meditation and energy exercises help immensely, as does pulling back the veil of the illusion and seeing ourselves and the world more clearly. Our experiences are exposing us to new ideas, and we need to take advantage of that knowledge. Stubbornly hanging on to old beliefs retards our progress.

Starting Our Travels[13]

The process of evolution is highly structured while at the same time allowing for a great deal of individual flexibility. Our permanent home is in the Tao where our spirit resides when it is not on an adventure. The Tao provides us a safe, comfortable and blissful existence throughout eternity. But eternity is a long time and our nature is to act. As such, our spirit wants to grow, explore and play. The desire to experience is akin to young adults who tire of living in the warmth and safety of their parents' home. The Tao has chosen to accommodate the desire for adventure and growth by creating universes and their assorted realities.

The untold number of spirits in existence are all at different evolutionary levels. It is virtually a continuum of capabilities. They vary from the newly-created consciousness units (CUs) existing within atoms that are virtually a blank sheet of paper, to the unfathomably wise spirits that are capable of conceiving universes. In order to service the needs of all the spirits, the universe provides a vast array of opportunities and challenges.

The six fields of the universe that we visit on our Grand Cycle are divided into many separate realities, each with unique characteristics. Our spirit decides which ones it wants to experience before it leaves the Tao.

The different realities that exist within a universe are simply different ways energy expresses itself. Each reality is a unique illusion, much like a fun house at a carnival. The fun house exists and is constructed with the same material as the regular world, but it gives us the impression or illusion of a different reality because of the way we perceive it. The various realities work in the same way. Their combined purpose is to allow spirits like us to have experiences where we can learn and play. Playing is far more important than one might suppose. It encourages us to create, which is the nature of being.

Cast from the Tao

Our spirit was cast from the Tao in a group called an entity, which encompasses ~1000 spirits. The other spirits in our entity are similar to us in nature and level of development. Because we plan to move through the Grand Cycle together, we need to be at about the same evolutionary level, but we will each be working on a wide range of issues. Many of the spirits will have plans compatible with ours so that they will work with us during our numerous lives. There are many other entities cast from the Tao with us and we work closely with them as well. We have a huge number of spirits in our normal working group who we incarnate with.

Spirit Ages
Our spirits are not 'newbies' when it comes to evolution. We are
by no means the most evolved, but we have been around a long
time, especially when we include the time we were a spark. The
Seth entity says our initial CUs have been around since before
our universe was formed.

We can get a crude idea of how long our spirit has been
functioning as part of a group soul if we look at 'plausible'
timeframes. The less evolved the spark/spirit, the more
cycles it will have had, but the shorter each cycle will be. The
more evolved we become, the greater the opportunities and
responsibilities each cycle provides, so the cycles last longer.
One can only imagine the age of the spirits responsible for
running a galaxy or a universe.

In a session I had with Shepherd Hoodwin, the Michael entity
provided some rough guidelines for how long our spirits might
have been around from the time our spark started having group
soul experiences. The Michael entity said that we can make a
very rough estimate for how many cycles our spirit might have
had in each phase and how long those cycles might have taken.
Let's say our spark had 11,000 cycles in mineral form, each
cycle lasting ~1000 years. Over time perhaps we had 1100 total
cycles in plant form, each being about 10,000 years. Of course,
there would be many different lives in many species in each
cycle. After that we may have wanted an expression into simple
animal forms to learn more about movement. Maybe we had
eleven cycles as amoebae, viruses and bacteria. Then we might
have started having experiences in increasingly complex animal
forms with a total of 110 animal cycles, lasting say 100,000 years
each. Again, we would have had many animal lives in each cycle.
Then finally assume we have had 10 sentient Grand Cycles, not
all on earth of course, and each lasted one million earth years,
which would include going through all the fields and the time
spent within the Tao between cycles. This all adds up to around

40 or 50 million years. This is an extremely rough estimate so it could easily be off by an order of magnitude or more in either direction for any one individual.

The point here is that whatever the right answer is for each person, our spirits have been around for millions of years and maybe many tens or hundreds of millions of years. Of course, this does not include the enormous amount of time we spent evolving before we reached the mineral level. We have all been evolving for a very long time. You are far older than you could possibly imagine. It takes a long time and an uncountable number of experiences to grow from a tiny 'speck' of energy to our level. You are much older, wiser, and greater than you think. Even our pets have been evolving for a long time and in the grander scheme of things they are not that far behind us. Some of them might be ready for a sentient experience in the next cycle.

Now I have portrayed all this in a linear order for simplicity, and it often happens that way, but it is not necessary. For example, we would not have to go through animal hive souls to be a sentient soul, but if we did, then we might bring more experience and capability to the table. There are no prerequisites for how we choose to grow. It is our choice. But generally, this linear development is common because it is a straightforward and effective way for the spirit to evolve.

The Sentient Grand Cycle

The soul's plan for this Grand Cycle is to have experiences in each of the universe's six primary fields. When we complete our Grand Cycle, we return to the Tao where we reside until we embark on another journey. The mystic Islamic term 'seventh heaven,' which implies the ultimate resting place and abode of God, probably originally referred to the Tao as this information has been available to select groups for a very long time. Each field offers unique lessons, and it is only by having multiple experiences in each field that we can adequately understand its reality.

Soul Age

The soul age is a key concept in understanding our own nature and the functioning of society in general. The number of Grand Cycles is an indication of how much sentient experience a spirit has had, wherein the soul age is an indication of how much experience the soul has had creating personalities in this Grand Cycle.

Our previous discussion of 'Spirit Ages' was in regards to how long our spirit might have been around before this Grand Cycle, which is many millions of years. However, our soul, which is a new creation in each Grand Cycle, is much younger than its spirit. The spirit uses its own energy to create the soul so the older and wiser the spirit the more evolved the energy is that creates the soul.

The Michael entity tells us there are seven ages that our soul will go through during a sentient Grand Cycle. The first five, which are completed on earth, are infant, baby, young, mature and old. There are two additional soul ages, the transcendental and infinite, but those are not achieved in the physical field.

Each age has seven levels within it, as shown in Figure 2, and we need to complete each level before we can move on to the next one. As such, there are 35 steps that we need to go through in order to complete the physical field experience. Although some steps can be achieved in a single lifetime, it would be unusual to complete every step in a single life. Practically speaking, it would take more than 50 lifetimes for a soul to complete a physical field cycle. Two or maybe three lifetimes for most levels would be more typical, however, if we are studying infant death, it might take 100 very short lives to get through a single level. If a soul finished one level in midlife it could change to another.

How long it takes to proceed through a level depends on what we want to get out of it. A spirit on its first or second Grand Cycle might choose to get through the process as fast as possible so it might spend less than a total of 10,000 years incarnating on earth, including the time between lives in the astral field. However, a spirit that has had 10 or 20 sentient Grand Cycles may spend >100,000 years and act as a teacher for the less experienced spirits. There are no requirements for how long it takes or what needs to be accomplished. Our soul decides what it wants to accomplish at each level and it evaluates each life as to how well it accomplishes it. No one judges our progress. We judge ourselves. We have guides who assist us in our evaluations, but we make the final analysis. Life is all about choice, and it is our choice to decide if and when we move on.

	Infant	Baby	Young	Mature	Old	Messianic	Buddhaic
Level 1	First Earth Life	X	X	X	X	Occurs after Death	Occurs after Death
Level 2	X	X	X	X	X	Occurs after Death	Occurs after Death
Level 3	X	X	X	X	X	Occurs after Death	Occurs after Death
Level 4	X	X	X	X	X	Occurs after Death	Occurs after Death
Level 5	X	X	X	X	X	Occurs after Death	Occurs after Death
Level 6	X	X	Average Human	X	X	Occurs after Death	Occurs after Death
Level 7	X	X	X	X	Last Earth Life	Occurs after Death	Occurs after Death

Figure 2: Soul Age in a Sentient Grand Cycle[14]

Figure 2 shows the progressions our soul goes through during the reincarnation cycle in the physical field. Each 'X' indicates a step, which may take multiple lives. We start at Infant Level 1. When we accomplish what we want to do there, our soul creates a personality that incarnates into Infant Level 2. This continues until it completes Infant Level 7, and then it creates a personality that incarnates into Baby Level 1. Note that soul ages have nothing to do with time. They are totally dependent on accomplishments.

Every human on this planet is at one of these levels. Our progress through the physical field would be expressed as '3rd level baby' or '6th level mature.' The Michael entity says that the average person on earth is at about 6th level young and that no new infant souls are entering earth now. Integrating additional infant souls onto earth is considered too challenging for our civilization at this time. If no new souls are incarnating on earth and humanity is maturing, then life on earth will continually improve, provided that we do not do something catastrophic. Note that there are many other planets where infant sentient souls can begin a Grand Cycle, so just because infant souls cannot begin incarnating on earth right now does not mean the process stops.

Changing levels is about changing our perspective. The infant stage is about learning to adjust to the physical field, working with small groups and keeping oneself alive. The baby stage is learning about structure and the focus is on 'me.' The young stage is when the ego takes over and the personality feels the need to be the star of the show. That is not saying that all success comes from young souls, but when social or financial success defines the individual, you can be pretty sure they are a young soul. The mature stage is focused on relationships and looks at the inner world. The old stage focuses on the meaning of things and they tend to be insightful. When we look at our civilization, it is pretty easy to see how strongly the young souls are influencing it.

Shepherd Hoodwin's book, *Journey of Your Soul*, is an excellent reference for this subject as he goes into much more detail for every level. If you have a personalized Michael

Reading chart from Shepherd then you can review the section on your particular age/level. It often helps explain why you do certain things and why things happen to you.

In every life, despite the level the soul is working at, the new personality starts out as an infant and progresses through all of the earlier levels until it gets to the soul's present level. In other words, if we are a 3rd level mature, we are born a 1st level infant, and during our childhood and early adult years we progress through all the steps until we reach our actual level. Our personality might be a 3rd level mature, but we would not function at that level until we reach our mid-30s or even 40s. This is why people in their 40s and older have such different views than they did in their 20s. Younger adults have not reached a level of maturity that enables them to make decisions that are as wise as those they will be able to make later in life.

When we know our age and level, we can better appreciate the type of challenges we encounter and the general criteria required to move from one step to the next. This helps us know what is important and how to live our life.

The impact of soul ages has a huge influence on our society. Our society assumes people are fully mature adults when they reach 21, and in some cases even earlier, but they are not. Even young adults graduating from college are functioning well below their soul age level. It takes life experiences and the burden of personal responsibility to fully mature us. We all know people who have struggled in their early adult years but have flourished as they got older. Maybe the Founding Fathers were on to something when they restricted voting to those that had reached a level of responsibility in life.

However, a serious problem can occur if people get so far off track in their early adult years that they can never recover. As a society, the onus is on us to continue working with and assisting the younger generation through their 20s and into their 30s if necessary. When we look at the terrorists and criminals, we see that they formed antisocial ideas at an early age when they were unable to properly evaluate the confusing world around them.

Evolving Goals

We create new goals for each life but these goals are heavily influenced by actions from previous lives. For example, maybe our recent past lives were unstable and we could never develop a sense of belonging or purpose. Our home or livelihood might have been destroyed in a previous life and we were unable to emotionally recover from those catastrophes. We might have lived a vagabond existence and had no real place to call our own. Those lives would have been characterized by fear and uncertainty, and we would never have felt in control of ourselves. In this case, we might have created our present life with the purpose of finding stability. Simply having a strong family and good friends to depend on might be a major goal of this life. Seemingly unimportant events like family gatherings and holiday meals might be extremely valuable to us in this life. Someone who created a huge company or had a famous life may not have accomplished nearly as much as a 'humble' homemaker. We all have unique and equally important goals.

We live in a competitive society and it is a natural tendency to compare lives and see how we are doing. However, comparing our lives to others is a fruitless effort because we do not have the information available to us. Besides, it simply does not matter. There is no competition in the spiritual realm. Every life has an important purpose no matter how grand or humble it may seem. Financial or social success is never a spiritual purpose. More likely these are roadblocks thrown in people's way for them to learn to overcome.

The Value of 'Mundane' Lives

Few people give themselves credit for the value of the lives they live. Although many people envy the lives of the rich and famous, a seemingly humble existence spent on helping others can be much more spiritually rewarding than lives of those who are trading karma for fame and fortune. The Michael entity noted that most people who are politicians and glamour seekers are younger souls who have not learned the importance of serving others or the downside of self-aggrandizement. Life is not as much about being better than others as it is about making others better.

The important experiences in life are much more mundane than most people would expect. Our experiences don't need to be record-breaking achievements or life-threatening adventures. Even when we think we are living a dull existence, it does not mean we are not learning a great deal. The endless performance of our day-to-day responsibilities enriches us. We can see this by looking at our own lives. The dull routine of holding a job, paying bills, making ends meet, keeping the house in order, taking kids to their activities, advising and consulting family and friends, etc. all requires a great deal of dedication, competence, and most important responsibility. Every day we see people struggle with these tasks because they really are not that easy. Each experience offers us something new, but when we put them all together, they require a high-level of organization, prioritization, and judgement. We are continuously confronted with new and different issues that create a raft of emotional and societal pressures, which we would not experience in the astral field. No two circumstances are ever identical. Every experience offers something new. We live very complicated lives, which we take for granted.

Ending the Reincarnation Cycle

After every earth life we return to the astral field where our soul absorbs the many lessons we learned in our last life, and plans for a future life. We have made a commitment to complete the Grand Cycle so our soul must complete the first five soul ages in order to end the reincarnation cycle. This is not to say that every soul must master the physical field in all its facets. The soul must have completed enough experiences to feel that this is the best it is able to do at its present level of development. Using the analogy of completing college, some will graduate summa cum laude and some will graduate with mediocre grades. But all have graduated. And that is all that is required to finish our lives on earth. We simply do the best we can. Continuing with the college analogy, we have at least had some experience with the various required and a few elected classes; and we feel we have learned enough for now. Again, let me stress that we do not need to master life in any one Grand Cycle, let alone in any one life. We just need to do the best we can.

We like to say that we are not perfect and to err is human. Spiritual beings are not perfect either. Even the Tao is striving towards perfection. We are all on an asymptotic path to perfection and we have eternity to achieve it.

I thought the Seth entity's comment about the soul's final departure from the physical field was interesting. He said that in our last life we try not to leave anything here on earth. It is unlikely that a 7th level old soul that was having its last physical experience in this Grand Cycle would have any children. The longer we are remembered here on earth the harder it is to break away from the physical field. It is not to our advantage to be remembered on earth as it continues to tie us to the physical field.

Leaving the Astral Field
When we die for the last time we return to the astral field, but we do not stay there forever. Eventually we will move on to the other fields. We are all part of a web of consciousness, which is a single united gestalt. But even when we are in the Tao, we never lose our individuality. Evolution needs to develop both our individual and group skills. The physical field focuses on our personal needs but as we progress back towards the Tao, we become more united with others.

The Michael entity says that we begin the integration process in the astral field after we complete our earthly incarnations. We do not move as an individual from the astral field to the causal field. We move as an entity of about 1000 souls. Our whole entity has to have completed both the physical field and the astral field before we can move on. When we are ready, we begin experiencing an increasing internal unity within our entity. The entity has to reach a coherence as an entity, where it effectively creates a working group mind. This does not mean that each member of the entity dissolves into the whole. But there is a new level of sophistication in the group experience. Because the astral field is focused on emotions, there has to be the ability to experience a group euphoria apart from the individual euphoria. There is a mutual agreement amongst the members which dictates that the entity is ready for the causal experience. This is not nearly as difficult to achieve as it is for all the fragments of the entity to be completed with the physical field. Apparently the physical field is usually the most difficult part of evolution for any sentient experience.

Multi-Life Influences

Past Life Issues
Although we view our existence from the perspective of a single lifetime, our life is really a continuous process of many lives. One life's problems flow into the next although we don't perceive it that way. We experience life as a series of chapters, where a chapter may be a job or a relationship or an interest. Each chapter consists of a series of events, and when it is over we think we are done with it. But in reality, each life is a chapter and the experiences we have are parts of various long-term investigations. We pause between lives to study and better understand our situations, however, the issues that we deal with are so complex that very little is completely resolved in a single lifetime. Most of our experiences are continuations of multi-life research projects that require experiencing them

from multiple perspectives. One way the soul does this is by providing the personalities with different energies, genders, nationalities and races so that it can experience different aspects of each situation. For a complete understanding, it may require a dozen or more personalities, all experiencing similar events but perceiving them differently. Having multiple viewpoints of the same issue greatly increases our understanding. One lesson rolls into another and only by looking at multiple lives would we be able to see how they are tied together. There is always more to learn about everything and our soul decides how deeply it wants to investigate each issue. Before each life, the soul decides which areas it wants to focus on and how it wants to proceed. Some issues may be skipped completely for hundreds if not thousands of years before the soul decides to readdress them from a more sophisticated personality's perspective.

It is possible to identify some of our multi-life experiences by looking at the issues we feel very strongly about. If we divide our life into eras, say maybe 5- to 10-year periods, we can identify trends of reoccurring issues. By selecting the more challenging periods we can see how we handled our problems and what we could have done better. If the problems recurred in multiple eras, we can see if we handled the situation better the second or maybe even third time around. Every soul has its own specific reasons for creating a personality. By closely examining our life experiences we can often identify some of those reasons.

Karmic Ribbons

Nowhere are multi-life issues more evident than with karma. Occasionally we have a feeling of unease or even dread when we meet someone new. We get a feeling that something bad will happen for no rational reason. This may be because we have a karmic ribbon with them.

Karma is an overused and misunderstood subject that is worth understanding. It is not an eye-for-an-eye punishment.

It is a teaching tool to show us the impact of our decisions. We are all part of the Tao. We are being taught that when we do something that harms another being, we are actually hurting ourselves. We are being taught to be responsible for our actions. When our selfishness interferes with someone else's life, we need to experience the impact we had on them.

A Karmic ribbon is created between two sentient beings when one of them prevents the other from achieving a significant planned event. Death is an obvious example. Although no one can actually kill someone else, they can certainly end their physical life. If that person missed the chance to have a planned experience, the perpetrator needs to experience a similar loss.

Karmic ribbons are created between two sentient souls but not between a sentient soul and a non-sentient soul like animals or plants. However, whales, and dolphins are sentient beings. Those who harm them would be wise to change their ways.

The soul usually accumulates many karmic ribbons during its various earth lives. All karmic ribbons need to be dealt with before the soul ends the physical portion of its Grand Cycle, and it is highly probable that we have been given one or more ribbons to deal with in this life. If we have experienced a very traumatic event, it may well have been karmic. The best way to deal with it is to simply accept it and move on. Ruing the situation is not useful and there is nothing more harmful for our ego than feeling like a victim. We deserve whatever happens to us and we are being shown the consequences of our actions. It is best to just move on knowing that we learned a very difficult lesson.

When a karmic ribbon ties two people together, there are two ways the offending party can repay it. The ribbon can be broken by either: 1) letting that injured person do an in-kind deed to the offender; or 2) doing something positive for that person. In other words, if we killed someone in one life, we could save them in another life. It is possible but unlikely to have a karmic debt dissolved but if it happens both parties need to agree to it on the soul level. This is only possible if both parties fully understand the implications of dissolving it. Both parties gain from completing the karmic experience so it needs to be a mutual decision.

Philanthropic karma can also be created. This is created when an individual does something positive for someone else and requires nothing in return; nothing meaning exactly that! For example, if a donor gets any type of credit for the deed, like having a building named after them or getting a tax deduction, then it does not count. The gift needs to be 100% altruistic and often anonymous. When this happens a debt can be created or repaid.

Also debt repayment has to be accepted by the recipient. If they choose not to accept the repayment in that particular circumstance, then the karmic ribbon is not dissolved and another experience will need to be created later.

Karma is a powerful tool for ensuring that our life is efficient. Although we can learn from every experience, some experiences are more valuable than others. Karma identifies specific lessons we need to learn and focuses us on high priority experiences.

Karma and reincarnation go hand in hand. Karma keeps track of the most important lessons we need to deal with and reincarnation provides us the opportunities to experience them.

We Have Come a Long Way

We ought to have a certain sense of accomplishment in how far we have advanced. Evolution is not easy. At the same time, we should note that the Tao has surely been around much longer than us, so some spirits are far more evolved than we are. Forgetting the math, I think it is safe to assume humanity is still in the very early 'adolescent' stage of development compared to the many other spirits in the Tao.

During this process, our spirits have amassed an immense amount of wisdom, which is critical to our success as a human.

It is not easy being humans on this planet. A young spirit does not all of a sudden decide to live a human life in a sophisticated culture like ours. It takes millions of years of learning, and even then, life is very challenging. It is easy to see how some people might have trouble as young sentient souls succeeding in this world. Although our ego cannot directly tap into our spirit's wisdom during our lifetime, our spirit is incredibly wise and helps advise and guide us throughout our many lives.

There are those who choose to have as many as 100 sentient Grand Cycles, because a sentient experience is very interesting. But there are other very interesting opportunities as well so after we have had say 10 or 20 sentient Grand Cycles, we may choose to do something different. For example, we could decide we want to be part of a planet's consciousness, which is much more sophisticated than being in a sentient life form. Or maybe our consciousness might decide to be part of an even larger cosmic form like a galaxy. Everything is choice!

Chapter 9

Creating a Life

New Beginnings are often disguised as painful endings.
Lao Tse

Key Concept: We plan our lives in great detail.

Choosing Our Options

The soul maps out every life in great detail before the personality is even formed in the 'prelife plan.' Great care is taken to maximize the benefits of each life and each experience. This is a detailed and complicated process because once the soul chooses the experiences, it then needs to create a personality that can perceive the experiences in the desired way.

This is more important than it might first seem. Two people can attend the same event, sit next to each other the entire time, eat the same food, etc. and still have very different experiences. Attitudes, expectations, emotions and many other considerations all play a large part in every experience. To do this the soul evaluates the key experiences it wants to have and then selects the biases that will most likely result in the personality having the desired experience. The soul inserts energies into the personality's gestalt, which enables the personality to be compatible with the plan. We can get a feel for how involved the planning process is by looking at what goes into it.

Initial Step
The first step is establishing the unique set of goals for the next life. In order to do this the soul needs to know:

1) The spirit's overall purpose in this Grand Cycle, which continually evolves depending on the experiences of the

previous personalities. New questions arise as fast as old ones are investigated. The deeper we search the more uncertainties we discover. Because the soul often has multiple personalities incarnating simultaneously, the status of the process is constantly evolving. The soul is working on many issues simultaneously. Balancing all the inputs and determining the next step for each personality is a challenge.

2) The status of the karma each fragment will deal with. Although we want to achieve as much as possible in each life, we don't want to create a plan that is so difficult for the personality that more karma is created.

Pre-established Relationships
All life experiences involve relationships with other people. Key relationships like parents, spouses, children, siblings and certain friends are often identified as options in the prelife plan. Other important relationships are established later in life when it is determined which paths the personality will follow.

If we desire a specific type of experience, then we need to find another soul who is willing to create a personality that will provide that particular experience. For example, if we want to be a parent, then we would need to find someone who is willing to be our mate and have children. Parental relationships are very common so finding mates is not difficult. However, some relationships are more specialized and can get pretty complicated. For example, if we were studying abuser/victim relationships and we wanted to be either the victim or abuser then we would need to find someone to agree to make that happen. There are always souls available but unless it is a karmic experience good choices are harder to find.

Free will complicates matters because the person we establish a relationship with may not be able to fulfill their agreement due to other circumstances, like if we agree to marry someone and they marry someone else. To account for these many conditions, we need to establish multiple agreements so that if one is not available then a 2nd, 3rd or other option could be chosen. Both people in an agreement need to benefit from the arrangement so some souls will not agree to a relationship if they are working on different problems. They also might not agree if they are concerned about our ability to carry out our end of the agreement. For example, if the other person was concerned about our previous history of alcoholism, they might not want to deal with that type of situation this time around.

Since we have so many options to consider, our plan soon becomes quite complicated. Each path we choose will lead to addressing different problems. As such, our plan does not describe a specific set of events we want to experience, but rather an array of options from which the personality can choose depending on the circumstances.

Exit Points

We think of death as not only unplanned, but controlled by external forces. However, this is not the case. Just because our ego is not aware of our planned death does not mean that it is left to chance.

As mentioned in Chapter 6, The 'Death' Experience, our life plan defines multiple exit points when we have the option of ending our life. Although the soul provides the personality with options for death at various stages of the plan, it never forces these upon the personality. When it comes to death, the inner conscious has the final decision.

Free will allows the personality to make choices that do not follow the life plan, especially in younger souls who have chosen difficult life circumstances. This is okay in principle except it can also lead to undesirable situations. If things are not going well and karma is being accumulated, our inner conscious might choose to abort our life, but in general we plan our death just like we plan our birth.

Soul Biases

The spirit's plan for each Grand Cycle is very comprehensive and detailed. This necessitates creating personalities that have the appropriate characteristics, which it does by creating soul biases.

The spirit chooses the high-level perspectives from which it wants to perceive its experiences during each Grand Cycle by selecting its role and positions in the cadence, cadre, and greater cadence as described in Chapter 4, Essence, Soul and Personality. These biases have been selected by the spirit, passed down to the soul, and remain in place for all personalities created during the entire Grand Cycle. However, the soul has access to its own set of biases, from which it selects to further fine-tune the process.

Personality Traits

The Michael entity tells us the soul chooses its 'overleaves' or what I refer to as biases from a predetermined set of options. These biases ensure our perspectives are different from those of our previous personalities. They make us who we are. The following is a short description of the personality biases or 'overleaves.'

Goals

We choose our 'goals,' which is our primary motivation:

1. **Reevaluation**, which is used to help integrate past lives
2. **Growth**, which is used to learn new things
3. **Discrimination**, which helps us think critically
4. **Acceptance**, which helps us make peace with what we cannot change
5. **Submission**, which helps us support larger causes
6. **Dominance**, which assists us in winning and helping others win
7. **Flow**, which helps us learn to surrender

Modes

We choose our 'modes,' which is how we release our energy.

1. **Reserve** draws our energy inward
2. **Passion** gives us boundless energy
3. **Caution** causes us to release our energy carefully
4. **Power** gives us a strong release of energy
5. **Perseverance** lets us release energy steadfastly
6. **Aggression** gives us a vigorous release of energy
7. **Observation** gives us a neutral release of energy

Attitudes

A personality chooses its 'attitude,' which results in why we do things and the way we do them.

1. A **stoic** has a serene view of the world
2. A **spiritualist** sees the world from its possibilities
3. A **skeptic** views the world with doubt
4. An **idealist** views the world as it could be changed for the better
5. A **cynic** views the world from what will not work
6. A **realist** sees the world factually
7. A **pragmatist** does what works best

Chief Obstacles

We choose our 'chief obstacles,' which is a negative feature or challenge that we want to learn to overcome.

1. **Greed**
2. **Self-destruction**
3. **Arrogance**
4. **Self-deprecation**
5. **Impatience**
6. **Martyrdom**
7. **Stubbornness**

Chief obstacles manifest as a child but do not solidify until late in our teens.

Centers

A personality also chooses its centers, which is where we get our ideas and where we process and store them.

1. **Emotional**
2. **Higher Emotional**
3. **Intellectual**
4. **Higher Intellectual**
5. **Moving**
6. **Physical**
7. **Instinctive**

Body Type

We even choose our body type:

1. **Lunar**
2. **Saturnian**
3. **Jovial**
4. **Mercurial**
5. **Venusian**
6. **Martial**
7. **Solar**

Although we choose a specific bias in each category, we also have secondary and even third level biases in some categories, which are not as strong but still influence us. The soul creates these biases by instilling the personality with certain energies.

Polarities

To add to the complication, each characteristic has what the Michael entity calls positive and negative polarities. For example, if the personality has selected the attitude of 'skeptic,' it will approach its experiences from somewhere between the positive polarity of investigation and the negative polarity of suspicion. If the experience is to be exposed to a new scientific concept, then the personality will choose to 'investigate' the details of the concept if it is working in its positive polarity or be 'suspicious' if it is in the negative polarity. Normally we would be somewhere in the middle.

The biases that our soul chooses from are truly infinite when we consider the variations between the extremes in each category. Selecting biases sounds like a very foreboding task but fortunately our soul is very wise as are the other spirits who assist in the process.

This has been a very quick overview of the biasing process. Again, Shepherd Hoodwin does a very thorough job of explaining the personality biases or what he refers to as 'overleaves' in his book *Journey of Your Soul*. In addition, Shepherd provides what he refers to as 'Michael Readings,' which is a personalized chart with all your biases, soul ages and other personalized data. These charts help us understand ourselves and why things are happening to us. They are available to order from Shepherd's website, shepherdhoodwin.com.

Further Refining the Process

After the soul creates our biases, it needs to deal with the practical issues of birth. Obvious things like gender, race, and nationality are chosen carefully. Gender is a key consideration. We go back and forth between genders but not necessarily altering between lives. Spirits have no inherent gender but they might generally prefer one over the other depending on what they are focusing on. Each culture has its own mores so some experiences are easier to have as one gender or the other. In reality, the inherent characteristics and capabilities of the genders are not as disparate as they appear in our society because many of the differences are culturally driven.

Race and nationality are key considerations. No one is forced to incarnate into a specific race or nationality. It is all choice. Most souls will move from race to race and country to country for diversification purposes. It would be unusual to stay with one race or nationality for very many consecutive lives. Some areas of specialization actually require having at least one life in each race and as many nationalities as practical. The whole idea is to give the soul many diverse experiences.

Of course, the family into which we incarnate influences possible experiences. Wealth, community status, available education and even job prospects are considered.

Personalities are also impacted by past life karma. Trying to deal with too much karma in a single life could be so difficult that the personality could not only fail to have its planned experiences but also create new karma. Past life karma is carried by all personalities but will only have an impact in a life when that karmic ribbon is active.

There could be negative energy that was created in a past life that is not karmic, but has become part of us. This can come down through our physical DNA if the energy is strong enough or from our own past life consciousness. Negative energy can have a very significant impact on the personality and may need to be dealt with if the personality is going to successfully complete its life tasks. Negative energy can interfere with relationships, and cause depression and general unhappiness if it is not released.

Finally, our personalities are impacted by the relationships of the nearby celestial bodies when we are born. The moon and planets in the solar system are large collections of energy, which have an impact on us at birth. Ancient civilizations understood the science of astrology better than we do today. Astrological effects bias our personalities and are part of the planning process. In my personal experience, I have found the Eastern Astrology to be more accurate than the Western Astrology, but I would not make life-changing decisions based on either.

Personalities are incredibly complex life forms. No two are identical and no two will react to a given experience in the same way. Lessons need to be learned by experiencing the issue in many ways. It is only when we develop multiple perspectives of a particular issue by feeling it from all vantage points that we can truly understand it.

We see life through a highly biased perspective, which we think of as truth. But we need to realize that our truth is not necessarily real truth, it is simply a point of view. The biasing process makes it very clear why there are so many different opinions between sane and intelligent people. We choose to see the world from a certain perspective because we want to understand the multifaceted nature of emotion. There are no right and wrong perspectives as long as our actions do not interfere with another person's choices.

There will always be a finer shade of gray for us to appreciate as we peel back the layers of truth. The wisest amongst us know that diverse opinions are needed to find more complete solutions.

Prelife Plan

After each life, our soul decides which portion of its master plan it wants to work on in the next life. It takes into consideration what it did in the last life but that is only part of the story. The soul creates multiple personalities and fragments that exist simultaneously and in multiple realities so planning the next life is more complicated than just picking up where we left off in the last life. All the inputs need to be taken into account.

Our soul consults with other advanced beings who assist in determining which experiences would be most beneficial. Our soul requests input from others, but it always make the final decision. If wiser beings make suggestions that the soul rejects, the personality may find that it is in a difficult situation, but no one will interfere.

Following the same concept, if we return to the astral field having made a mess of our last life, no one will judge us. Our soul will simply pick up where we left off and all involved will offer their best guidance for the road ahead. The soul is ultimately responsible for resolving any karma the personality creates. Clearly it is in the best interest of everyone to heed these sages' advice as they always have our best interests at heart.

The planning process is extremely thorough. With every personality and fragment having free will, it is impossible to predict all the potential outcomes and experiences that will be available to us. We incarnate in groups with similar interests, life after life. We continually change roles, relationships and goals, and it is common to be surrounded by many close spiritual friends in any given lifetime. We have been comrades in arms, lovers, family members, business partners and every other relationship imaginable. We have even been rivals and able adversaries when called for. We have been there for other souls when they needed us and they have been there for us. If we meet a stranger and instantly like or dislike them, then it is likely that we knew them in another life.

As we look back at our lives we can see people who have been important to us and feel sure they are our close spiritual friends. We can also see the antagonists that heavily influenced our life. They may even be our closest spiritual friends who have agreed to incarnate with us and play the role of our adversary so that we could have a needed experience. They may have sacrificed a good deal in this life just so they could help us. We can be frustrated, but still not hate them. Life is short so we need to deal with the difficult experiences as best we can. Life's problems can be frustrating but they should not make us miserable. Forgive, forget and move on!

Agreements
During the planning process, we make agreements with souls who may be in our lives, especially with close relationships like

parents, children and siblings. Free will forces us to take many contingencies into account so we make numerous specific non-binding agreements with many souls. We may have a dozen or more agreements with potential spouses, parents and siblings. Each agreement, if followed through, would lead to different experiences.

Agreements are a two-way street. Both parties need to benefit from any relationship. Some agreements might simply be as a mentor or teacher or advocate lasting for a relatively short time. Naturally an agreement between a married couple might be fairly complex because of its long-lasting nature. However, even marital agreements are not always meant to last a lifetime. In fact, some people plan to divorce each other and then deal with the consequences.

We pick our parents and they pick us. It is common to have an agreement with one parent but it is less likely to have agreements with both parents because it is difficult to tell who they will marry. However, it is highly likely we will have known the other parent in a previous life even if we do not have an agreement with them.

We often have agreements with our siblings and other family members. These agreements are lifelong so they may be more complicated than with friends. It is highly likely that we have much in common with our brothers and sisters, which may go back thousands of years. Grandchildren and other relatives are usually part of our group as well.

In addition to family, we can also have agreements with friends and coworkers. These can be agreements that cross multiple lives and result in great accomplishments. Groups of four or six souls might agree to work together for a common goal. Groups may be dispersed around the world yet come together to achieve a specific goal, such as a new creation.

Agreements are generally short, easy to understand and broad in nature. For example, someone may want to understand how the universe works and grasp some of the more intricate aspects of metaphysics in order to be a teacher. The agreement with their parent might simply be to introduce them to concepts that will awaken their curiosity. Again, life is a series of choices and an agreement never forces anyone to do anything. They are meant to awaken an idea within us or create an experience.

Monads

A complete experience is known as a monad, which simply means a single unit or in our case a single experience. A monad would be experiencing both, if not multiple, sides of an issue. It allows us to see the validity of different points of view. We have a tendency to think of our perspective as better than those who disagree with us, which is short-sighted. Every view has its valid and invalid aspects. We will only gain a complete understanding when we experience all sides of an issue. Occasionally that could happen in a single life but often monads are multi-life events.

The Michael entity explains that there are intra and inter monad experiences. The intra monads are experiences we have with ourselves and the inter experiences we have with others. A full life which runs to completion has the following seven intra monads: 1) our birth; 2) when we are two or three and become aware of our individuality and realize we are independent of others; 3) when we are in our late teens or early 20s and become responsible for ourselves; 4) when we are about 35 and reach the full potential of our age level; 5) when we become a senior citizen and start viewing our accomplishments versus our early life's expectations; 6) when our physical body begins to decay and starts dying; and 7) is our actual death. Clearly lives which are cut short will not experience all those monads.

Inter monads require at least one other person to accomplish. There are a huge number of these types of monads. Student/teacher; liberal/conservative; attacker/victim; boss/worker;

caregiver/patient; activist/pacifist; soldier/civilian; parent/ child; etc. Literally any other relationship we can conceive of is probably a monad. Of course, many of these relationships are subtle enough that we need multiple experiences to truly appreciate the complex aspects of the issues. Some monad experiences like ones that involve race and nationality, where there are far more than two sides to experience, for example, might require numerous opportunities to appreciate even the most rudimentary aspects of the issues. Some monads like student/teacher and parent/child can be seen from both sides in a single life. But most of these relationships are complex enough to require many lives to understand. Monads are tracked from life to life to ensure we will have complete experiences.

Guides

Even with a detailed and intricate life plan that includes many agreements, and a personality that was created and attuned to the jobs at hand, there is no assurance that the experiences will proceed as planned. Taking a personality created by a soul, especially a young soul, and placing them in an environment with so many uncontrolled influences makes success a risky proposition. To improve our chances of success there are spiritual workers in the background assisting us throughout life.

Our spirit guides are always with us. Some guides are with us for many lives, and they know us and our plan very intimately. Others are specialists in some area and are only called in to assist in especially difficult and complicated circumstances. Guides are often identities that have finished their lives in the physical field and are waiting for others in their entity to finish their lives so the whole entity can transition from the astral field to the causal field together as a whole. Some guides might be close friends who are between lives but have agreed to support us in this life. It would be common for a personality to have about a half dozen guides at any one time.

Our guides often interface with us during our sleep. Our inner conscious will interact with them, discuss things, and be given guidance. I suspect most of us have had revelations in a dream that helped resolve some complex issue we were dealing with. This may have been an input from our spirit guides. Occasionally we might remember dreams of our spiritual contacts, but most of our spiritual inputs will come from our subconscious in the form of gut feelings or intuitions. Also, the ego is assisted by our soul/spirit during our sleep. They provide information, and ask our opinion on certain things.

Angels

The angels play an important role in allowing us to achieve our experiences. Their role is to remove roadblocks in our lives such that we can have the experiences we chose. However, the angels will never actually interfere in our lives unless it is critical. A catastrophic event would have to be about to happen to us for an angel to actually change something on the physical plane, but it does happen. An example of this would be: when a person does not board an airplane on a doomed flight, then an angel may have interceded. If it was our time to die, we would have made the flight.

Other Aspects of Evolution

Nature's Caretaker

Mankind's purpose is no different than any animal, plant or mineral. We are here to expand our consciousness and enjoy the process. Despite the greater consciousness of sentient beings, mankind and cetaceans are no different than other species on earth. At one time we were all at those various levels of consciousness and eventually they will be at our level. We are all equally worthy and we are all part of the Tao. We are all one entity. However, unlike the other species, mankind has more control on whether to help or hurt the planet, which is an onus we need to assume.

One of man's responsibilities is to enrich the quality of life for the entire planet. We are not meant to compete with nature or replace it with our creations. We are meant to create a symbiotic relationship with it. Everything on earth has a consciousness. The nonhuman world knows we are all part of a single conscious entity and continues to assist humanity. No matter how poorly we treat nature, it always tries its best to help us. It is our responsibility to protect the earth and all the flora and fauna on it.

Judgement

All spirits are evolving and evolution is the process of learning to expand our consciousness, and every belief system is important. For example, in our society we like to classify people by category and then judge them. The positive side of this is it allows us to generate difficult emotionally-driven issues to deal with. Biases against race, gender and nationality are typical issues we often use. Religious and political beliefs are other common areas we use to judge others. The negative side is that we usually hold our beliefs up as the only right ones and we don't understand why everybody else does not follow suit because the issues seem so clear to us.

Our continuing evolution requires us to see the important issues in as many ways as possible as we change perspectives life after life. Our actual opinion during this life is much less important than we think during our most zealous moments. For the truly difficult issues like prejudice, abortion, intolerance, etc., our spirit creates the opportunity for us to experience all sides of the issue. This can be a multi-life effort. We are seeking understanding, not preeminence. Success is not measured by winning the argument but by discerning the complexity and subtleties of all sides of an issue. When we shut down opposing arguments, we slow down our learning.

The key to successful experiences is how we perceive them. We approach our experiences from a preselected biased perspective, and it is our perspective that allows us to fine-tune our experiences. It is critical that we view our experiences the way our spirit chooses. As we experience, we are adding subtle wisdom to the universe. Judging others for their different views is counterproductive.

Playing

I mentioned this before, and I will again, as it is incredibly important. It may seem strange but one of the biggest reasons we are here is to play. Playing is a very creative activity that begins during infancy and continues throughout life. The Tao is no different than us in thinking that all work and no play makes life pretty dull. The Tao likes to play and we should also.

There is no reason we should not enjoy our life. It is easy for life to become a burden but everything inevitably will work out for the best. We need to keep our problems in perspective. We are here to learn and we are supposed to make mistakes. The key to happiness is to stop ruing the past and stop worrying about the future. Just do our best, treat others as we would want them to treat us, and appreciate nature and the wonderful world we have all created together. People can be annoying because they are struggling to deal with their own issues. We shouldn't let their problems become our problems. If we are not happy with our world, we and only we, have the power to change it.

Section IV

The Power of Thought

Chapter 10

Our Unique Reality

Knowledge is learning every day. Wisdom is letting go of something every day.
Zen Proverb

Key Concept: Our world is not as it appears to be.

Illusion

A reality is not how things are, but how things appear to be. Hollywood creates special effects that make us believe a situation is different than the actual event we are watching. The purpose of each reality is to provide a unique experience. Our world is no different. What we perceive to be real is only a special effects presentation. It is real and it does exist, but for some reason its true nature is different than how we perceive it.

We are so attuned to our environment that we think the world around us is typical across the universe. We cannot imagine that what we are experiencing is not the norm because we don't know anything different. But what we accept as universal reality is only a highly sophisticated illusion.

The purpose of the illusion is to give us the experiences we desire. In the long term this is extremely positive because it teaches us the lessons we came here to learn. However, in the short term there is a downside. If we get off track and confused, we can cause ourselves a great deal of unnecessary suffering, which we do. However, if we can understand the nature of the illusion and see how we are affecting ourselves, then we can change our ways and reduce the suffering.

Two of the greatest minds in mankind's history, Plato and Einstein, both believed we live in an illusion. Many of the ancient

Greek and Egyptian philosophers seemed to have had access to metaphysical information. It is worth repeating Plato's thoughts on life's illusion, which I also included in *The Endless Journey*. In *The Republic* Plato explained that (I paraphrase): "life is as if we are sitting in a cave with our backs to the light. As we gaze upon the shadows on the wall, which is all we can see, we search for truth. But the real truth is the light source behind us that we don't see. We simply see the illusions on the cave walls." Plato's example, he viewed the world from a macroscopic perspective. The figures on the cave wall are the projections from a three-dimensional source onto a two-dimensional surface. He was alluding to a phenomenon in the real world where all we see from the multidimensional spiritual realm is our projection into the three-dimensional world. For Plato, the real truth was the inner spiritual world, which was the light behind the figures.

Einstein looked at our world from a microscopic perspective. He saw that matter was not solid and consisted of mostly space. He viewed matter as energy held together by various forces, which from our macro perspective gives us the illusion of solidity. He noted that not only was this world an illusion, but a persistent one at that. The reason that it is persistent is the odd nature of time, which we will get into shortly.

Both of these two great minds realized that the world was not as it appears to be. How we see ourselves and our environment is a special circumstance, which turns out to be a 'self-created reality.'

Our Perceived Reality

Dimensions

In order to describe a reality, we need to have a way of defining it. We do this by selecting characteristics that are inherent to its nature, which we refer to as dimensions. We say our world consists of three-dimensional space, where each dimension is a linear measure of distance, orthogonal to the other two.

When we refer to other realities as having different dimensions, we are saying that their nature is best characterized by their own unique set of parameters. In other words, width, length and height may not be the best way to describe them.

Energy and Its Perception

A reality is created by a combination of two things: 1) the actual configuration of the energy within it; and 2) how the energy is sensed. The combination of the two creates the perceived reality.

Both the energy configuration and the sensed data are required to create a reality. If the energy is not configured properly, the perceiving mechanism, which in our case are the outer senses, cannot view it in the form it was intended. In other words, if we were supposed to see a tree, but the energy of the tree was not in the shape of a tree, then we would not perceive that energy as a tree.

We assume that our perceived reality is the true reality, but the deeper one looks into the nature of our perceived reality, the stranger it looks. If Plato and Einstein were correct, then it is worth looking at our reality to see what might be an illusion versus what might be a true reality or what we have been calling a Universal Principle behind the illusion. To better understand the true nature of our reality, we need to look at some of its characteristics or dimensions.

Very few objects in our life remain the same when viewed over a wide range of parameters. For example liquid water looks like a solid (ice) when it is cold and a gas (steam) when it is hot. Our world would appear very differently to us if it were observed outside its ambient environment. We can use that same analytical approach when investigating our reality.

The majority of our physical reality is created from a combination of space, time, and matter. Looking at the nature of these parameters at their extremes helps us get a sense of their true nature. Science tells us that space, time, and matter can act in some pretty strange ways. Metaphysics tells us that they are even stranger than science presently suspects.

Space

We live in what science calls a four-dimensional space-time continuum. We think of space as simply something that just is: a fact of reality. It does not seem to have any distinguishable characteristics. It appears empty and a place where matter does not exist. But metaphysics disagrees with that perspective, and science is beginning to think otherwise as well.

Einstein tells us that matter warps space. He says that gravity does not really exist, and that what we perceive as one body being attracted to another is no more than the bending or warping of space. This means that planets are not orbiting the sun because they are attracted to it by gravity, but because space is warped around both the sun and the planet in such a way that the planet is actually moving in a straight line through a curved space. Therefore, Newton's formulas describing the motion of planets does not describe the gravitational pull between two bodies, but the degree in which space is warped.

Science also tells us a spinning black hole is so massive and dense that it can actually twist the space nearby. In February of 2016, the Laser Interferometer Gravitational-Wave Observatory (LIGO) reported the discovery of what they called 'gravitational waves' when two black holes collided. If Einstein was correct, then LIGO's detected ripples were not ripples in gravity but ripples in space. So if space can be warped, bent and twisted then it must be a substance or fabric of some sort.

Science is telling us that space has a malleable nature and therefore cannot be 'nothing.' It has to be 'something.' Metaphysics goes even further by saying that space is a construct of consciousness. Space appears to be unique to our portion of the physical field. If space only exists in our reality then it must be limited. It must stop somewhere, so our reality must have sides.

Space appears transparent. We think of transparency as something we can see through but true transparency is something we can move through, which space certainly is. This transparency gives space an appearance of being nonexistent, but space is anything but nonexistent. We note that light slows down when traveling through water and becomes even slower when traveling through glass because of the different resistivities in those substances. We note that the speed of light is limited to 186,000 miles/second in the 'vacuum' of space. We consider this a universal physical constant, but it turns out that it is only valid when light is traveling through space. All this implies that space is a 'material' with an internal friction or viscosity, which acts on matter and other substances like light.

Space appears to be an energy field that acts on everything within it. It seems to be a place that allows us to put physical objects.

Time

Time is a subject we take for granted. Our clocks run our life. Nobody questions the reality of absolute time. In fact, we even call it a dimension. If there is anything in our life that seems to be constant and predictable, it would be time. Every day we see its steady effects on the aging process, or so it appears.

Time is one of the great metaphysical mysteries. To understand the nature of time we need to know what it is. Unlike space and matter, time does not impact any of our senses. You cannot see it or feel it or touch it, even with instruments. We think a clock records time but the clock only displays a predefined duration. It does not actually measure anything physical.

Science gives us our first hint that there is something wrong with our concept of time. We think of time as being constant and one directional. Einstein predicted that time in our space-time continuum is related to motion. The faster an object moves through space the slower time moves, and if we reach the speed of light (186,000 miles per second in space) time stops completely. At first this might seem like a theory that has gotten ahead of reality. But in October 1971, Joseph Hafele and Richard Keating put two atomic clocks on commercial airliners and flew each around the world and then compared the clocks against another that remained at the United States Naval Observatory. When the clocks were compared the three sets disagreed with one another by an amount consistent with Einstein's prediction. The clocks on the airplanes had slowed down. Time had not changed for the rest of the world, just for the airplanes and their passengers.

Space contributes to the appearance of time by limiting the speed of objects within it. Time appears to 'lapse' as we slowly move through space. Physics tells us Time=Distance/Velocity. For a fixed distance, the greater the velocity the shorter the time. If velocity is extremely high or instantaneous then time becomes zero, or in other words, time would not appear to exist. It is the 'slow' movement of matter through space that gives us the perception of time.

Mankind has arbitrarily defined time using the earth's rotations on its axis and around the sun, which we assume to be constant. We have taken the earth's rotations and divided them into years, days, hours, minutes, and seconds. But if time can change with motion then it has no absolute duration. Clearly time is malleable.

Metaphysics goes even farther and says that time as an absolute measure does not exist. In fact, it is a phenomenon that is created as a byproduct of space. Admittedly this is a hard concept to grasp, but if we are to understand the strange nature of the universe, we need to better grasp the strange nature of time.

However, fully understanding the true nature of time is probably impossible for most of us and it is certainly not required to understand the concepts in this book. All we need to know is that although time exists in our reality, its true nature in our reality is elastic.

It turns out that time is expanded or shortened by the parameters of each reality. Time is certainly a good dimension to use to describe our reality but its variability keeps it from being a Universal Principle.

Matter

If time and space are not what they appear to be then where does that leave matter? Again, we need to look at the extremes of matter to understand its real nature. In our reality, matter is intended to be presented to us on the macro level. Our eyes cannot perceive the microscopic so it is the composite perception of matter that we are familiar with. Quantum Theory is the study of the microscopic behavior of matter. It has been around for over 100 years and physicists are still trying to understand what it means. Between entanglement, the quanta of electromagnetic energy, the uncertainty principle, the Pauli exclusion principle, and the wave theory of particles of matter, quantum mechanics tells us some pretty strange things about matter. Metaphysics goes even further and tells us that physical matter is not only a special form of energy, it is a special form of matter.

Science is aware of at least a portion of the electromagnetic spectrum,[15] in which it uses the wavelength of the radiated energy as the dimension to define its characteristics. The Seth entity says that matter has a material spectrum that corresponds to the electromagnetic spectrum. Whereas the electromagnetic radiation spectrum uses wavelength or frequency as its dimension, the material spectrum uses dimensions like intensity, density, pulse amplitude and duration.

There are literally an infinite number of states matter can be in. These different states of matter are the building blocks of all the fields of creation.

In order for matter to appear in our physical reality it needs to have specific characteristics. For example, if a particle's fluctuation is too fast or too slow it will not appear in our physical field. The particle may well be in a reality that is collocated with us, but our senses and our instruments will not be able to detect it because it will not be in our energy reality.

CUs Create Matter

The Seth entity says that our thoughts cause energy to materialize, and consciousness forms matter in a very specific way. There is nothing accidental or coincidental about the forms matter takes. Here is a simplified version of how the Seth entity explains it.

Consciousness exists in what Seth calls consciousness units or CUs, which were mentioned earlier. A CU can grow to any size, but despite its size, a CU creates its own thoughts and emotions.

Consciousness creates thoughts with emotions, which are unique vibratory patterns or waveforms of energy. Each thought is like a personal signature of energy consisting of pulses varying in frequency, duration, amplitude, polarity, density and intensity. Each of these dimensions of the thought is further modified by the emotion that goes with it. The characteristics of these dimensions are so finely differentiated that there is literally an infinite number of possible unique signatures. No two thoughts or emotions will ever be identical. However, similar thoughts and emotions have common characteristics so they can be grouped together and 'coded.' Note that at this point in the process the conscious energy does not have electrical properties, even though it has frequencies, pulses and other characteristics we associate with electrical energy. It is somewhat akin to energy in the form of acoustic or light, which are not electrical in nature either, but have waveform characteristics.

When a CU creates a thought, which by definition has emotion behind it, the resulting waveform immediately enters a 'mental enclosure' that exists within the CU. The Seth entity calls this the "Capsule Comprehension" process. The mental enclosure is a cube-like structure the size of which is determined by the size and capability of the CU. The energy enters through a single side, which functions as a gate that then closes and encapsulates it. Mental enzymes use the energy provided by All That Is, which exists everywhere, and transforms the waveform into Electromagnetic Energy units or EEs. As the name implies these are electrical in nature. After a minuscule delay, the EE is released through a gate. The result is an identity in the form of pseudo matter. This is not the matter that we know, but it is a building block of physical matter. If the intensity and emotion of the thought is right then the process will cause the energy to become physical matter. If not, which is the case for human thoughts most of the time, it forms 'pseudo matter.' Pseudo matter is similar to physical matter except it does not have the proper energy to enter the physical field. However, both matter and pseudo matter will follow the laws of the reality they are in, but once they transition into another reality they will follow the laws of the new reality.

Because every thought and emotion is unique, then every EE is unique. Like all energy, EEs are self-aware and will immediately manifest into a reality in which they are compatible, usually ones that are less dense than our physical field. There are millions of different realities and our space-time continuum is only one. Due to the principle of Value Fulfillment, EEs have a propensity to join other similar EEs in order to create larger and more significant self-aware structures or gestalts. The critical characteristics of an EE which allow it to combine with another EE are positive and negative poles. By alternating its polarity between positive and negative, an EE can align or misalign its poles with other units. They either attract and attach to like structures, or repel and detach from unlike structures.

However, even if the new EEs were not initially intense enough to be categorized as matter, they are the seeds of matter and the building blocks of all the realities. These vague objects are invisible to our present instruments because they are below the level of matter that we can presently detect.

When the strength of an EE (pseudo matter) reaches what the Seth entity calls a "Critical Intensity Level," it is able to enter the physical field by virtually exploding into physical matter. This occurs when other lower energy EEs join together and form a more energetic gestalt. Although EE energies never cease to exist, they change strength, move in and out of our physical field and other realities, join existing structures, and continue to evolve.

The initial level of intensity in each EE is determined by the emotion behind it. We think of an emotion as no more than a passing feeling, but strangely, emotion is what activates everything in the physical field, and it does this through our thoughts. Emotion acts as a catalyst by making our thoughts more energetic and powerful. Even at its lowest level pseudo matter is energized enough to become an object in less dense and less energetic realities.

There are many different stages or levels that pseudo matter can go through before reaching the level that we call physical matter. These pseudo matter stages are as valid as the ones we are familiar with, just not as intense. We are surrounded by this subordinate energy but we don't perceive it because it is either outside of our frequency range or below our other detection levels. Our senses are simply not attuned to them.

Matter and pseudo matter do not last as separate units forever. The patterns that they form decompose and the energy joins other EEs and creates new patterns. However, the energy in an EE never ceases to exist or degrade in strength.

Both matter and pseudo matter have a self-directed life. Like everything in existence, they are conscious identities making their own decisions. As strange as it may seem to us, our thoughts are alive and have their own existence. Our thoughts have far more consequences than we realize. They create objects and events not only in our reality but also in other realities. Our thoughts literally have a life of their own. For example, the Seth entity says that our thoughts create objects that might appear as stars to the inhabitants in some realities. CUs generate thoughts, which create EEs that are the creators of all objects and realities, not just in our portion of the physical field.

Our Perception

Let's take stock of where we are: space is a fabric woven together by some form of energy field that is transparent to our outer senses; time is malleable and has no absolute duration; and physical matter is itself a unique form of energy that is created by consciousness. This strange configuration of energy needs one more thing to make it a reality. Since realities are based on perceptions, it requires a unique interface that will perceive the space, time and matter in a certain way.

Our universe's elaborate illusion is based on the principle of vibration. The 'conscious portion' of our psyche is created to interface with our reality through our five senses. These senses are based on perceiving energy in very narrow frequency bands. Our vision is limited to the wavelengths of about 300 to 750 nanometers. Our hearing is limited to circa 20-20,000 hertz. Our smell appears to occur because of our nose's sensitivity to RF frequencies. Our taste buds sense five flavors (sour, sweet, salty, bitter and umami), which appear to be related to acoustical frequencies. Touch is even more complicated as electrical impulses are sent from our skin to our brain when we impact something. We interface with the physical world through these limited vibrations, which combine to present us with a very specific view of the world. Our outer senses, in combination with the unique energy formations that we perceive as matter, combine to create our perceived reality!

We take our reality for granted but it is more unique than we might at first realize. There are many other frequencies not in the 'visible light' spectrum that our eyes are not sensitive to like infrared, radio frequencies, microwaves, X-ray, etcetera. If our eyes were sensitive to those frequencies the world would be presented to us in a very different way. For example, X-rays penetrate soft tissue like flesh and clothing. If we could see X-rays, we would see our skeletal form and other structural components, but not see outer skins. If we could see infrared, we would see temperature differences like the hot body of an animal at night. In addition to the select frequency bands, we have a very limited ability to discern small or distant objects. With our lack of granularity, everything seems to blend together, which gives us a composite picture of our surroundings. There is no reason we could not have been given the capability to see what we think of as microscopic or distant objects, except that our creator did not want us to have that capability in this particular reality. In the same way there is no physical reason our ears could not hear colors and our eyes could not see music, except that is how the Tao chose to present the world to us. Many animals can hear much higher and lower frequencies than we can. Dog whistles are based on the concept of their sensitivity to higher frequencies. Our nose, taste and skin are sensitive to specific energy frequencies as well. Except for taste and touch, our three other senses were created to detect the world in space away from our body. And none of our senses detect the internal workings of our bodies. The senses we have to measure our well-being are pain and discomfort, which come to our attention through our nervous system.

We have been put here on earth and given very limited perception so that we could see the energy around us in very specific ways. As such we create our reality by the way we perceive certain energies. If our consciousness did not focus on the frequency band in our physical field, then we would not be able to see matter, let alone its solidity even though we were amidst it.

The senses of every species on the earth are also fine-tuned to allow them to experience their physical environment in a very specific way. Whether it is a bat's radar, or dolphin's sonar, or a dog's smell, each species perceives the world from their own unique perspective. Their illusion and therefore the reality that they experience is very different than ours even though we all live within the same space-time-matter backdrop in our reality. If we had different senses, it would be the same world, but we would not perceive it the way we do. What is presented to us is an elaborate illusion customized for our benefit. This allows virtually an infinite number of identities, each functioning at their own level with their own needs and expectations, to coexist simultaneously in the same locale and in the same creation field. The matter we look at is the same, but how we perceive it is very different.

Because of our limited perception, our reality is very focused. We cannot see the bacteria living in our body and digesting our food. We cannot see the viruses working for our common good and in some cases assisting our antibodies in the process. We simply experience the universe as the Tao and our spirit want us to. When we look out the window and see trees and lakes, we think that is reality, but it is only our perceived reality. It is only a picture created by our senses for our consumption. It is not that what we perceive does not exist, but it is just a unique perspective of the energy used to create our reality.

EEs create the objects that we perceive whether they are in the physical field or other spiritual realms. They take the form of objects that we see, hear, taste, touch, and smell. They also include the psychological objects like dream and hallucination forms, and every other type of perception. What we call telepathy is when EEs are directly transmitted between two identities and bypassing the outer senses.

It is impossible for us to conceive of the magnitude and sophistication required to create this illusion, and what we can see is not even the tip of the iceberg. By using different combinations of the electromagnetic and material spectrums, combined with unique devices of perception, similar to our five senses, the Tao is able to create different realities.

All this may seem like mass chaos, but there is great order behind it. The consciousness creating this process manages the creation of the objects that they form down to their smallest detail. Everything has its place and its role. Even though consciousness has free will, miraculously nothing is left to chance. Our environment that appears so normal to us is really a unique combination of vibrational energy, which is so finely tuned that even science's most precise experiments can barely detect the illusion.

Science's View

Science says matter is energy but it does not tell us how or why energy forms matter. Quantum physics sees matter functioning in very strange ways. But the spooky world of quantum physics is not nearly as spooky when seen from a metaphysical perspective. For example, quantum physics perceives particles appearing and then disappearing and then reappearing. Having no understanding of different realities, this is a difficult concept to explain. In his book *Wholeness and the Implicate Order*, quantum physicist David Bohm[16] proposed the possibility of a plenum type structure that our physical universe rests above. This is actually pretty close to what the Seth entity describes. The parameters of matter oscillate. Therefore they go in and out of our physical reality depending on if they are compatible with our reality. When the particle's energy is not compatible with our reality, they disappear from our view and become pseudo matter in other realities, which may well be spatially collocated with us. Although they disappear from our perspective, they do not go out of existence, they just change states.

As an aside, I find it interesting that the Gospel of John begins with, "In the beginning was the word, and the word was with God and the word was God." The problem with the scriptures is that they have been translated inaccurately (all too often intentionally), which makes it difficult to decipher the original intent of the writer. However, scholars have analyzed the Gospel of John and many of those scholars who are familiar with metaphysical principles have concluded that the writer of the Gospel of John was a mystic. Scholars agree that the John who wrote that Gospel was not the Apostle John, a fact many Christian organizations seem to ignore in their teachings. It was another individual who wrote it some 50+ years after Jesus had supposedly died and even well after the Apostle John had died. As such, this phrase can be understood from a metaphysical perspective. We cannot have a 'word' without a thought behind it, and 'the Tao' is a less biased term than the word 'God.' Thus, we could read John's opening phrase as, "In the beginning was thought, and thought was with the Tao and thought was the Tao." Indeed, the Gospel of John had it right. The universe started with thought and it is thought that maintains and grows it. This can be a hard concept to accept at first because it is so foreign to what we are used to believing. The Tao, or God if you will, is a mind, and the only product of a mind is thought.

Other Realities

If our reality is unique, then there should be other realities just as unique as ours but totally different and there are.

Parallel Realities (Compartmentalization)

There is only one true reality that is not an illusion and that is the reality of the Tao. It encompasses our universe, every other universe, and all the places not in a universe. Within that reality, all the other realities exist.

There are an untold number of realities in existence, each one inhabited with spirits that want to experience their unique characteristics. Each reality has specific purposes. How identities perceive a reality and how it impacts their lives is key to the nature of the experiences they can have in it.

Because each reality is different from the others they have been compartmentalized, which separates and to some extent isolates the realities from each other. Some are spatially separated while some are collocated, but separated by other parameters like frequency, intensity, density, polarity, etc. One reality abuts and flows into another in what the Seth entity calls a spiral-like pattern, similar in shape to a spiral galaxy.

The Tao has created a set of natural laws that apply everywhere, but manifest differently in each reality. If we looked at multiple realities, we would expect to find some overlapping similarities in the implementation of the various natural laws, although many of their specific dimensions would differ. All the natural laws that science has identified in our reality, which we consider sacrosanct, function very differently in other realities. For example, the speed of light would vary among realities.

Because the natural laws respond differently within each reality, it gives each reality a distinctive feel or appearance. Energy is able to go from one reality to another, but when it does it is immediately transformed into the form it takes in that reality. For example, when energy enters our reality it is transformed into matter. If energy is unable to reach the energy levels of our reality then it cannot enter into it.

The Structure of Realities

A reality is created whenever enough collaborative spirits have a need for it. An untold number of realities have been created and a huge number of them are still in existence. The characteristics of each reality would depend on the attributes the Tao decided to incorporate into it. Ours is only one of an endless number of realities.

Although the overall structure is multidimensional, to get a feel for what it is like we can picture a three-dimensional honeycomb structure of virtually an unlimited height, width, and depth. In total our make-believe structure would have many millions of honeycomb-like cells. Each cell represents a single self-contained energy reality with four sides, plus a top and bottom, like cubes but with irregular shapes. Now imagine that the sides of the realities are invisible yet impenetrable to the inhabitants. In other words, inhabitants on the edge of one reality could not move into the other reality without a transformation of their energy to make them compatible.

Since the energy realities are transparent to the inhabitants whose senses are not tuned to it, on occasion the realities can actually move through each other without either reality being affected or the inhabitants being aware of it happening.

Different realities create different illusions. In some realities a car would not be visible unless it was moving; and in other realities it would not be visible unless it was stopped; and in other realities it would only appear as a shadow. Emotions can cause colors and smells to appear. By altering the parameters of perception, it is possible to create any type of effect we can conceive.

Personal Reality
Within the structure of the energy reality, and the perceived reality created by our five senses, there are personal realities. Personal realities are unique to each individual identity. We use space, time and material objects as a backdrop and then we add personal items like our home life, work, family, friends, politics, religion, and especially our health, abilities and opportunities. These all combine to form the reality in which we live.

Probabilities

We have seen how different our actual reality is than how we perceive it. The unique aspects of our time, space and matter present our spirit and the Tao with options that are not intuitively obvious. Before we discuss those peculiarities, we need to understand the concept of probabilities.

Because we have free will we live in a world of choices. But speaking from your and my perspectives, these choices are not unlimited. We can divide our options into three categories: 1) the possible choices we can make, by far the broadest category; 2) the probable choices we can make, a subset of the possibilities; and 3) the actual choices that we make, which create the path our life takes. As we actualize our choices, each set of remaining options becomes more and more restricted because of the ever-expanding limitations that we put on ourselves.

The first set of restrictions are the physical limitations, which are caused by the physical environment. For instance, humans cannot fly or live under water without assistance. Although these are obvious there are other limitations not nearly as obvious that will be discussed later. Closely aligned with those are the practical limitations of our culture. Most people cannot be the President of the United States or the Pope. Each of us has our own set of practical limitations, which are generally out of our immediate control because of past decisions that we made. These significantly reduce our personalities' possible choices.

However, there are other possible choices of action that for all practical purposes we will voluntarily not do. It would be possible for us to dive into an empty swimming pool, or leap off a building, or jump in front of a moving bus. Although these are possibilities, they are not real choices, even though we could do them if we wanted to. So unless we were like stuntman Evel Knievel, these are possible but not probable choices.

This leaves our personality to select its actions from probable choices. But even this is not as wide a selection as one might imagine either. We have chosen a specific set of circumstances for us to be born into. As such, our choice of race and nationality were previously chosen when we selected our parents. The process of selecting our parents also includes selecting many of our family members, social and economic status, etc.

Because the soul created a prelife plan for us to follow, it endowed our personality with various energies that bias our choices on things like aptitude and attitude, and has given us latent abilities in areas like sports, arts and crafts, and music, which we can choose to develop. It even gave us specific energies that impact our views on cultural issues like religion, politics, society, etc. Even things like being a liberal or a conservative, or a type A or B personality are heavily influenced before we begin to guide our own life. It is possible to change some of these during our life, but it is not easy and it is not likely unless one is a very experienced soul.

But in the end, our personality is still left with an enormous number of probable choices to select from. We choose our mate, friends and adversaries, vocation and avocations, where we live and how we live, etc. The choices that we actualize are selected from our probable choices. We weave our own path through life by the probabilities that we actualize.

The reincarnation process is a series of events actualizing probabilities stretched out over multiple lives. After each life, the soul decides which events it wants the new personality to experience so it selects the biases and birth conditions that are most likely to make that happen. This results in the events of one life at least partially determining the basis for another life. It is a continual process that is somewhat open-ended but follows a general plan.

On the surface the concept of probabilities seems rather obvious, until we realize that the Tao and our spirit/soul are always interested in what might have happened had alternative choices been made, and as we will see they find out.

Aspects of Our Unique Reality

Spontaneity
We briefly went through the Seth entity's explanation of how consciousness creates matter and pseudo matter. Our thoughts,

along with the thoughts of many other identities in the universe, create them. We are co-creators of our world but we do not notice it because of 'time,' one of the strangest and most unique phenomena that is inherent in our reality. We take time for granted and therefore do not notice that the effect of time is to slow down everything that happens. If time did not exist, then everything in our world would happen the instant we thought of it, which is exactly how many other realities work. This is known as the Universal Principle of Spontaneity, which states that thoughts, which manifest objects and events, do it immediately. This principle is concealed from us because of the nature of time, but the effects of this are significant and widespread.

'What If?'
The Universal Principle of Free Will goes hand-in-hand with spontaneity and probability, and the three have some far-reaching implications, especially in our reality. Did you ever wonder what your life would be like if you had made other choices. Maybe picked a different career, had a different spouse, or taken a different job. You are not the only one who wonders. Both our spirit and the Tao wonder, but the difference is, they do something about it.

We have many opportunities in life that we can either take advantage of or ignore. When we make a decision, we actualize one of our probable options. When we look back at our life, we see a string of choices that we made that appear to follow one after the other. This gives us the feeling of 'cause and effect' where one choice leads to another. It also gives us a sense of being an individual experiencing a single life. Each choice would probably have given us a completely different set of experiences, and a very different life. Understanding what might have been an optimum path and what we should have done differently would be interesting to know. Time is the key to finding out.

Time as we know it is a creation of the Tao that seems to be somewhat unique to our reality, and it can be used anyway the Tao wants to use it. Although time does not exist in the same way that we perceive it outside our reality, events do have a duration. But the length of that duration compared to our timeframes is variable. In our physical reality the duration of events is slowed in comparison to the speed of activity that takes place in the inner universe. We can think of it like a clock whose second hand jumps rapidly from one second to the next and then stops for what we perceive as a second, and then jumps again. To identities operating in the inner universe our pauses between seconds seem much longer because so much more can be accomplished in that duration. It is as if a moment happened, then there was a long pause before the next moment. The result is that our life happens in slow motion compared to the inner universe.

From our soul's and inner conscious's perspective, it appears that our ego makes a decision, which actualizes a probability. At that point our inner self (soul and inner conscious) perceives everything coming to a halt and it is as if life stops for the rest of that moment. In the next moment we continue the process of actualizing a probability, at which time everything stops again, at least from the perspective of the inner self. In other words it is like everything is happening in slow motion.

This gives the inner self time to do other things beside actualizing the ego's choices. The inner self wants to maximize its experiences so it would like to know what would have happened if a different probability was actualized. Instead of wondering, it effectively examines the other choices. The inner self has a staggering amount of processing power. It is able to determine what would 'probably' have happened if a different choice had been selected so it is able to run through other scenarios and determine what would have been the likely outcome. For example, say we were considering accepting a new job. Our inner conscious knows who would be our new supervisor and colleagues. It knows the likely tasks we would be given, who we would work with, and how well we would do our job. It knows the impact that the job would have on the family, our existing friends, etc. In other words, it knows the probable outcome of that decision.

The physical world is so slow in comparison to the inner universe that the inner conscious can examine and experience all the important probabilities before a decision is actualized by the ego. The inner conscious has plenty of time to work through all the various probabilities of interest. Although this is an interesting exercise for the inner conscious, it has an extremely useful side effect. The analysis of the likely outcome of any decision the ego might make is performed before we make a decision. The inner conscious actually looks into the future and determines which of our options would work out best.

We can think of this process as exploding each moment in time and experiencing all the probabilities available to it. Since the inner conscious is us, to some extent we actually experience all our probable choices, not just the ones we actualize. After we die, we remember all those experiences.

When the inner conscious sees a clear advantage, it sends that information to the ego via the subconscious in the form of 'gut feelings' and 'hunches.' We think of this as intuition. At one time or another most everyone has gone against their 'gut feelings' and usually regretted it.

At a higher level, elements within the Tao are also interested in maximizing their experiences only they do it on a grander scale. For example, the Tao would likely be interested in world impacting situations like if the South had won the United States Civil War or if the Germans had the A-bomb first in WWII. Certain events, although not necessarily these, are experienced in alternative realities that we discussed earlier. These alternate realities are not constrained by our time so a lot can happen in a short period of physical time. These realities might last for what we would perceive as anywhere from moments to eons. They are special purpose events and the beings acting them out would not be the same as the ones who remain in our actualized reality. However, they would be thought forms created to act very similarly. These realities would be dissolved when the Tao is finished with them and the energy would go elsewhere. The Tao wants to experience as many probabilities as possible. The examination of alternate probable choices plays a much greater part in our civilization's existence than we expect.

Individuality

Although our true nature is both group and individual, in this life we are focusing on aspects of our individuality. Specifically, we are being taught to accept personal responsibility for our actions. Our reality is self-created as our thoughts create our environment. However, it is obvious that our thoughts are not spontaneously manifested into objects and events. The delay between the thought and its implementation gives us the impression that our thoughts are not connected with the events, which enhances the illusion. However, it is a safety device.

Due to our immature nature, if our every thought was immediately implemented, we would soon destroy each other and the world around us. Both individually and as a civilization we make a lot of mistakes so we need a safety measure to prevent chaos from reigning. Our world results in the average of our thoughts spread out over a duration or what we perceive as a 'period of time.' Our thoughts create our world but they do it slowly.

Despite the delayed reaction, we still create our world and the events that we encounter. The implication of this cannot be overstated. We and only we control our lives. Chapter 11 discusses how this affects our dreams and Chapter 12 discusses how this affects our physical life.

Chapter 11

Dreams

Dream experiences are as real as our awake ones.
The Seth Entity

Key Concept: Dreams are critical to our physical existence.

Dream Reality

The Seth entity gives us a whole new concept of dreams and their purpose. They are not the mindless wanderings of our psyche that they appear to be. They are actually a well-planned process in which the inner conscious resolves many of the ego's problems. In fact, Seth says that dreaming is so critical to our life that if we did not dream we could not function in the physical field.

There are many other realities in the universe besides our space-time continuum that we do not have any conscious contact with or even the slightest conception of their nature. However, the dream reality is an exception. It is a totally separate reality from the one we know, but one we regularly perceive. The dream reality is an actual reality, although we don't think of it that way. It is a permanent psychological structure that always exists, even when we are not involved with it. It no more stops existing when we are awake than the physical field stops existing when we are asleep. The only thing that changes is our awareness.

We think of dreams as just our thoughts running around our brain, but dreams are actually mental experiences in a totally separate reality. Just like in the physical field, our inner conscious actually enters the dream reality and creates experiences. The dream reality is not part of the physical field but parallel to it.

We view an experience as a physical action. It is an event that we attend or some circumstance that happens to us and we define 'us' as our physical bodies. But experiences are mental and the physical parts are just the 'wrappings' in which we cloak them. We are a mind and experiences are psychic events. The physical world sets the scene but all of our experiences take place in our consciousness. In our 'awake' experiences this is an irrelevant point as the physical body accompanies the psyche. However, it is highly relevant in our dream experiences because our physical body is not participating in the dream experiences.

Both the physical reality and the dream reality are independent realities, each functioning under their own laws. However, the dream reality has some very different characteristics than the physical reality. Because it exists outside of our physical reality it has no time constraints, and instead of using physical space as its medium it exists in a psychological space.

Dreams have forms just like the physical field and those forms also consist of molecular structures. However, they differ from our physical matter in that they use a type of pseudo matter that follows very different physical laws than the matter we are familiar with. For example, the particles are less dense, move faster, and do not exhibit the 'permanence' or staying power of physical matter. We experience this when we perceive dream objects instantly changing form: houses turn to fields, people morph from one person to another, and time does not exist. Dream reality does have rules but they are very different than the rules we operate under in the physical field.

When we are dreaming, the portion of our consciousness having the dream thinks the experiences are happening to it. The dream-created emotions are as real as our waking emotions. In fact, one could argue that we are more aware in our dreams than in our physical life because in our awake life we are so focused on the physical field it is like being in a deep trance, unaware of the other spiritual realms around us.

An interesting aspect of the dream reality is that it gives us a glimpse at how other realities operate. Dream reality is much like the reality of the astral field in that things change very rapidly in accordance with our wishes. In fact, many of our dreams actually interface with entities in the astral field. Of course, other realities are not as haphazard as our dreams appear to us, but then our dreams are not really as haphazard as they appear to us either.

Our inner conscious dreams all the time. But when we are awake our ego focuses its attention on the physical field, which consumes our awareness to the point that we do not realize anything else exists. When we sleep our ego stops focusing on the physical field and our inner conscious takes over the personality's awareness. However, a part of our inner conscious is always focused on the dream reality. We just do not notice it when we are awake.

We think of dreams as our own personal experiences, but the dream reality is a shared field just like the physical field. We interface with others in the dream field just like we interface with others in the physical field.

The structures we create in dreams do not exist in our physical space, but they do exist in psychological space. They are as real as the objects in our waking lives.

Validity of Dream Experiences

Although dreams exist in a psychological reality, they provide experiences that are as valid as any waking experience. The thoughts we have when we are asleep are as important as the ones we have when we are awake. Our mind never stops thinking, even when we sleep. During sleep the inner conscious is the personality's decision maker, not the ego. Upon waking and before refocusing on the physical field, for just an instant our ego becomes aware of the inner conscious's focus and control. It quickly retakes control and our dream awareness rapidly disappears. The ego is afraid of losing control to the inner conscious so it ignores its activities upon awakening. The ego is only interested in what it focuses on and fears what it does not understand.

Dreams cause us to feel emotions that are as powerful as any we feel when we are awake. We learn as much, if not more, through dream experiences as we do through our daily activities. Dreams have the advantage of being faster and more controllable, and not being actualized means we do not need to deal with their consequences.

We have adventures when we are awake that we perceive through our physical senses. Our awake reality is constructed so that we experience the events in a physical way. Dreams are no different except in the ways we experience them. They are every bit as sophisticated, objective and real as our physical experiences.

Dream reality consists of energy that takes different forms, just like the physical field. The objects and events that take place in our dreams are created by our inner conscious, just like the objects and events in the physical field. As far as our psyche is concerned, an experience is an experience. Both physical and dream experiences have equal validity.

Physical Importance of Dreams

The dreams of the inner conscious are not only more important than we suspect, they are essential to our health, livelihood, and existence in the physical field. Issues in our daily life that the ego is unable to resolve are addressed by dreaming. During dreams we learn, play, have new experiences, cure illnesses, communicate with our existing friends and family, solve problems, and even inspire ourselves. Every dream has a meaning, every dream fragment has a purpose, and every dream is formulated by our inner conscious with great care.

Dreams connect physical reality to spiritual reality, which enables us to get direct knowledge from the spiritual realm. For example, we are given pertinent genetic information that guides our growth throughout our life. Our prelife plan describes how we should appear at each stage of our lifetime and some of that information is received in dreams. Reincarnation experiences and expertises come to us in our dreams. Our prelife plan defines the experiences our soul wants us to have and that guidance is available in dreams. Karmic details can also come to us this way. We even interface with those who have died and experience many of the things we will encounter in the afterlife.

Dreams also provide many physical benefits. The stresses in our lives cause chemical imbalances in our bodies. The emotional impact derived from our dreams enables the body to release substances that counter these toxins.

All Consciousness Dream

Dreams are a critical part of the existence of any being experiencing the physical field. We have all watched our pets when they were sleeping and occasionally their movements made it pretty obvious that they were dreaming. Dreams are a property of consciousness when it is manifested in the physical field. Since everything on earth is conscious, then everything dreams. Animals, plants, minerals and atoms all dream to some extent. However, the less sophisticated the consciousness, the less complicated the dream.

The Dreaming Process

Portions of our inner conscious are always operating in the dream reality. Since dreams are not encumbered with the time delays of our space/time reality, events happen much more rapidly. The Universal Principle of Spontaneity, where what we think of is instantly created, can be clearly seen in our dreams. As a result, a great deal can be accomplished in a short period of time.

We think of our life as a single continuous saga, but it is actually a series of different event fragments. We go to work, participate in social activities, and settle family issues. We do them in segments. We stop and do other things until we return to a specific activity, continuing where we left off.

Similarly, we experience dreams in fragments. The inner conscious has multiple topics it wants to deal with so we have multiple dreams every night. Most dreams run in about 20 minute segments, so the inner conscious will deal with a number of issues in a normal night's sleep. Deep complicated dreams operate in fragments like a TV serial. When the fragment ends nothing happens until the inner conscious returns to it and continues where it left off. Although our inner conscious is always working on dream episodes, it temporarily stops one episode and starts another.

Our ego is only aware of a tiny portion of a dream experience when it awakens. We only remember the last few moments of the Rapid Eye Movement (REM) portion of our dreams, which are the least important portions of our dream activity. The deeper into our consciousness we go, the more impact the dream has on our psyche.

Dreams do not end or even disappear when we wake up. The inner conscious may continue the dream during our waking hours. However, when we are awake our ego focuses on the physical world and we generally ignore the inner conscious's activity.

Dreams are the creation of the highly controlled and focused inner conscious. It is because our ego only views the tail end of our dreams that we think they are uncontrolled and random. To add to the confusion, our dream experiences happen extremely rapidly compared to our daily life. The ego is not used to that pace of activity, especially when it gets such a short glimpse of the experience.

An interesting aspect of dreams is that they are a peek into the hidden reality in which our inner conscious exists. Because our ego is consumed by the physical field, we do not notice the behind the scene work of our inner conscious. Occasionally we have a dream that either solves a nagging problem or predicts a future event or seems to have some other impact on our daily life. However, in general, few people would say they understood their dreams or that their dreams had much effect on their lives.

Although our ego rarely remembers much of our dreams, our inner conscious remembers all of them. It seems strange that we cannot remember our dreams when we are alive, but have total recall of them in death. The inner conscious always has access to all our physical and dream experiences, but the ego does not have access to the inner conscious during life.

Resolving Issues

Our inner conscious, which never sleeps, uses the dream reality to resolve issues and provide guidance to the ego. It chooses the topics with great discretion from both unresolved issues during this life and issues that arose in previous lives that are still unresolved. There is no shortage of topics for our inner conscious to draw from.

Some of the problems the inner conscious addresses are the choices we are struggling with in our waking hours, which we discussed in the last chapter. The inner conscious is always helping the ego have the experiences it wants so it assists the ego in making choices. The inner conscious's incredible processing power enables it to select potential options, process complete scenarios covering our probable future choices, and then determine the likely outcomes. This enables the inner conscious to understand the likely consequences of each choice before we commit to it.

Another area our inner conscious works on is unresolved past life traumas. The inner conscious has access to all the past personality's issues. The inner conscious is able to recreate a scenario that happened in a past life and rerun the experience with a different ending. Because dream experiences are as valid as physical experiences, the trauma created in a previous life can be resolved in a dream. Studies have revealed that during past life regressions trauma experienced by past personalities can be brought forward during hypnosis for resolution. This is only required for the most severe circumstances where the past life issue has surfaced and is negatively affecting the personality. However, most past life issues never reach this level as they are resolved in our dreams.

Dreams also allow us to perform actions that would be difficult for us to accomplish in our physical life. For example, we might have a need to have either a dependent or dominant relationship in order to release a certain type of energy. If we cannot release these energies, then illness is likely to follow. Dreams allow actions to occur without physically experiencing them.

Dream Personality

We are incredibly complex beings and dreaming is yet another aspect of our nature. We have a dream personality just like we have a physical personality. The ego is the 'I' we know by day, but the inner conscious is the 'I' of our dreams. The personality of our inner conscious is much fuller and richer than the one we know because it has the benefit of knowing and drawing on all the soul's previous personalities. But, of course, both the ego and the inner conscious are different parts of the same entity. They are both 'us.' It is like our business persona and our home persona. Both are us but operating under different conditions.

In our dreams we have very real interfaces with other personalities. We work with the inner selves of people who are in our present life, like business associates, friends, family, and strangers. We also work with souls and personalities in the spiritual realms like our loved ones who have died, and souls who have been or will be in our past and future lives. In addition our spirit guides use this opportunity to provide us guidance and make suggestions. We might even communicate with animals, plants and other life forms, as these are also beings with a spiritual nature that have incarnated into different bodies. From the apparent chaotic structure of our dreams comes our ordered physical life.

Interpreting Dreams

Understanding our dreams is extremely difficult because we do not understand the context of the images that we perceive. The images are symbols that have very complicated and often changing meanings. A quick glimpse of a dream event that the ego perceives as nonsense, will make great sense to the inner conscious. To better appreciate this it helps to understand the nature of dream images.

Realities consist of objects, which are symbols representing some aspect of a thought. In other words, the thought is real and the object is the symbol of it, which is just the opposite of how we think of it. For example, we see houses and boats and we think they are real. Although those objects do exist in our reality, they have a very limited lifespan. Their only purpose is to give us experiences. However, the idea of those objects is eternal but the experiences that we have with them stay with us forever. It is the eternal nature of a thought that makes it real, and it is the temporary nature of an object that makes it a symbol. This concept is true both in life and in dreams.

In our reality, objects are symbols of things or events. But in other realities objects might represent emotions. The emotion might be a feeling about an object and not the object itself. Apparently, this is how the mental field of creation operates.

We spend our early education learning the meaning of symbols in an effort to understand our culture. But even common symbols will mean different things to different people. For example, fire can represent a feeling of warmth and comfort or danger, depending on the experiences we had with it. Symbols will often change their meaning as our experiences with them change. Of course, across our planet a symbol will often mean different things in different cultures.

To add to the confusion of the meaning of dream objects, the inner conscious controls the dream process and selects topics from past or present personalities. Each past life occurred in a different era, and dealt with different issues in different ways. Cultures have changed a great deal over the centuries, so each past life symbol might have a different meaning for a similar object, event, and emotion, which makes them multitiered.

It is easy to see how this can complicate interpreting our dream images, which consist of symbols from multiple periods and sources.

The inner conscious is the only portion of the psyche that truly understands the meaning of every symbol in each past life. If we had a dream that was intended to deal with a past life issue, the images may be familiar to us but have very different connotations than how we would interpret them.

For us to understand a dream we would need to use our inner sense and become part of the thought creating that dream. This would be an extremely difficult task for the ego. However, under special circumstances, hypnotism could possibly be used to understand a given dream.

There are many books providing guidance to help us understand the meanings of our dreams. These can be interesting and also assist in interpreting recurring dreams that seem to refer to our present day issues. But because of the huge variability in the meaning of symbols, the interpretation of dreams should not be relied on for major life decisions. In addition, we only remember a small portion of a dream, so even knowing what a symbol means does not necessarily tell us the full context of what a dream means.

However, the true value of dreaming is not for the ego to understand or interpret them, but rather for the soul to resolve our problems. If an action is deemed necessary, the soul will provide that guidance to the ego and we will receive it through intuition and gut feelings.

Controlling Our Dreams

Understanding our dreams may be more work than it is worth, but controlling our dreams is not that hard and can be very rewarding. The inner conscious is always trying to assist the ego. It carefully chooses what it considers the most important issue to best assist the ego. But it is possible for our ego to direct the inner conscious to create dreams that will actually perform specific tasks for us. For example, depression is a common affliction many people deal with. If our depression is not too severe, we can simply ask our inner conscious to create a dream that will leave us happy and upbeat upon awakening. The key is to wait until we are ready to fall asleep and make our request the final thought of the day. Repeating it several times is good insurance. Writing down our request and putting it under the pillow is another good approach.

Another advantage of controlling dreams is to have experiences that would be difficult to have physically. If we are frustrated and want to have an experience of aggression without actualizing it, then we can do it through our dreams. This can be very therapeutic as it can prevent us from causing harm and still release us from the aggressive urge. However, we need to be very careful not to focus our dream aggression against anyone in particular. Our telepathic abilities can actually impact the psyche of that individual and cause them to respond. It is conceivable that they could react so negatively that we could create a karmic ribbon. Any aggression we create in our dreams or otherwise needs to be nonspecific.

Dreams appear chaotic because we only remember a tiny piece of them and we don't understand the symbolism. It is possible to train the portion of our waking conscious that is not the ego to be aware of our dreams while we sleep. This allows us to learn more about our dreams by having our non-ego consciousness witness them, but it requires training and is not easy to learn.

Dreams are a critical element of our physical existence. Learning to interpret them is not easy but learning to better control them can make our lives happier and more successful.

Group and Mass Dreams

Group events are the result of desires from all the individual inner consciouses who want to participate in that event. These discussions and planning sessions are done with each other during the dream state. Dreaming allows us to work through group problems with our family, friends, community, etc. When we are working in groups, each inner conscious has its particular skill or interest which it focuses on. For example, people who have many nightmares are often the guardians of the group. In order to protect the group, they agree to look into the future and deal with potential issues, which can cause them to suffer through bad dreams.

Sometimes we are involved in issues that are much bigger than the personal world we have created for ourselves. We occasionally participate in planning large group events, even to some extent global ones. In mass events, everyone gets their say, even if their ideas are very unpopular.

Mass dreams cause the most significant events in the world to take place. Major storms, famines, plagues, pandemics and conflicts are all organized and implemented in the dream world. We have an input into every event that affects us. However, we can also choose not to participate in an event, and our inner conscious will ensure we are not involved.

Chapter 12

Expectations

Watch your thoughts... they become your destiny.
Lao Tse

Key Concept: The importance of our thoughts cannot be overstated.

The Extended Nature of Thought

We think of thoughts as intangible wisps of nothingness as we cannot see them or touch them. At the same time we view matter as the substance of the universe, but it is just the opposite. Thoughts are not only the greatest power in existence, they are the only power in existence. They form the universe, create every circumstance we encounter, and cause every emotion that we feel. They can heal every sickness we encounter, change our financial situation, and determine how we spend our day. Our thoughts control who we are, the life we lead, our happiness and our suffering. The implications of this are unbounded. Mastering the control of our thoughts will allow us to change any and all circumstances in our life, bar none. Thoughts create our life and everything in it.

Beliefs Create Events

By forming EEs, consciousness creates both pseudo matter and physical matter. Different realities use different types of matter but they are all created by thought. Thoughts create realities and our thoughts create our reality. The form energy assumes in our personal reality is a reflection of our psyche. However, the space-time illusion that we perceive makes it difficult for us to see our interrelatedness with our environment. The illusion makes it difficult to realize that we can change our life by changing our beliefs. The impact of our beliefs is not only the source of all our earthly difficulties, but the basis that allows for our rapid evolution.

Personal Belief System

Everyone creates a personal reality and they base their belief system on it. What we think is real and absolute is based on how our five outer senses perceive the illusion. The nature of space, time and matter are ingrained root assumptions caused by the illusion. But also our abilities and limitations, our perception of others, our political and religious views, and an array of other opinions are also part of our belief system. We create concepts about these things and then synthesize those ideas into an all-encompassing belief system.

Our belief system is not based on fact or absolute truth but on truth as we create it. Because we perceive our life through a distorted lens, our personal reality is also distorted.

It is easy to see how events around us will impact our beliefs. If we are chronically ill our view of life will be very different than if we are a world class athlete. The question is: how did we become chronically ill or a world class athlete? What we don't see is the impact that our thoughts and decisions had on creating our life.

The integration of our reality and our beliefs gets even more intricate when we realize that our reality creates our beliefs, and in turn, our beliefs then change our reality. This creates a loop that can work in our favor if our beliefs are constructive, but can cause us problems if our beliefs are destructive.

Impact of Our Beliefs

If you only take one thing away from this book it should be that **we cause everything that happens to us**. We create ourselves, our life, and every event that we experience; the good, the bad, and everything in between. There is no such thing as a victim. If our life is not working the way we would like it to, it is because of the decisions that we have made. The best part of this is that because we created our problems, we have the power to fix them, all of them.

Thoughts are more real than the observable universe because thoughts created the universe, and will be around long after the universe is gone. Nothing can exist in any reality that is not first created by a thought. Matter does not just miraculously come into existence and create the objects we see. Without exception every object, which includes every human in existence, is a result of a spiritual thought. All of nature, to include mankind, is being taught how to use this immense power, which is our birthright.

Responsibility

Until we began our first sentient Grand Cycle, we incarnated as group souls. Group souls had a shared responsibility for their actions. As we evolved past that stage, our evolution became more challenging. Our group soul days are over and we are now being taught to accept responsibility for ourselves as an independent consciousness. Individual consciousness is a sacred concept and consciousness needs to learn to use its energy wisely. Part of that process is learning to work in a supportive manner with others and indeed all of nature.

We learn this lesson by experiencing the effects of our decisions. We are the creators of our life and everything that happens to us. When our life makes us unhappy and we feel downtrodden, it might be time to examine our expectations.

Our ego creates our beliefs and the emotions that energize them, but it is our inner conscious that manifests those beliefs, which then become our experiences. It means that we, and only we, create our experiences. If an experience is positive, we caused it. If an experience is negative, we caused it. There is no one else to praise or blame for our lives. We and only we are responsible for who we are and where we are.

Ego vs Inner Conscious

The inner conscious is responsible for enacting our long-term plans. The ego can plan long-term events, but only the inner conscious can make them happen. The communication between the ego and the inner conscious is critical, and that is where the problems occur.

Our ego is the ultimate authority on what experiences our inner conscious will create for us in the physical field. This sounds like we simply decide what we want and our inner conscious will create it for us, but it is not that simple. The ego and inner conscious have a limited communication link. The inner conscious knows the role of the ego, and knows it is supposed to manifest the experiences that the ego wants. On the other hand, the ego does not even know the inner conscious exists so it has no idea the inner conscious is manifesting its thoughts.

The ego's decisions for short-term movements, like deciding to stand up, are rapidly responded to by the subconscious, so it appears the ego is in control of itself. The ego assumes its long-term plans are simply a series of short-term actions that it controls. However, it is the inner conscious's focus on the long-term events, like those taking weeks, months, years, and even decades, that makes them occur.

Trying to decide what the short-term focused ego wants to do in the long term is not that easy. The inner conscious is forced to look at the ego's deeply-held assumptions and beliefs. The inner conscious assumes that the ego wants to experience what it thinks about. It is the ego's long-held 'truths' and expectations that become manifested, which have far more subtle implications than it first appears.

Take the simple example in which someone is a devout Christian who dutifully follows the Church's doctrine and truly believes he and the rest of humanity have original sin. This concept now becomes a part of his belief system. If that person also assumes that sinners should suffer, then the inner conscious ties them together and sets up events that will make him suffer. Now that may not really be what he wants, but it will be what he gets. In this situation he is trying to live a good life by following the Christian tenets, and all he gets is unnecessary hardships. 'God' does not want him to suffer, and even the Church does not want him to suffer. However, this belief causes an unintended consequence because neither he nor the Church understands how life works.

Our beliefs shape our lives. Mankind is in an evolutionary stage where we are learning to accept responsibility for our actions. Our thoughts have great power and our expectations direct that power. Over time and after many experiences and multiple lives we eventually realize the impact of our beliefs and change them to be more constructive. We are not being punished for those beliefs, we are being shown their power. We will accept responsibility for our life once we realize that we are the creators of it!

'Catch-22'

The term 'Catch-22' is a phrase referring to a dilemma where no matter what choice we make, we keep aggravating the problem and the situation keeps getting worse. This is a common occurrence for people whose lives are not going as well as they would like, which is typical for many. The choices they make to improve their lives only make the situation worse.

Our beliefs and our reality are meant to have a positive symbiotic relationship. How we see reality has a huge impact on our beliefs, and in turn, our beliefs create our reality. Ideally this is a positive situation, but false beliefs cause problems.

If we envision ourselves with a good job, healthy family, adequate finances, nice home, etc., then our soul will create that life for us. The universe is biased to give us an enjoyable life providing we do not do something to change it. When we view these experiences negatively, then life can become unpleasant. We might view ourselves as inadequate, not smart, or a poor family provider. Whatever the situation, we begin to limit ourselves. If this feeling persists, we will start changing our beliefs, which causes the inner conscious to think this is what we want, and it creates more difficult experiences. For example, we might have originally lost our job, which was part of a larger plan intended to inspire us to change our career focus towards something more conducive to our prelife plan goals. But instead of accepting this as a positive new opportunity, we view it as our failure. If we let this shake our self-confidence enough, we may begin to believe we are not worthy of a better job. It is easy to see how this could begin a long downward spiral.

This distorted belief will foster other self-imposed limitations on us, which the inner conscious will begin manifesting. These limitations can cause considerable problems to include poor health, financial problems, and added stress, all of which reduces our quality of life. Once we get on this downhill slope it can be difficult to turn things around.

However, unlike a true Catch-22, this situation is reversible if we change our expectations, which are driven by our two main self-imposed inner 'truths': root assumptions and core beliefs.

Root Assumptions

Root assumptions are beliefs we take for granted. We don't think about them or analyze them because we simply assume they are true. We have been told these 'truths' by parents, teachers, religious and political figures, and other sources that we respect and believe. They are buried deep in our psyche and we base our reasoning on them. Often, we don't even realize they exist. Religious beliefs are a good example of root assumptions.

Religions have been modified so much from their founding principles that they purport a multitude of contradictory beliefs. It is not as important which religion we choose as the tenets we adopt. For example, the three great Abrahamic religions, Judaism, Christianity and Islam, all have a long history of violence and negative aggression as well as affirming the value of love. We each have a choice as to which tenets, love or violence, we will adopt as our root assumption. We should choose wisely because our beliefs create the world around us and are responsible for our experiences. Obviously, if we choose violence our life will likely be short, unproductive and full of new karmic ribbons. Terrorism is an obvious example, but the results from a choice of violence can have much more subtle effects on our life than overt crime, as our previous example of humanity's original sin indicated. If we see violence as an answer to our frustrations, we will attract it to us.

Everyone has root assumptions and there is nothing wrong with that as we do not have the time or interest or capability to analyze everything we encounter. Many root assumptions are instilled in us from early childhood and impact us throughout our life. Most of our root assumptions are harmless, so even if they are faulty, little damage is done. A problem only occurs when our assumptions are self-limiting and we base our life on them, which is very common.

Some of our most fundamental beliefs, which we consider truths about life, are simply ideas about life. But by believing them we manifest them into our lives. Our self-limiting 'truths' are only true because we make them happen. We might tell ourselves that we are poor because the world is stacked against us. If we believe we will always be poor, then our inner conscious will give us that experience. We cause things to happen and then we reaffirm them by telling ourselves this is the way life is.

The best way to deal with root assumptions is to not be dogmatic about things we are not fully familiar with. Who says mankind is born with original sin? We don't have to decide if that is right or wrong. If we set aside or 'park' the information that we are not sure of until further knowledge becomes available, then it does not become part of our root assumptions. Simply telling ourselves that we do not know and leaving it at that resolves the issue. We can tell the world whatever we like, but the damage occurs when we fool ourselves.

Core Beliefs

Our core beliefs are similar to our root assumptions except we have consciously thought through a scenario and arrived at a conclusion, which we then live by. Many children are convinced they are dumb and cannot do well in school. This may be caused by a learning disability but often it is caused by comments from parents, teachers or friends. Whatever the cause, they give up on education at a very early age. This haunts them all their life, affects their family and financial status, and damages their self-respect. If you think you will fail your inner conscious will give you that experience.

Core beliefs are more obvious than root assumptions because they are more a part of our awareness. Although they are easier to identify, they are not necessarily easier to remedy. The easiest way to identify them is to determine which beliefs are self-limiting. When we look at our society, we see numerous situations that negatively affect our beliefs. Our cultural organizations continually stress our dependency on others. Religions tell us we are at the mercy of a demanding deity, the government tells us they need to run our lives because we apparently cannot, the media tells us we need their sponsors' products to be happy and healthy, etc. Even when we recognize the nonsense and resist it, we still fall prey to the constant bombardment. The result is to become convinced we are a pawn at the hands of the powerful, instead of the master of our life.

It is our responsibility to decide which thoughts to believe. In many cases it is not important which ones we choose to believe, even if they are wrong, because there are no serious consequences. For example, it does not make a difference if we believe in a divine entity or not. Unlike what some of the religions tell us, everyone has an afterlife no matter what they believe and there is no damnation to worry about. However, if we let our beliefs in a specific divine entity cause us to act poorly towards others, then we will have negative repercussions. Our misconceptions begin to make life difficult for us when they are self-limiting. We manifest what we believe, and when we think the worst will happen, that is what our inner conscious will create for us.

Our root assumptions and core beliefs drive the events of our lives. If we think we will fail, then we will. If we think there is evil in the world then we will find evil. If we have been told all our life that we are a loser and will not amount to anything and we come to believe it, then we will make it happen. Our expectations become self-fulfilling prophecies. We literally hypnotize ourselves into believing our root assumptions and core beliefs. We are so focused and convinced of our 'truths' that we are unable to see how they shape our life.

Victimhood

No one forced us to come here. In fact, sentient life on earth is an opportunity that we aspired to. The prelife plan we created spelled out our goals. We chose our biases, which determine how we view life. We chose our parents, which gave us our start in life. We chose our culture, nationality, gender, race and initial social status. We chose it all! We are not a victim of our circumstances. We created our circumstances. So if we control all life's variables, what is it about life that makes day-to-day living such a struggle? Why would we choose to experience all these problems?

The conditions under which we were born don't cause our problems or the actions of others, but the decisions that we make after we are born. The choices that we make cause all our problems, and a major purpose of our life is to learn how to make wiser choices.

We don't realize that our thoughts are actually making choices for us. We don't see the connection between our expectations and our experiences. Life gives us what we expect to get. If we expect trouble, then we get it. If we expect to be healthy, then we are. Unfortunately, our true expectations can be very different from our desires and even the superficial expectations that we proclaim to others and even ourselves.

The good news is that we have the power to change our life because we create our experiences. But only we can change it. No one else can change it for us. We waste a lot of time and effort trying to get other people to change our life when they cannot.

Because our thoughts create our world, our world is a reflection of who we are. The world we live in is a personal reality that we created, which is a mirror image of us. If our world is in chaos, then that is the state of our psyche. We live in a self-created bubble, and even if there is chaos all around us, it will not impact us unless we let it.

We have free will to do as we please and the ability to create any life we want. If we are not happy with our life then we need to change it. Blaming others for our problems simply creates another roadblock for us to hurdle before turning things around. Victims are only victims of their own beliefs. If we don't like the way the world is, then we need to change ourselves, not others.

Unintended Consequences
Poor health is not caused by misfortune. In one way or another it is caused by our beliefs. Unless we are dealing with a karmic issue or are a highly advanced soul looking for a special experience, we are designed to be healthy and will remain so unless we do something to change it. Like all the circumstances in our life, our beliefs create our physical and mental conditions.

Like Attracts Like
When we continually focus our thoughts in a particular area, we create what the Seth entity calls a 'Characteristic Emotional Climate,' which is another way of saying like attracts like. This is

a psychological environment that results from the types of ideas we constantly think about. If someone teaches the same topic over a prolonged period or works in a particular field of research, he may create a climate receptive to ideas that are compatible to his own way of thinking. When we work intensely on a difficult problem, we will attract the type of energy that will assist us in resolving it. Many of the great discoveries have been a result of the inner conscious receiving thoughts from others who are also working in closely related areas. Generally, this enables us to have a positive attitude towards new ideas that will help us achieve our goals and even find major breakthroughs.

Unfortunately, this can be a doubled-edged sword. The nature of the 'characteristic emotional climate' is to encourage us to entertain ideas that are similar to ours and reject ideas that are different. This might sound like a reasonable approach to life, but if our idea is wrong, constant reinforcement of a bad idea only reinforces our mistaken core belief.

Fear

Sickness is often a case of attracting what we fear. It is a common belief that many sicknesses are genetic. If our parent or sibling or other blood relative has suffered from a disease, then we often believe we are at a higher risk of getting it. So we start to worry. The more we focus on the disease the stronger our belief becomes. To make matters worse, drug advertisements bombard us with fears about diseases and our ego tunes in to the symptoms that we are most worried about. We discuss it with our friends and family, study it in the periodicals, and worry about it in our spare time. Our preoccupation with the disease causes our inner conscious to believe that the ego wants to experience it. We literally make it happen.

Our phobias can also cause us to attract negative events. If we are afraid of being in a car or plane accident, or having our house robbed or are even being germophobic, then we can attract the very situation we fear. Just not wanting something to happen is not going to attract it to us. It has to be part of our core beliefs and we need to continually focus on it. If it is a deep-seated fear, even if we consciously try to ignore it, it will eventually become a reality.

Negative Emotions

Pent-up negative emotions can also cause illness. The world we create is an image of our beliefs. How we feel about others is a reflection of how we feel about ourselves. If we dislike another person it is usually because what we think we see in them is what we dislike about ourselves. If we get upset when we see arrogance or prejudice in others, it is because it reflects the arrogance or prejudice we see in ourselves. We create our lives around our self-image.

When we dwell on emotions like hate, anger, rage, grief, blame, sorrow, depression, etc., we create more negative energy than our body can release. Our body is well equipped to deal with immediate and specific threats. It has numerous defenses at its disposal like white blood cells, helpful bacteria and viruses, and untold numbers of fluids and secretions, which react immediately to defend the body from foreign threats. But when the threat doesn't exist, and the ego tells the body something is wrong, it does not know how to deal with it. Over time this wears down the body's defensive system. Our response towards vague general threats can result in diseases and general deterioration. For example, our body does not know how to deal with long-term despair.

When we drive ourselves to the point where the emotional burden is too great, our inner self will do something to relieve it. Sometimes our body's only way to release energy is through illness. Sickness slows us down and changes our focus away from our obsession. Sickness can be an outlet for the accumulated negative energy. Of course, excess drugs, alcohol, smoking and eating are obvious potential causes of disease but they are symptoms of our negative thinking.

Although it is possible that experiencing a disease or debilitating event was part of our prelife plan, in most cases it is simply suffering that we do not need to experience.

Changing Our Beliefs

The solution to all our problems is to change our beliefs but there is nothing more difficult than changing our belief system. Our root assumptions and core beliefs are so fundamental to who we are that it is very difficult to be objective. However, we do not need to change everything immediately. The initial step is to accept responsibility for our difficulties and stop blaming others for circumstances we caused.

We should think of all the ways we might be limiting ourselves. If we think we are bad at math or science it will become a fulfilling prophecy. If we see ourselves as being prejudiced against, or unpopular, or a poor athlete, or a poor dancer, then so it will be. When we focus on what we do not have, we get even less of it!

It is important to take action. Changes in our life only happen by having new experiences. We need to give our inner conscious a chance to help us. If we stay home and wait for our life to change nothing will happen. It reminds me of the story of a very pious man who was stranded on his roof in a flood. A man in a raft came by and offered him a ride, but he turned that down explaining that God would save him. A powerboat came by and he turned down the offer for a ride saying God would save him. Then a helicopter came by and he said the same thing. Eventually the water rose and he drowned. When he died, he asked God why he did not save him. God said, "What do you mean. I sent you a raft, a powerboat and a helicopter."

We cannot wait for the world to solve our problems; we need to take action. Our actions go hand in hand with our beliefs. If we want more money, we cannot hibernate in our home waiting for it to be delivered. We need to take positive actions so that the inner conscious knows what we really want. If we want to truly convince our inner conscious we are serious about wanting something, we have to make an effort to obtain it.

Of all the many untruths that we now take for granted as core beliefs, the most harmful is that others can solve our problems for us. We blame our issues on our government, our boss, our spouse, our parents, our adversaries, our relatives or whoever, but we ignore the fact that all our troubles are self-made. We create a dependency on others in hopes they will solve our problems. But because only we create our troubles, only we can solve them. Personal responsibility is the only solution to our problems.

We have many thoughts and we need to decide which ones we want to incorporate into our beliefs. If we could convince ourselves we are ten years younger than we really are and acted upon it by doing physical activities that align with our new beliefs, like acting younger, our body would respond with the strength and agility of a younger person.

It helps to take some alone time and look at what we do not like about ourselves and our life. Then examine our beliefs about those issues. Brutal honesty is required.

Self-affirmation means accepting our own unique individuality and knowing only we have the ability to create our own reality. If we want to change our life, we need to affirm who we are and commit to changing our self-limiting beliefs. Just desiring something is not enough, we need to expect it.

Obstacles to Good Health

There are several things which determine how successful we will be in healing ourselves. First and foremost, we need to believe we can be cured. If way down inside we are convinced we will always be sick, then we will always be sick. We need to believe we can be cured and want to be cured. Some people just don't want to be cured. We may feel we deserve to be sick because of the things we have done. Or we may enjoy the attention we get or the excuse not to do things we would rather not do. If we do not have the desire to be cured, we won't be no matter what we do.

It also depends on how strong the purpose for the disease is. If our body is trying to make us change our lifestyle, then we will need to find that cause and change it before we can get well. It also depends on how capable we are of mobilizing our defenses. If our willingness to be cured is not strong it will be more difficult to heal ourselves.

Power of Positive Thought

Ever since 1952 when Norman Vincent Peale published his book *The Power of Positive Thinking* people have been taking this concept more seriously. When we realize that we are what we think, this concept becomes critical to our happiness and success.

We see it in people who have reached the pinnacle of their careers. The differences between outstanding athletes near the top of their field and true superstars are often the differences in their belief in their abilities. Champions are convinced they will succeed. When an injury or something else derails their career, after the incident is over their biggest hurdle is convincing themselves they can do it again. Tiger Woods is a good example. In his early career Tiger thought he was invincible, and he was. When he succumbed to the scandal, which was not directly related to golf, he lost his feeling of invincibility. He battled more than just injury and age, he had to regain his self-confidence.

Believing in ourselves and our abilities is critical to improving our life. When we doubt ourselves, it means that we believe we will fail, and when that happens our inner conscious sets up situations that will give us that experience. This fear is especially common with children, teenagers and young adults. It is important that parents find ways to allow a young person to excel at something. Everyone has a gift, they just need to find it. Academics, sports, music, and the arts are some of the common areas for young people to gain self-confidence. But there are many other characteristics that need positive reinforcement like being a good friend, a good listener, a good helper, having a positive attitude, being compassionate, never giving up, etc. It is important that we see ourselves as worthy or our fears can divert us into destructive causes.

It does not matter what we choose to do as long as it helps us believe in ourselves. Self-confidence helps us to succeed in all areas of our life. We wear many hats and it is important that we establish a belief system that allows us to create a successful and happy life. We cannot change our beliefs if we do not have a positive attitude about ourselves and what we are trying to accomplish.

Many people would like to change the world for the better but are not sure what to do. The best way to help the world is to create a strong positive energy system within ourselves and focus that positive energy on the world's troubled areas. If all the people in the world living comfortable lives would focus their positive energy on the world's distressed areas, that would do far more to resolve the issues than sending money or troops.

Visualize Life as You Want It

We all contain a 'self-image' or 'blueprint,' which was originally used to create our physical form. The blueprint describes how we will change throughout our life, which allows us to maintain our body when atoms, molecules and cells are replaced with other particles. Our blueprint continues to be used throughout our life. The blueprint defines everything necessary to keep us alive and appearing the way we were intended.

Illness and injury occur when unwanted energy enters our body. There are many reasons why this happens but to get well our energy needs to be rebalanced. The 'illness energy' is a system just like breathing, digestion and walking. Although the blueprint does not include the sickness, the ego sometimes recognizes the sickness as part of itself and tries to retain it because it fears losing anything that might diminish itself. The key to getting rid of the sickness is to convince the ego that the ailment is not a necessary part of the body. The ego has added the ailment to its core assumptions, and that thought needs to be severed.

Our inner conscious can greatly assist with our recovery if we tell it what we want it to do. We need to think of ourselves the way we would like to be. Closing our eyes and picturing our self without the affliction tells the inner conscious how we want to be. We should not picture ourselves becoming healthy, as that just reinforces the problem. We should picture ourselves as being healthy, walking, running, happy, and loving. By picturing ourselves the way we want to be, not the way we are, the inner conscious can work with the subconscious to make the required changes. We might visualize this for about five minutes at a time and repeat it half a dozen times a day, especially when we are just getting started. We need to refocus our mind and rid ourselves of negative thoughts. Visualization can heal us faster and more permanently than any medicine can. All we are is energy, and when it gets out of balance, it needs to be corrected.

I find the test for new drugs very enlightening. When a drug is tested, they have a control group, which gets a placebo. Inevitably large portions of people taking the placebo respond positively as well. These people believe they are taking a drug that will help them. In both cases, the body is really doing the healing. The soul realizes the ego wants to be cured and accommodates it. I am not suggesting that we should not see a doctor. We have great faith in our medical system, and if we do not wholly believe our inner conscious and subconscious can cure us, it is better to rely on our belief in a doctor. Of course when it comes to trauma the medical system is absolutely required. Broken bones, serious cuts and severed parts need immediate medical attention. But for conditions that the medical system considers terminal, if we work diligently to convince our mind that we want to be healed, it is possible that we will be able to train our mind to heal our body.

The key is to get the ego to recognize the problem so it can get the inner conscious to deal with it. Sometimes our illness is caused by long-held beliefs, even from previous lives. If we can bring the problem into our conscious mind, recognize it for what it is, and deal with it, then the inner conscious can resolve the problem. There are many stories about people who have cured deadly diseases like cancer after the medical community had given up on them.

Real Life Applications

Although this may sound theoretical, there are real life applications that are proving extremely successful in helping people change their beliefs. On January 8, 2016, I had the pleasure of interviewing Dr. John McGrail on my radio show. He is the author of *The Synthesis Effect: Your Direct Path to Personal Power and Transformation*. Dr. McGrail not only supports the concept of changing your life through changing your beliefs, but he has spent years doing it with amazing success. He works with people around the world and can be contacted through his websites: hypnotherapylosangeles.com or drjohnmcgrail.com.

Positive Aspects of Suffering

The inner conscious is the cause of all diseases. No medication can heal us until we resolve the true cause of the disease. There is a reason for every disease, even the deadly ones. Everything has a purpose. Our inner conscious creates diseases when we need them as part of our evolution.

Although no one is being punished for their beliefs, it certainly can seem like it. Ultimately, the purpose of suffering is to teach us not to suffer. It is only by feeling what suffering is like, that we can understand the value of happiness and contentment. No one is meant to suffer longer than it takes to learn the lesson. But we have free will so we determine how long and how deeply we suffer. We need to accept life as it comes and not resist it. Deal with life's issues then move on and don't focus on the negative.

Some illnesses may be deflecting a catastrophic event. This is true on a personal basis and equally true for major world events. When energy is accrued it eventually needs to be released. A body can only handle so much imbalance. A minor illness now may prevent a major problem in the future.

It is important that we experience some suffering because true understanding only occurs when we have personal experiences. We can witness an event or read about experiences of others and even get a glimpse of the excitement or sorrow they may have felt. But without experiencing the associated pain of the tragedy or the joy of the victory, it is impossible to learn the same lesson as those who actually went through it.

Defects

Birth defects are an interesting phenomena. No one is born with a defect that they did not choose in their prelife plan. In fact, we create our own bodies so we actually create the defect. There are many reasons why someone might want to live with a defect. Advanced spirits often want to experience life from a different perspective and the defect allows them to do this. Or maybe someone has done something in a past life that they are unhappy about so they create a defect that will prevent them from repeating that mistake. Whatever the cause, no one is being punished and we should be sympathetic and supportive to the individual as they are learning lessons that will benefit us all.

Mental Illness

Mental illness is an example of how reality is created by the perceiver. Mental illness occurs when someone's reality is so different than the norm that they have trouble functioning in society. They simply live in a different reality than we do. But reality is in the eye of the beholder. A person with what we call mental illness is not sick, their reality is just different than the norm.

Our mental abilities are a balance between reasoning and imagination. In our society reason is much more important than imagination. We encourage the importance of reason early in a child's life by doing things like disapproving of our children's imaginary friends, and we talk about 'dreamers' as people who struggle to survive in 'the real world.' Instead of stressing the importance of imagination we focus on reasoning and dealing with physical events.

Autism is an example of someone who is born with an unusual amount of imagination. The Seth entity says that these people are usually more advanced individuals choosing an alternate way to experience the world. It is hard for these people to function in our world of reason or even interface with us, but they are not sick, just different.

People born with 'mental disorders' chose that condition to experience life differently. Also, it is likely that the parents had agreed to this experience in their prelife plan. One state is not better than another but one state can function more easily in our culture, and the less capable need our assistance to have the experiences they have chosen.

Our dreams are far more imaginative than rational, but we accept them as normal. It is only in our waking or 'conscious' state where imagination needs to be so subordinate to reason. But the Tao wants to experience life in every possible way. It wants to experience all the different balances between imagination and reason. Within every entity there is a divine element that chooses to be the way it is. There is no right or wrong way to experience the world.

Our society relates to the universe through the reason of science and technology, and we rarely value imagination unless it has a practical end. Before the Industrial Revolution imagination played a greater part than reason for most of the population. It was the imagination of musicians and artists that entertained the rich and famous, and local art and oral stories were a big part of everyday life for the common people. Our focus on material objects has shifted the balance from imagination to reason. It is interesting that the more we find out about the spiritual world, the more we realize that mankind's focus on reasoning has led us further astray from the truth. Like science, mankind's reasoning capabilities are also in their infancy.

The Seth entity says that dementia is a slightly different case. During dementia key elements of one's consciousness have left the physical field and are already transferred to the next existence in the astral plane. This often occurs when there is a fear of death. By doing this they are more prepared when they get there and it makes the transition easier.

Obviously, the people that we label as 'mentally ill' may need our assistance to function in our society. But their experiences are just as valid and real as ours. Our society would benefit tremendously if we could learn to get into their world with them. If we could learn to use our inner sense and travel back and forth between these realities, we would learn a great deal about the strange nature of consciousness; and just think how much better the life of the 'mentally ill' would be if they could learn to travel between realities.

Mass Events

Because our consciousness is part of a huge web, our beliefs do not only just impact our individual lives, they join together with the beliefs of others and jointly influence the entire planet. If we watch or read the news it is irrelevant to the world. But what we think about world events is critical, because our thoughts contribute to making the events happen. For example, wars and pandemics are not caused by a single individual or event. They are caused by a group of people focused on a single mass event, which they jointly make happen. It may be a protest for a perceived injustice or an awakening of some kind.

Natural events like hurricanes, tornados and earthquakes are caused by group beliefs. The inner world provides constant communication between all living entities, including animals and plants. Every species involved with a mass event participates with its creation. All those who are impacted by the event agreed to participate at the inner conscious level.

Psychological energy builds up and needs to be rebalanced. In fact, a major climatic event may prevent a war by releasing pent-up psychological pressure. It is hard to accept this if we think we are a victim of such an event, but we see such a small glimpse of the big picture it is impossible to understand the reasons behind events of such a large scale.

Thoughts even impact our local weather. Our weather has an effect on our moods and surprisingly our moods have an effect on our weather. Our beliefs impact everything.

Mass events occur at all levels of society. Religious popularity, political events, and technological innovations are all mass events. They can occur at the local, state, country or worldwide level. Even when a business flourishes, it is a localized mass event. The employees, customers, and suppliers all participate in the event.

Our Power Is in the Present

It is well known that history is not necessarily what actually happened, but how it was recorded by biased historians. Our past is no different. Our memory is based on events as seen from our biased perspective. If we went back to check the facts of our past, we would learn that the circumstances of our life were not how we remember them. However, the only thing that is important about our past is how it has affected our present by influencing our views and creating the lives we are living.

The significance of our past is not what happened, but how we remember it and how it affected us. It is our memory of the past that influences us today. In circumstances where we were negatively impacted by past memories, if we could have seen our life in a more positive way, then our deterioration related to it would not have occurred.

But if we can change our attitude about ourselves and see our past as a series of accomplishments as opposed to failures, the damage that we did to ourselves can be reversed. Because of the laws of our reality, a loved one that we may have lost cannot be brought back into our life. However, if we are able to view this incident as a positive learning experience, and change our negative attitude about life to a positive one, we can change the cumulative negative impact that it had on our life.

Although we may think that the impact of our past cannot be changed, our past experiences are controlled from the present. It is our present attitude about the past that is causing our problems, not the actual past events. Only the lingering effects that our conscious mind keeps alive are our problems. Everyone does things they wish they hadn't, but we learn the most from our mistakes. The Tao has no interest in how we learn things. It only cares about what we learn. We should feel the same.

Past, present, and future are all controlled from the present. If you insist on searching your past, focus on the positive. Remind yourself about all the good decisions and wonderful deeds you have done. Leave your mistakes in the past where they belong. We need to remember that it is our attitude about the event that is causing our problem, not the event itself.

Conclusion

*The two most important days in your life are the day you were born
and the day you find out why.*
Mark Twain

The source of everything that exists is an infinite supply of
conscious energy known as the Tao. It exists in a psychological
domain, which is the ultimate reality. Our universe is a unique
reality within this domain. The Tao consists of everything that
has ever existed or ever will exist. The ultimate purpose of the
Tao is to evolve to the highest level possible, as fast as possible,
and as efficiently as possible.

To this end, within the Tao there are an infinite number
of conscious identities clustered together into countless
configurations. The Tao is a continuously changing web of
consciousness that constantly forms and reforms itself into
gestalts. Amongst other things, these identities take the form of
what we perceive to be physical objects from atoms to galaxies.
The gestalts also take the form of beings like sparks, spirits,
greater spirits, and of course, you and me.

Spirits evolve by learning about themselves. They do this by
creating domains with different dimensions and characteristics,
which are known as realities. The world we live in is a portion of one
of those unique realities. When multiple realities are combined they
form what we consider to be a universe. Our universe is a Research
and Development (R&D) center and it consists of seven fields of
creation, which are divided into a multitude of realities. Because it
is R&D oriented, all beings within our universe are experimenting
with new and better ways to evolve. These experiments are not
limited to our earth, or even our galaxy. Multiple civilizations exist
that are experimenting with unique evolutionary processes, and
mankind is one of those experiments.

The Tao allows every being to have the free will to evolve as it chooses. As such, the Tao created the universe such that the beings incarnating into the various realities would also be co-creators of those realities. This means that each individual is responsible for its own circumstances because it controls its own destiny.

Mankind is the big experiment on this planet and many higher-level spiritual beings are working hard to help us succeed. With this in mind, we can address our original questions that we posed earlier.

Who Are We?

The Tao is the only entity in existence and we are part of it. It consists of an enormous network of conscious energy clusters, tied together by highly complex communication channels. The Tao's gestalt nature allows it to be divided into groups of varying degrees of complexity. We are one of those groups and a unique part of this eternal, divine entity.

The Tao has created a system that allows every being to experience continuous evolution at their own pace. We are relatively young consciousnesses learning to take responsibility for our actions.

The psyche, which is a combination of the ego, subconscious, and inner conscious, is the individual identity that we can identify as 'I.' Although we appear to be our body, it is not part of our eternal existence, and it is only the ego that believes it is one with the body.

Mankind is only one form that spirits assume on earth. Every object in nature is part of the Tao from the smallest cells to the cosmos itself. Over a period that spans tens of thousands of years, our soul continually returns to the physical field in a process known as reincarnation. It accomplishes this by manifesting small portions of its energy into various forms. Each manifestation is a single personality living a single life, e.g., you and me.

Our time on earth is precious so a great deal of planning is involved, both before we incarnate and while we are living our life. Although we have free will, nothing is left to chance. We create a prelife plan that guides us through life. If we do not follow the plan it is because we choose not to. It is not because someone else interfered or fate got in the way.

I refer to each one of us as a personality, which is a subset of our soul. To form a personality the soul selects multiple groups of its own energy that it permanently gives to the personality. It chooses the energy that will most likely help the personality accomplish its prelife plan.

Once established, the personality becomes an independent identity in its own right, and is not under the soul's control. Initially it agrees to accept the challenges it will face during its physical life, and to that end it can develop its energies in any way that it chooses. If the soul decides the personality needs additional energy during its life, the soul has the option to supply it.

The soul creates many personalities in each cycle. The soul acts as a mini Tao in that it continually breaks itself into different combinations of energy and then allows this new identity to grow and evolve in any way it desires.

After the personality's life is over it remains independent and is free to evolve as it chooses. The personality always has a special connection to its soul through a psychic bond and they both support each other forever despite each pursuing their own independent evolutionary path. The soul gains wisdom from each personality it creates and in so doing becomes greater than it was.

Our soul is a subset of our spirit, which has had an untold number of incarnations into a myriad of different species over literally millions of years, and we are the beneficiary of those valuable lessons. The wisdom gleaned from those experiences is the source of our current creation. The wiser the spirit, the wiser the personalities it creates.

Our Nature

Each of us has a group and an individual nature. But because this life is focused on our individual nature, it is easier for us to identify with those characteristics.

Each soul has its own unique combination of characteristics. Even though each personality has a unique set of aptitudes, attitudes, viewpoints, and other biases, there is a recognizable thread through all a soul's creations. This endows the soul's various personalities with similarities or what we might call family resemblances, which we could recognize if we were familiar with our past reincarnations. There are endless ways the soul's energy can be used to create a personality, and each personality's experiences will be different from any other.

We think that our beliefs and root assumptions are not only sacrosanct but are the essence of who we are. However, they are simply the perspective of the controlling energy within our ego, and they certainly are not the perspective of our soul. They are more like 'accessories' that we wear in each lifetime, only to be exchanged and modified in later lives.

We are building the foundation that will support the grander versions of ourselves. However, no matter how much we change, there will always be part of us that will remember every aspect of the life we are currently living.

Our Greater Self

Our personality is part of our soul, and our soul is part of our spirit. But our spirit is also part of a greater spirit, and our greater spirit is part of an even greater spirit, and so forth up to the Tao Itself. We are all One Being, functioning both separately and as a group. It is only the illusion that makes us think of ourselves as individuals.

Our next greater spirit is like an older sibling in a close-knit family. It develops on its own, chooses different realities to experience, but always stays in contact with us, and offers advice and support. In exchange, we provide a special expertise for our greater spirit, and we both understand what that is. Whenever either one desires assistance, it is always provided.

Our greater spirits help guide us in our development. They each have their own goals and they encourage us to support their efforts as well as our own. The roots of our prelife plans could be traced back to our greater spirit's plans. Our spirit is not pursuing independent and unrelated goals. We are all part of a highly organized system. We could relate it to designing an airplane. We might be designing a small part in the landing gear, but as insignificant as our part may sound, it is a critical part for the plane's operation and needs to be coordinated into the overall design. Our soul is supporting goals that our greater spirits are pursuing.

We may seem like a tiny, insignificant being in the immense scope of the Tao, but we provide an invaluable perspective that no other entity has and our contribution will increase as we evolve. Our uniqueness is more important than just being different. We provide our greater spirit with valuable wisdom, and our greater spirit does the same for its greater spirit and so forth up to the Tao itself. Therefore, all consciousness is interdependent, one upon the other. Every consciousness provides value to the whole.

Death
When trying to understand who we are, it is important to remember who we are not. We are eternal beings, not mortals. Death is no more than a transition from one energy field to another. The only thing that dies is the physical body and even then, the body's energy simply realigns with other creations. The ego that we perceive as 'I' is released by the body at death and transitions back to the astral field. Nothing is lost and we gain total recall of every event, thought, and emotion that we had during our lifetime, including our dreams. We reconnect with all our friends and loved ones who have passed, and there

are even ways that we can stay connected with those we leave behind in the physical field. The dying process can be painful, but there is no pain at the moment of death and the pain of life subsides immediately. It is much easier and less painful to leave the physical field than to be born into it.

Once we understand the nature of life, we realize that death is a necessary step in our evolution. Death allows for the regeneration of the species. Life wears us down so death gives us a much needed rest and restoration. It allows us to evaluate our achievements and shortcomings, and refocus our goals.

I like the comparison of a life to a business trip. On a business trip we plan the objectives that we want to accomplish before we start the trip, then we do the best we can to accomplish them. Surprises always occur during the trip that we need to deal with, so we readjust our goals and expectations in accordance with what we encounter. Finally we return home and evaluate what went right and what went wrong, and prepare for our next excursion. Life is no different, and death is the inevitable trip home.

Where Are We?

After millions of years of slowly evolving, we have finally reached a level where we are ready to accept responsibility for our actions. We are in a training session where we are learning to responsibly transform the emotional energy of our thoughts into actions. To do this we have chosen a reality where the consequences of our decisions directly affect our physical well-being. We are learning the consequences of our thoughts.

The universe is comprised of many specialized psychological domains that are manifested by the Tao. Our universe is the Tao's research and development sector, or at least one of them. The Tao created our universe and divided it into seven primary fields of creation. These fields are spatially collocated and separated by unique parameters, like frequency bands and types of matter. Except for the akashic field, each of these primary fields is subdivided into a multitude of realities, with ours being only one of probably millions.

We think of the earth as a solid structure positioned in a vast expanse of 'nothingness' that we call space. But space is no more a 'nothingness' than the roads we drive on. Space, matter and time work together with our outer senses to present us with an illusion of physical reality. Our physical reality is only one of many unique manifestations of the Tao's psychological reality. We are living in a psychological reality that appears physical to our senses.

When we 'die' or more accurately cross over, our psyche relocates to the astral field by merely refocusing away from the physical and onto the astral field. This happens because we lose our outer senses and our inner sense takes over. Because the astral field is collocated with the physical field, we don't actually go very far. We just change states. Where we reside in the afterlife is in a realm that is very close to our frequency band. This means that our family and friends who have crossed over are often still with us and that is why it is so easy for mediums to contact them. Although they are no longer focused on the physical field and have other primary interests, they have not really gone away.

The spirits, souls, personalities and sparks within each reality join together to co-create the environment that they choose to experience. There are universal laws that each reality must contend with. However, the realities appear different because the universal laws manifest differently under different circumstances. For example, in our reality the speed of light is limited to 186,000 miles per second and EEs appear as matter. Using our thoughts, we select a portion of the reality, incarnate into it, and then alter the environment to create our own personal reality to experience. In our slow responding reality it is difficult to see how our thoughts are manifested, but we actually co-create the world we live in. Our 'self-made' reality includes things like our home, family, friends, job, etc., which all function in accordance with the universal laws as they apply in our reality.

You create your life. If you are not happy with your life, you and only you can change it. No one else is responsible for the conditions that you are living in nor can anyone else change them. Only you create and control your life.

Why Are We Here?

We are here because we chose to be here. No one forced us to live this life. Our spirit chose to come here because it believed the hardships and joys were worth the rapid evolutionary progress we would attain. There are certain lessons that we need to learn before we can experience the more advanced realities. This reality provides a fast and efficient evolution for those willing to accept the hardships. It is an extremely difficult place to live because there is so much suffering connected to it. But suffering has a purpose, and in the end we are being taught to make wiser decisions so we don't need to suffer.

The human condition is clearly no accident. Nothing as complicated as this universe could be an accident, and nothing as difficult as our life would be undertaken without a need and a plan. As we become more evolved, an ever-widening universe of excitement and fascination opens up to us. The more we evolve, the more interesting and enjoyable existence becomes. As such, consciousness desires to evolve as efficiently and quickly as possible.

Evolution does not occur by simply waiting for an experience to happen. Although life seems pretty haphazard, it is not. Our soul creates our prelife plan, which delineates the specific experiences it wants us to have. It then selects the type of energy that will assist us in experiencing the events in the way the soul has chosen. Anyone can participate in an event but having that event impact them in a particular way requires an immense amount of planning.

Our prelife plan included selecting our abilities, goals, experiences, parents, and friends, which we did long before we were born. We are now deciding how we can best utilize those choices. No one did this to us nor did fate play a role. We chose this life and created all the circumstances that surround us.

In *The Endless Journey* I said that the purpose of life from an individual's perspective was part of the process of perfecting our soul. We accomplish this through the concept of Value Fulfillment, which is the prime consideration for every spirit in the Tao before it selects a new experience. If we will not benefit from an experience, then we will not undertake it.

We learn through our emotions. Vicarious knowledge is always available to us but real understanding and wisdom is only gained through the emotions of first-hand experiences.

Each person is trying to attain the maximum benefit that this life can offer. Everyone has specific goals they want to accomplish in each lifetime, which are unique to them. By looking back over our life we can see periods where our life took a sudden turn. The events just before that change were probably the culmination of a set of preplanned experiences. The change often starts with a rest period where things seem to go smoothly as we prepare for a new set of experiences.

Although each of us has very specific and unique goals, there are broader lessons that mankind as a whole is learning, which are embedded in all of our life plans. The following lessons are intertwined throughout our lives as they need to be learned before moving on.

Lesson #1: The Sacred Individual
When we are not in the physical universe, we function as part of a group or web of consciousness. We see ourselves as team members more than as individuals. But we have two aspects in

our nature, group and individual, and we need to understand and appreciate both aspects.

In this life we see ourselves as separate from each other, and apart from the rest of nature. Every object appears to be an independent identity unrelated to each other. We don't see the ties that exist in the inner universe that connect us together. Separation helps us understand that although we are closely connected with others, we have an individual existence that is our own.

As we leave the physical and astral fields for the last time and progress through the higher fields, our individuality will become less and less important. By the time we return to our permanent home within the Tao we will again be fully integrated.

However, no consciousness ever disappears or morphs into another consciousness. Once activated, an identity always remembers where it came from, the experiences it had, and the gestalts it took part in. Nothing is ever lost. Although we are part of a web of consciousness, the individual nature of consciousness is sacred.

Lesson #2: Personal Responsibility
Seeing ourselves as independent beings has another purpose. It teaches us that we are responsible for our actions. Spirits have immense power at their disposal but this power needs to be used responsibly. In this life the power available to us is limited because we have not learned the implications of its misuse.

Our soul lets us experience anything we want. What we concentrate on and obsess over is what we will experience. If our thoughts are constructive then life will be positive and rewarding. But when our thoughts are negative, we create stumbling blocks that we need to overcome. Our inner conscious creates these obstacles when this is the guiding message our ego sends it.

Our thoughts create our world and manifest our experiences. Because of the time delay created by our space-time reality, we rarely notice the connection between the two. But the implication of this is clear. No one is a victim of fate or of the actions of others. We are only a victim of our own poor judgement. The world offers us many opportunities to make choices, and it is our choices that cause our problems, not the behavior of others.

If we create our life and our environment, then we, and only we, have power over our lives. No one else is responsible for our problems. Others can present us with challenges, but only we control how we react to those situations. When we understand how the world functions, we realize that what seems like an unfair and cruel world is actually a completely fair world.

Lesson #3: Managing Energy
Part of taking personal responsibility for our actions is learning how to deal with energy. The energy of the universe is available to us and we have the power to do anything we want with it. But before we are given complete access to it, we need to understand the consequences of our actions. The simple solution is for us to experience the effect of both our good use and misuse of this power. Learning to be responsible custodians of this immense power is an important element of what life on earth is all about.

Our world may look like it is out of control and isolated from the rest of the universe, but it is not. Our planet is participating in many experiments that are occurring across the galaxies and in multiple realities. In conjunction with many other planets, our civilization is examining how much freedom is appropriate when learning how to manage energy. Our planet has been given a great deal of freedom compared to some civilizations on other planets with similar levels of maturity. The Seth entity says that other civilizations at our level of development have restrictions on their use of energy to include being programmed to become totally passive if they reach a certain level of aggression. We have no such restrictions, and as a result these other civilizations are learning more slowly than we are, but our risks are higher.

The nature of energy is that it cannot get too far out of balance before it corrects. When the world's energy becomes unbalanced, which is caused by our society's collective poor decisions, it builds to a level where it needs to be released. This can take the form of wars, epidemics and pandemics. Because mankind is tethered to the rest of nature, rebalancing the energy can also include earthquakes, hurricanes, and other natural disasters.

Humanity is slowly learning many lessons, and the capabilities we are allowed to have correspond to our maturity level. For example, atomic weapons were not given to us until we were judged to be responsible for their use. Other technologies like efficient space travel are also being kept from us until our society is more mature.

We can use the energy that we have been given as we please, to include destroying ourselves and our planet. But if that happens, mankind will just continue evolving on another planet, and both we and the Tao will have learned from it. No matter what the consequences, all the affected spirits would survive unharmed and wiser for it. We are an important part of the universe and there are many wise beings like the Michael and Seth entities assisting us. The hope is that our experiment is successful, and from it we will learn better ways for future spirits to evolve.

Lesson #4: One with Nature

An important part of this life is learning how to live with other species. We are part of this planet, and so are all the flora and fauna. Physical life is a gift to be shared by everyone. Before we are granted the ability to interface with less developed planetary civilizations, we need to develop a respect for all living things. As a food source, animals were created to eat other animals, and we are part of that food chain. Nothing really dies when the body dies, there is only a transfer of energy. But we need to do it humanely and efficiently. Mankind's habit of wastefully killing both plants and animals is a travesty that needs to be corrected.

We are learning that the quality of our life is more important than just surviving. We need to take care of the environment and all living things. Plastic in the oceans and pollution in the air and ground are unacceptable. Our environment needs to be pristine, for our sake and for the sake of the other species we share the world with. We need to make this planet a paradise for all of nature.

Lesson #5: Love
Many of the 'new age' practitioners speak of love as the critical emotion humanity needs to focus on. I have not stressed the value of love in this book because so many others have. I wanted to concentrate on the overall processes that influence our existence. However, if we could base our thoughts and expectations on love for all of nature, to include mankind, our lives would improve exponentially. The higher frequency energy of love will eventually overcome the lower frequency energy of fear. It is impossible to go wrong if the decisions we make are based on love and compassion for others. Justifying the mistreatment of others in the name of our 'righteous' causes is never an act of love.

Hate is by far the worst emotion we can have. When we hate others, it is because we also have hate for ourselves. We see in others things that we dislike about ourselves. When we learn to overcome our hate, then our reincarnation cycle will end and we will move on to other things.

There are many conversations in the metaphysical communities in regards to the importance of raising our frequency, but what that means and how to do it is seldom articulated. In a discussion with the Michael entity in regards to raising the frequency of the earth, he said, and I paraphrase: "Frequency refers to vibration. The phrase 'raising our frequency' reflects a greater refinement of consciousness. The frequency of the planet is rising but the people who are stuck in the old consciousness feel the pull of the higher consciousness and are screaming bloody murder. So there is a sort of separation going on where the obstinate people are becoming more entrenched. The higher frequency people are moving to higher levels and there is a large middle ground of people who have not made up their minds yet. The more you can raise your vibration through living with greater love each day the more you are inviting the undecided people to join you. It is a little bit like your political landscape where you say it is the undecideds who determine the election."

Lesson #6: State of Grace
We are meant to live in a state of grace, which means having a life of comfort, health, and gratifying experiences. But that doesn't mean we will not have difficult challenges to deal with. We should take them in stride, accept the results and move on. We should not rue the past or fear the future, but rather accept and enjoy life as it comes. When we live in grace we evolve by following the experiences outlined in our prelife plan.

As a global civilization, many communities are struggling. But the suboptimal living conditions are teaching us many lessons, and we need to learn those lessons before the conditions will go away! For example, one of mankind's biggest challenges is to learn to stop killing each other. When that occurs our civilization will evolve in leaps and bounds.

How We Can Improve Our Life
Expectations
Thoughts are not only the greatest force in existence, they are the only force. Our expectations determine our experiences because our inner conscious will manifest those expectations. If we live a life feeling sad and lonely then our inner conscious

will think that is what we want to experience, and it will make us sadder and lonelier. If our life is full of happiness, our inner conscious will increase those emotions. Our emotions create our expectations and our expectations create our life.

Our space-time reality's inherent slowness makes it difficult for us to see the connection between our difficulties and our beliefs. If we think we are unable to do something, like make money or be healthy, then circumstances will be created to make that come true. We are inadvertently self-limiting ourselves. If we don't like our life then we need to change our expectations about life.

We and only we are responsible for ourselves. We should not expect others to change our life for us because they cannot. It is not up to the government, our boss, our spouse, or our doctor to change our life. We need to take personal responsibility for our situation, and stop blaming others for our poor decisions.

If we believe we are a victim, then our inner conscious will give us the opportunity to experience being one. We get caught up in the easy dialogue that we are a victim, which provides an excuse that allows us to ignore our contribution to the problem. We are who we are and where we are because of the decisions that we have made. Our root assumptions and core beliefs are the basis of our expectations. If we don't like something about our life, then we need to break that cycle, or life will just become more difficult. Victims are self-created.

However, we can change our life. We are not dependent on anyone else, even God, to improve our life. We have the power to do it, we just need the understanding and the will. Changing a belief requires soul searching and honesty, which most people are not used to or not willing to do. Root assumptions and core beliefs are so ingrained in our thinking that we base all our logical reasoning on them. But, if our assumptions are wrong, our conclusions will be wrong.

Another difficulty is that as we get older and have success in life, we find that we base our self-image on the beliefs that we espoused. Changing them seems to be admitting that we have been wrong, which requires self-confidence and humility. However, if we go through life without evolving our beliefs, then we have gained nothing.

Modern societies spend billions of dollars attempting to change the circumstances of people's lives, whether their health, poverty, antisocial behavior or whatever society wants changed. But those changes rarely succeed because we don't address the real cause. We don't teach people that their beliefs are causing their problems. Instead of encouraging them to blame their problems on others, we need to help them gain the self-confidence to take control of their lives, and solve their own problems. There is no shame in needing support as occasionally we all need help. But any assistance that does not leave the individual with a renewed and expanded sense of self-confidence will ultimately fail.

Ethics
Understanding how the universe works is not a requirement to live a good life. Knowing the key principles can make our life easier and reduce our suffering, but we will all transition to the astral field when our life is over no matter what we believe. However, what is important is how we treat both each other and our nonhuman co-inhabitants on this planet.

Our culture fails to provide us with an ethical rationale for why we are here and how to live our life. Science is a major culprit because it has such a great influence on society. Science's view that the creation of the universe was an accident and there is no higher power behind it presents mankind with a materialistic philosophy in which life itself has no meaning, and therefore, no lasting value. With its focus on the physical world and pretense of being the ultimate source of knowledge, science leaves us with a belief in a Godless universe that has no purpose. There is nothing wrong with using the tools of science, but they need to be applied with the concept of Value Fulfillment. We need to act in such a way that is not only good for us, but also for the rest of mankind and indeed all creatures. Consuming plants and animals for our sustenance is consistent with nature's ways. But the inhumane treatment of living creatures for the sake of sport, convenience, or excess profit, is unacceptable.

Science's lack of understanding of the nonphysical universe leaves mankind without a purpose or guidelines on how to live our life, or even a reason to live it. Unfortunately, philosophy, the once preeminent source of morality in the ancient world, has followed science down a path of logic where it is trying to find reason in a senseless world of material objects.

Over the millennia Krishna, Buddha, Christ and others have offered mankind insight into the spiritual world, but their teachings have been misunderstood and misrepresented to a level where now they are hardly recognizable. Despite this, religions have provided ethical guidelines, which were certainly better than nothing. But society has grown too sophisticated for these rules. We need to move forward and begin by teaching our children the intricacies of ethical behavior.

Metaphysics is the only body of knowledge that provides a coherent explanation for mankind's purpose, and provides a basis for an ethical standard.

Spiritual Ignorance

The Seth entity says that the single biggest problem with our society is spiritual ignorance. If we knew why we were here and how the world works, we would have very different opinions about right and wrong.

The human population has reached a point where there is an acute need to be more responsible for our actions. Pollution and neglect are damaging the world's resources at a level never seen before. If this continues, the earth will not be able to support the vastness of life that it now does. The Seth entity says that mankind is at a turning point and that is why we are being given so much spiritual guidance.

We also need to stop treating each other so poorly. We fret over racism, but it would be irrational for a person to be prejudiced against a race if they knew they had experienced it in the past, and will again in the future. Race is a choice and we cycle through all of them, and the same holds true for nationalities. Gender prejudice is foolish when we realize that we spend half of our many lives as the other sex, and indeed our true self is neither one. Things like sexual preference, social status, education, and occupation are choices we make before birth in order to have certain types of experiences. Judging others against those standards only diminishes us.

The mores passed down to us through our religious heritage have played an important part in mankind's evolution, but they need to be reevaluated in light of metaphysical principles. We need to separate the dogma from the reality. Imposing our beliefs on others is not only counterproductive, but it instills an unjustified pecking order of moral superiority.

The Tao does not care about our religious beliefs, only how we treat each other. Those who interfere with another person's life in the name of a perceived injustice are no better than those they object to. The ends never justify the means no matter how 'holy' we think we and our causes are.

As more people accept responsibility for their own actions, laws will be fewer and fairer. Drugs, alcoholic addictions, crime, terrorism and fear will be significantly reduced. We all came here with a purpose and no one came here with the intention of mistreating others.

I mentioned earlier that the ancient Egyptians stressed the importance of knowing ourselves. Wisdom is all about knowing who we are. Nature and the spiritual universe are a reflection of ourselves. Until we know ourselves we will be living in ignorance; and it is ignorance that causes our problems.

New Paradigms
In order to improve our life, we need to change our beliefs about life. We are accustomed to getting our ideas about life from either science or religion, but both are stuck in their own convictions.

Scientists need to realize that there is a mind behind the material world and stop the charade that this universe is just a fortuitous combination of particles. Science's understanding of the physical world would be greatly enhanced if it focused some of its attention on the inner source that created and sustains it.

Religions would make great strides forward if their proponents would return to their founders' principles. Religious leaders need to realize that the search for truth is a journey in which no one has the final answers and new information is always becoming available.

Both science and religion need to combine their efforts and a good place to start would be to consider the metaphysical principles. Down through the ages we have been told that many of the great figures responsible for scientific, religious, and philosophical discoveries received their insights from spiritual sources. We need to heed their wisdom.

Enjoyment
Wisdom is the goal and endless growth, creativity, and amusement is the reward. But nothing worthwhile comes easily. Mankind is learning from very wise souls, and we are making good progress despite the bad actors highlighted in the media. However, eternity is a long time and we are meant to enjoy the journey. We learn the most from our mistakes, but then we need to let them go.

Living a physical life is about experiencing a wide variety of events. We make mistakes, say things we regret, have aches and pains, fear change, and struggle with day-to-day activities. All this is okay as we learn from these challenges. The self we know is a small part of our true self, and our purpose is to gain wisdom so that we can move on to greater things.

This book is an attempt to provide you with a more rational explanation of the human condition than either science or religion offers. My hope is to help you better understand your life. At the end of every session with the Michael entity, he makes it clear that we are not to take anything he tells us as the final word. Although the Michael entity, the Seth entity and the other spiritual sources that communicate with us know a great deal more than we do, the Tao's Truth is so complex that even these entities can only understand a portion of it, and even then in a simplified form. It is our responsibility to discern truth for ourselves, to the best of our ability. No one else can do that for us. The Tao's Truth is not an opinion, it is the way things are. However, this book is my opinion of truth, as best that I have been able to discern it.

Notes

1. Both the Michael entity and the Seth entity like the word 'play' as opposed to joyful living or enjoyment. It stresses that life should not be all work, and no matter how difficult our situation is, life can be viewed as a game.
2. From a private session with Shepherd Hoodwin on July 25, 2017.
3. *Seth Speaks*, pp. 212-214.
4. The Seth entity used the concept of Frameworks to explain the difference between the inner and outer universe. Although I use a different example, the concept is the same.
5. From a private session with Shepard Hoodwin.
6. For further OBE travel experiences see Robert Monroe's book *Journeys Out of the Body*.
7. The Michael entity refers to biases as characteristics like roles, male/female ratio, overleaves, etc.
8. Personalized Michael Reading charts can be obtained at shepherdhoodwin.com.
9. *The Seth Material*, Chapter 19, p. 251.
10. David Gaggin, *The Endless Journey*, pp 46-49.
11. Joe Fisher, *The Case for Reincarnation*, p. 107.
12. Joe Fisher, *The Case for Reincarnation*, p. 114.
13. See Shepherd Hoodwin's book *Journey of Your Soul* for more detail on this process.
14. Sourced from Shepherd Hoodwin's *Journey of Your Soul*.
15. The electromagnetic spectrum is a description of the range of wavelengths or frequencies over which electromagnetic radiation occurs.
16. David Bohm's book *Quantum Theory* was published in 1951 and may still be the quintessential book describing the basis of quantum theory as we know it. Bohm worked closely with Albert Einstein on relativity for a number of years at Princeton until they parted ways over a disagreement on the nature of quantum theory.

Bibliography

Bohm, David, PhD
Quantum Theory, New York, NY: Dover Publications, 1951
Wholeness and the Implicate Order, New York, NY: Routledge and
    Kegan Paul, 1980

Gaggin, David
The Endless Journey, North Charleston, SC: CreateSpace, 2013

Hoodwin, Shepherd
Journey of Your Soul, Berkeley, CA: North Atlantic Books, 1995

Long, Jeffrey, MD and Paul Perry
Evidence of the Afterlife, San Francisco, CA: HarperOne, 2011
God and the Afterlife, San Francisco, CA: HarperOne, 2016

McGrail, John, PhD
The Synthesis Effect, Pompton Plains, NJ: Career Press, Inc., 2012

McMoneagle, Joseph
Remote Viewing Secrets, Charlottesville, VA: Hampton Roads,
    2000

Monroe, Robert
Far Journeys, New York, NY: Doubleday, 1971

Montgomery, Pam
Plant Spirit Healing, Rochester, VT: Bear and Company, 2008

Peale, Norman Vincent
The Power of Positive Thinking, New York, NY: Touchstone, 1952

Pike, Albert
Morals and Dogma of The Ancient and Accepted Scottish Rite of Freemasonry: First Three Degrees, New York, NY: Kensington Publishing, 2004

Roberts, Jane
Dreams, "Evolution," and Value Fulfillment, Volumes 1 and 2, San Rafael, CA: Amber-Allen Publishing, 1986
The Early Sessions, Volumes 1-9, Manhasset, NY: New Awareness Network, Inc., 1997-2002
The Seth Material, San Rafael, CA: Amber-Allen Publishing, 1970
Seth Speaks, San Rafael, CA: Amber-Allen Publishing, 1972
The "Unknown" Reality, Volumes 1 and 2, San Rafael, CA: Amber-Allen Publishing, 1977

Stevenson, Ian, MD
Where Reincarnation and Biology Intersect, Westport, CT: Praeger Publishing, 1997

Tse, Lao
Tao Te Ching, London, UK: Penguin, 1963
The Texts of Taoism, New York, NY: Dover Publications, Inc., 1962

Weiss, Brian, MD
Many Lives, Many Masters, New York, NY: Touchstone, 2012

Glossary

Absolute (The): The psychological domain of dormant energy that the Tao initially emerged from.

Akashic Field: One of the seven Fields of Creation. Its frequency band resides between the causal and the mental fields and contains the records of the universe.

Aliveness: The measure of a spirit's evolution. Everything is alive, and the more aware a consciousness is the more alive it is said to be.

All That Is: Another name for the Tao or Universal Consciousness or God.

Apparition: The portion of the consciousness of a deceased being that has not fully transitioned into the astral field, but instead remains in one of the higher levels of the physical field.

Astral Body: The vehicle that our soul uses to experience the astral field.

Astral Field: One of the seven Fields of Creation. Its frequency band is between the physical and causal fields, and is where we reside before and after death during the period that we are reincarnating on earth.

Aura: Our ephemeral body that we use to experience the higher-level physical fields.

Awareness: The ability of a consciousness to understand its nature and the environment around it. Awareness expands as a consciousness evolves.

Beliefs: The opinions that we consider to be truths. These are the thoughts and actions that are manifested by the inner conscious.

Bias: The energy that is incorporated into an identity that causes it to perceive and interpret events from a predetermined perspective.

Blueprint: The detailed design of the personality that guides its growth throughout its life.

Buddhaic Field: The highest frequency of the seven Fields of Creation. During a Grand Cycle it is the last field we reside in before returning to the Tao.

Capsule Comprehension Process: The steps in which a consciousness unit (CU) transforms a thought into pseudo matter, which then takes the form of electromagnetic energy (EE).

Causal Field: One of the seven Fields of Creation. Its frequency band is between the astral and the akashic fields.

Characteristic Emotional Climate: The tendency for thoughts and emotions to attract similar thoughts and emotions. Like attracts like!

Chi: Another name for conscious energy or vitality.

Consciousness: An attribute of spirit that can function in both an individual and weblike manner.

Consciousness Unit (CU): Consciousness's smallest indivisible subdivision.

Core Belief: An opinion that we consciously accept as an undeniable truth.

Critical Intensity Level; The energetic level that pseudo matter needs to reach to become matter in the physical field.

Death: The transformation of a spiritual entity out of the physical field and into the astral field.

Dimension: A measurable extent of an object or event that in some meaningful way describes its nature.

Dream Reality: A psychological realm that our inner conscious experiences.

Ego: The portion of our consciousness that focuses on the physical field. It is what we think of as 'I.'

Electromagnetic Energy (EE): The building blocks of matter and pseudo matter that are created by consciousness through the Capsule Comprehension Process.

Entity: A group of ~1000 spirits that travel together through the Fields of Creation during a Grand Cycle.

Essence: A subset of a spirit that has inherent biases that are passed down to the soul. It can be thought of as the greater soul.

Evolution: The eternal process of a spirit's psychological growth.

Expectations: The beliefs of the ego that the inner conscious manifests into objects or events.

Fields of Creation: The seven primary energy fields that form our universe. In a Grand Cycle we transition through six of those fields: physical, astral, causal, mental, messianic, and buddhaic. The seventh is the akashic field, which we do not reside in.

Fragment: A spiritual identity that is not complete. This usually refers to a partial personality with a special but limited purpose. However, technically it could be any spirit within the Tao as only the Tao is complete.

Free Will: The ability of a consciousness to choose its own experiences. However, it is always subject to the limitations that have been imposed on it by its greater spirit and the characteristics of the reality it is in.

Gestalt: The combination of two or more consciousness units (CUs) in which the sum is greater than its individual parts.

Grand Cycle: The period starting when a spirit is first cast from the Tao, continuing its transition through six Fields of Creation, and ending upon its return to the Tao.

Greater Spirit: A spirit's larger spiritual entity.

Group Soul: The soul of lower level animals, plants, and minerals in which multiple identities incarnate into a single soul.

Hive Soul: The soul of a higher-level animal.

Identity: Any subjective or objective item or group of items acting together for a common purpose.

Illusion: The perception of energy that creates a reality that is different than the true nature of the Tao's reality.

Inner Conscious: The portion of a soul that is dedicated to supporting an ego during a physical experience.

Inner Sense: The capabilities inherent within all beings to perceive and communicate with other identities.

Karmic Ribbon: The agreement between two sentient beings to have a joint experience, which is caused by one being having prevented the other from having his/her planned experience(s).

Life Analysis: Unlike the life review, this is an in-depth review of a past life performed between incarnations and after the being has become adjusted to the astral field. All the important decisions are analyzed to see how they impacted that life and the effect different decisions would have made.

Life Review: A cursory overview of the most recent past life, which is performed in the astral field shortly after we die. This allows the personality to experience the feelings it caused in others.

Material Spectrum: The range of characteristic states matter and pseudo matter can assume. Each state is defined by parameters such as density, intensity and polarity. This corresponds to the electromagnetic spectrum, which is based on matter's emitted frequency.

Mental Enzymes: The catalysts that cause the transformation of thought energy from its initial state into a material state during the Capsule Comprehension Process.

Mental Field: One of the seven Fields of Creation. Its frequency band is between the akashic and the messianic fields.

Messianic Field: One of the seven Fields of Creation. Its frequency band is between the akashic and the buddhaic fields.

Metaphysics: A philosophy of reality that encompasses spiritual, physical, and ethical considerations. I often use it synonymously with spirituality.

Mind: The nonphysical aspects of ourselves. It is synonymous with spirit.

Monads: The major experiences that we have in a life. Inter monads are experiences with others, such as parent-child or teacher-student relationships. Intra monads are personal experiences like birth, old age, death, etc.

Out-of-Body Experience (OBE): The process whereby the main portion of the consciousness leaves the physical body.

Past Lives: The previous personalities that our soul created.

Perception: The method used for sensing the surrounding energy.

Personality: The unique set of energies that form individuals like you and me. It is composed of the ego, subconscious, inner conscious and body.

Prelife Plan: A detailed description of experiences that a soul wants a personality to have during its lifetime.

Pseudo Matter: The state that energy is transformed into before it becomes matter.

Psyche: The mental and emotional aspects of a personality.

Psychological Domain: An area where mental and emotional energies exist.

Reality: The way energy is perceived.

Reincarnation: The process in which a soul creates multiple personalities.

Root Assumption: An opinion that we unconsciously accept as an undeniable truth.

Sentient Soul: The human or cetacean soul, which is more evolved than an animal, plant or group soul.

Seven: The number our universe is based on.

Soul: The spiritual identity that creates a personality. It is the lower portion of the essence. It is our greater 'I' that remains in the inner universe during our physical life and experiences our events.

Space: The fabric or field that permeates our reality and gives us the illusion of time and distance.

Spark: The spirit nature inside an identity, no matter how small or undeveloped, that has not evolved to the level of the sentient soul.

Spirit: The eternal gestalt energies within the Tao.

Spirituality: The process of a sentient soul living in the physical world. I use it synonymously with metaphysics.

Spontaneity: The universal principle that causes matter to create instantly. Due to the time delay in our space-time continuum, this phenomena is not apparent in our reality.

Subconscious: The portion of the psyche that manages the physical body and contains the past life memories. It consists of the body management and material management consciousnesses.

Synchronicity: The apparent random circumstances that are encountered that change one's life in some significant way.

Tao: The all-encompassing spiritual consciousness that we are part of. Also known as All That is, the Universal Consciousness or God.

Telepathy: The inner sense that allows communication directly between consciousnesses without the use of language.

Time: The apparent dimension that is unique to our reality, which is caused by the slow movement of objects through space.

Universal Consciousness: Another name for All That Is, Tao or God.

Universal Principles: Fundamental Truths that hold true in all realities.

Universe: The seven Fields of Creation.

Value Fulfillment: The innate desire within everything to have experiences that benefit both itself and all other identities.

Victimhood: The illusion that someone else is responsible for our troubles.

Vitality: The energy of the Tao that has been activated from its previous latent condition in the Absolute. It is the only substance in existence. Everything else is a derivative of it.

Web of Consciousness: The universal principle that states all consciousness is connected together.

Index

About the Author

I received Bachelor of Science and Master degrees in Electrical Engineering and a Bachelor of Arts in Mathematics. I spent 16 years designing and managing flight control systems, avionics and cockpits for The Boeing Company. I then joined the US Government's Senior Executive Service where I spent nine years in various director positions for the US Army and NASA research and development organizations. For the last 16 years of my business career I was the CEO of Cobham Defense Electronic Systems Corp, a company I founded and grew into the world's leading defense microwave corporation, which at my retirement had a billion dollars in annual sales and over 3500 employees.

However, throughout my business career I spent my spare time seeking answers to questions like: who was I, where was I, and why was I here. I studied all the great religions in an attempt to learn the nature of their origin and their founding principles.

Philosophy seemed like a fertile source of wisdom so I started in the West with the ancient Greeks like Plato and Pythagoras and worked my way up to Emerson. I then studied Eastern philosophies, which offered excellent insights. Curiously, it seemed the older the philosophy the more enlightened it was.

Mainstream science was part of my education so I was exposed to those tenets early in life and often. But science focuses on the physical world and I figured if the source of the physical world is spiritual, then finding reality's truths without considering its spiritual aspects would be a futile effort.

I concluded that if religion, science and philosophy could not construct a rational view of reality, then the answers needed to come from elsewhere.

I found that for centuries psychics, mediums, channels, remote viewers, near-death experiencers, etc., had been offering a fascinating and consistent perspective on the spiritual world from first-hand experiences, and usually by highly reliable sources. But like any source, verifying the reliability of ESP reports was paramount.

After sifting through reams of data, a consistent pattern of potential truth began to emerge that separated itself from the rest of the information. After retiring from the business world I wrote *The Endless Journey* and for two years I hosted *The Common Sense Spirituality Show*, which was a weekly Internet radio program, where I was exposed to a group of fascinating people. I also did a weekly podcast called *Aspects of Spirituality*, and hosted the Sanibel Metaphysical Meetup Group.

After a lifetime of study not only did the multitude of disparate information begin to make sense, it turned out to be a truly good news story. I always had the feeling that truth would be positive, but the answers I found were far beyond my wildest dreams.

6TH
BOOKS

ALL THINGS PARANORMAL

Investigations, explanations and deliberations on the paranormal, supernatural, explainable or unexplainable. 6th Books seeks to give answers while nourishing the soul: whether making use of the scientific model or anecdotal and fun, but always beautifully written.
Titles cover everything within parapsychology: how to, lifestyles, alternative medicine, beliefs, myths and theories.
If you have enjoyed this book, why not tell other readers by posting a review on your preferred book site?

Recent bestsellers from 6th Books are:

The Afterlife Unveiled
What the Dead Are Telling Us About Their World!
Stafford Betty
What happens after we die? Spirits speaking through mediums
know, and they want us to know. This book unveils their world...
Paperback: 978-1-84694-496-3 ebook: 978-1-84694-926-5

Spirit Release
Sue Allen
A guide to psychic attack, curses, witchcraft, spirit attachment,
possession, soul retrieval, haunting, deliverance, exorcism and
more, as taught at the College of Psychic Studies.
Paperback: 978-1-84694-033-0 ebook: 978-1-84694-651-6

I'm Still With You
True Stories of Healing Grief Through Spirit Communication
Carole J. Obley
A series of after-death spirit communications which uplift,
comfort and heal, and show how love helps us grieve.
Paperback: 978-1-84694-107-8 ebook: 978-1-84694-639-4

Less Incomplete
A Guide to Experiencing the Human Condition Beyond the
Physical Body
Sandie Gustus
Based on 40 years of scientific research, this book is a dynamic
guide to understanding life beyond the physical body.
Paperback: 978-1-84694-351-5 ebook: 978-1-84694-892-3

Advanced Psychic Development
Becky Walsh
Learn how to practise as a professional, contemporary spiritual medium.
Paperback: 978-1-84694-062-0 ebook: 978-1-78099-941-8

Astral Projection Made Easy
and overcoming the fear of death
Stephanie June Sorrell
From the popular Made Easy series, *Astral Projection Made Easy* helps to eliminate the fear of death, through discussion of life beyond the physical body.
Paperback: 978-1-84694-611-0 ebook: 978-1-78099-225-9

The Miracle Workers Handbook
Seven Levels of Power and Manifestation of the Virgin Mary
Sherrie Dillard
Learn how to invoke the Virgin Mary's presence, communicate with her, receive her grace and miracles and become a miracle worker.
Paperback: 978-1-84694-920-3 ebook: 978-1-84694-921-0

Divine Guidance
The Answers You Need to Make Miracles
Stephanie J. King
Ask any question and the answer will be presented, like a direct line to higher realms... *Divine Guidance* helps you to regain control over your own journey through life.
Paperback: 978-1-78099-794-0 ebook: 978-1-78099-793-3

The End of Death
How Near-Death Experiences Prove the Afterlife
Admir Serrano
A compelling examination of the phenomena of Near-Death
Experiences.
Paperback: 978-1-78279-233-8 ebook: 978-1-78279-232-1

Where After
Mariel Forde Clarke
A journey that will compel readers to view life after death in a
completely different way.
Paperback: 978-1-78904-617-5 ebook: 978-1-78904-618-2

Harvest: The True Story of Alien Abduction
G. L. Davies
G. L. Davies's most terrifying investigation yet reveals one
woman's terrifying ordeal of alien visitation, nightmarish visions
and a prophecy of destruction on a scale never before seen in
Pembrokeshire's peaceful history.
Paperback: 978-1-78904-385-3 ebook: 978-1-78904-386-0

The Scars of Eden
Paul Wallis
How do we distinguish between our ancestors' ideas of God and
close encounters of an extra-terrestrial kind?
Paperback: 978-1-78904-852-0 ebook: 978-1-78904-853-7

Readers of ebooks can buy or view any of these bestsellers by clicking on the live link in the title. Most titles are published in paperback and as an ebook. Paperbacks are available in traditional bookshops. Both print and ebook formats are available online.
Find more titles and sign up to our readers' newsletter at http://www.johnhuntpublishing.com/mind-body-spirit.
Follow us on Facebook at https://www.facebook.com/OBooks and Twitter at https://twitter.com/obooks.